Teach[...] to Read
Letter by Letter

Teach Me to Read Letter by Letter

A Fun Way to Learn Reading through Hands-On Experiences

Bernice B. Green, M.S.

BookWorld Press
Sarasota, Florida

Published by:
BookWorld Press, Inc.
1933 Whitfield Park Loop
Sarasota, FL 34243
941-758-8094

Printed in the United States of America

ISBN 1-884962-18-1

Publisher's Cataloging-in-Publication
(Provided by Quality Books, Inc)

Green, Bernice B.
    Teach me to read, letter by letter : a fun way to learn reading through hands-on experiences / Bernice B. Green. -- 1st ed.
      p. cm.
      Includes bibliographical references.
      Preassigned LCCN: 97-75155
      ISBN: 1-884962-18-1

    1. Reading readiness--Handbooks, manuals, etc. 2. English language--Alphabet--Study and teaching (Early childhood) 3. Early childhood education--Activity programs--Handbooks, manuals, etc. 4. Reading--Parent participation. 5. Snack foods. 6. Cookery.
    I. Title.

LB1050.43.G74 1997   372.4'14
                                        QBI97-41290

I am dedicating this book to the following people who have supported, encouraged, reinforced my idea and helped me: my husband, Michael, my daughters Suzanne and Michelle, my first teaching partner, Maryanne and her husband Joe and son John, my mother, Bessie, may her soul rest in peace, my dad Howard and my brothers and sister who promised that they would buy a book, and janice@bookworld.com.

Table of Contents

Introduction

To parents and educators:

Research shows that children retain the most when they see, hear, "hands-on" manipulate, or touch, the lesson, letter or concept. It further shows that as teachers, at any level, we must not keep using the method that is the most comfortable for us, but must use the method/style/technique that meets the child's needs.

Teach Me to Read, Letter by Letter is an exciting collection containing activities that are needed to strengthen any reading/writing approach for students enrolled in English as a Second Language, Special Education, or any student who has not cemented that all important step of associating sounds with symbols.

Teach Me to Read, Letter by Letter is an A-a through Z-z exciting, clever collection of recipes, activities and word lists, geared toward hands-on, total body utilization activities, which have been classroom tested and proven to help the child/student learn best. This collection can strengthen the Whole Language Approach, or any reading program used at home or in the classroom. It is designed to offer many "pick and choose" activities that parents or teachers may select to best meet the child's needs. Some activities and recipes the teacher may have to start at home and then bring to school. If the students can associate letters (symbols) with sounds (phonemes), he or she can then learn to manipulate sounds and blend the letters into consonant-vowel-consonant words, which will immediately produce reading success. These activities also will help with recognition of sight words.

This collection differs from those currently available because it contains many features not found in other books: an extensive word list, six or more recipes, at least ten activities, and a recommended book list for each of the 26 letters.

I presently hold a Resource Specialist Teacher Credential with a Master's Degree in Special Education. I also hold a Language Development Specialist Credential and have been a teacher for over twenty years. I am currently employed by the Los Angeles Unified School District as a Resource Specialist Teacher and Mentor Teacher. I have recently returned from a Reading Teacher's Delegation to Russia, as one of 50 teachers selected by People-to-Peoples to take this trip. While in Russia, I observed how much effort it takes to develop materials to teach manipulation activities, reinforce language development, and provide the basis for formal reading and writing activities.

I have found that cooking is a great motivator for learning and even changing/modifying behavior. These recipes can be copied and then taken home so that students can teach parents about good health and healthy foods. Many strategies/techniques found in the appendix can help teach reading by just using the recipes.

Beware! Children will want to learn to cook and read!

Bernice B. Green

A Note About this Collection:

This book was designed and written to help *you* teach all of your students in:

- following directions
- sequencing
- reinforcing sound/symbol association—which helps decoding and encoding
- associating by seeing, hearing, feeling, and tasting
- modifying behavior
- learning/reinforcing sight words
- increasing sight vocabulary
- bridging information learned from classroom to the home
- teaching parents and children how to cook, measure, and use kitchen safety rules
- teaching phonemic awareness

How Parents and Teachers Can Modify Behavior
A Special Note from the Author

I have found that food is a very powerful reinforcer. If the child has completed his assignments, or if the targeted behavior has been lessened (not displayed or not in evidence as often), or if the targeted behavior has been replaced by a more appropriate behavior, then the student is invited to "cook" today. I used to allow my students to copy the recipe from a chart, as it made the recipe "theirs" and they then shared this recipe with their family. I had many parents tell me how they made the recipe several times. I have made these for you to copy and give to your students or they can be used on an overhead to underline the vocabulary you want to expand upon. Do what is easiest and most meaningful for you.

I found myself searching from cookbook to cookbook, modifying/enhancing each recipe to work for a classroom. *You* do not have to do that. Many recipes are from several cultures, so you can use these recipes for your multicultural component.

Today, skills have so many parts to address, so many themes, and concepts that many of the techniques/strategies are either not taught, overlooked, or have been forgotten. So please, look in the Appendix for ideas and have fun with the recipes and activities.

Recently, I took a trip with other reading teachers to Russia, where students learn by using a lot of manipulatives and many activities are called "games." If it is fun for a student, then he or she will retain the information. If they see the importance and application, they listen. So please model and explain the reason and make it fun. (My students in high school come back to see if we are still cooking and doing the activities and to say they are still in school and doing well!) My first students in Special Education were *Educationally Retarded* and they were reading—which totally surprised the principal and school psychologist. I made everything fun, a game, modeled and kept the lessons short. The material is here for *you* to use as *you* want and *need*.

Several of my students have been in the bilingual program and transferred into English. These students need English readiness activities or games to assist the transition. This collection is designed to "pick 'n' choose" depending on your program and your students' needs.

How important is teaching phonics? According to _Becoming a Nation of Readers_, "teachers of beginning reading should present a well-designed phonics instruction." After teaching Phonemic awareness, research has shown that letter identification and sound/symbol association are the first steps for success in reading. The readiness games/activities and recipes supply ready and easy identifiable objects to stimulate the sound/symbol association. The recipes also make a parent/school connection, which provides parent/home/school connection. The activities and flash cards made from each word list can also provide sequential memory and letter recognition necessary for decoding/encoding and computation. Also, by using art, movement, and many games, a child remembers or associates it with the letter because it is personal or it belongs to him/her. "Taking turns" is another important reinforcer in many games. This book is full of powerful reinforcers.

A-a — Recipes

ADORABLE APPLES

Materials:

toaster oven

aluminum foil

spoons

apple peeler

plates

tray

1/2 teaspoon sugar per apple

1/2 teaspoon margarine per apple

1 baking apple per person

water to cover the tray

"stuffings": raisins, walnuts, cinnamon and sugar, cinnamon candies, marshmallows, ice cream (put in after cooking), peanut butter or cheese.

Directions:

1. Clean hands, area, and equipment.
2. Line tray with foil. Preheat oven to 400 degrees.
3. Cut core out of each apple with peeler.
4. Put 1/2 teaspoon of margarine and sugar into each apple.
5. Stuff apple with "stuffings" of your choice.
6. Pour enough water to just cover bottom of the tray.
7. Bake at 400 degrees for 30 minutes.
8. Spoon liquid over apples every ten minutes.
9. Apple must cool down for a few minutes before eating.
10. Adorable.

APPEALING APPLE FACES
(No Cooking)

Materials:

raisins

apple wedges

peanut butter or cream cheese (as "glue")

1 bread slice per child

marshmallows

Directions:

1. Clean hands area and equipment.
2. Use peanut butter or cream cheese to glue parts to the bread.
3. A marshmallow can be used to make the nose.
4. Two raisins make the eyes.
5. An apple wedge becomes the mouth.
6. Appealing and delicious.

ALLIGATOR APPLESAUCE

Materials:

sauce pan
4 apples
cups or bowls
1/3 teaspoon cinnamon, 1/4 teaspoon nutmeg, or almond or vanilla extract

1/2 cup granulated or brown sugar
apple peeler and potato masher
stove or cooking unit

Directions:

1. Clean hands, area, and equipment.
2. Peel 4 apples with peeler.
3. Cut apples into fourths and cook in saucepan with 1 cup water and cook until tender: Older apples require more water. This should take 3 minutes.
4. Mash with potato masher
5. Stir in sugar, nutmeg, cinnamon, and almond/vanilla extract.
6. Children could also add dried apples (crushed) or avocados (chunked).
7. Cool and anticipate. The taster could decide which flavoring they liked best.
8. It could be cooked at home and tasted at school or where the lesson is presented. It could then be heated.
9. This looks like alligator skin.

AMAZING ALMOND APPETIZERS

Materials:

1 lb. of cream cheese
1/2 cup crushed almonds, walnuts, and/or peanuts.
1 stalk of celery per student or crackers
knifecutting area
alternative additives—crushed dried apples or chunked avocados

Directions:

1. Clean hands, area, and equipment.
2. Soften 1 lb. of cream cheese.
3. Add 1/2 cup crushed, chopped almonds or walnuts/peanuts.
4. Spread on chopped celery/crackers.
5. Add 1 cup raisins/dried fruit.
6. Compare/contrast the taste of almonds with walnuts/peanut, dried apples with chunked avocados.
7. Chart students' preferences.
8. A-mazing.

CARAMEL APPLES

Materials:

1 apple per child
2 tablespoons water
saucepan
hot plate or approved portable unit

1 Popsicle™ stick per apple
1 package of caramels per 6 apples
aluminum foil or wax paper

Directions:

1. Clean hands, area, and equipment.
2. Wash and dry apples.
3. Twist off the stems.
4. Stick Popsicle™ stick into each apple.
5. Melt caramels in saucepan and add 2 tablespoons of water.
6. Dip apples carefully into caramel mixture.
7. Cool on aluminum foil or wax paper.
8. These apples are "caramelly."

APPLE JUICE
(No Cooking)

Materials:

1/2 cup seeded apples
1 teaspoon sugar

1 cup water
blender

Directions:

1. Clean hands, area, and equipment.
2. Liquefy all ingredients in blender.
3. Drink and enjoy.
4. Different fruits/juices could be added, like raspberries or cranberries.

ALARM AVOCADO

Materials:

butter

salad dressing

1/2 to 1/4 ripe avocado per serving (peeled & dropped into lemon & salt water to keep it from turning brown)

4 tablespoons butter

4 tablespoons ketchup

2 tablespoons sugar

1/2 teaspoon salt

2 tablespoons water

1 teaspoon vinegar

1/2 teaspoon cumin

1 teaspoon lemon juice

1/2 teaspoon ground red pepper

season to taste with Tabasco sauce

Directions:

1. Clean hands, area, and equipment.
2. Add all seasonings with butter into saucepan and heat on approved hot plate or approved heating unit until boiling.
3. Place avocado on lettuce leaf & garnish (tomatoes, celery, carrots, & olives).
4. Pour small amount of butter/dressing over it.

ALMOND COOKIES

Materials:

1/2 cup margarine

1/2 cup brown sugar

1 teaspoon vanilla

1 egg

1/2 teaspoon salt

1/4 teaspoon nutmeg

waxed paper

foil wrapped cookie sheets

3/4 cup granulated sugar

1/2 cups finely ground almonds

2 cups all purpose flour

2 teaspoons baking soda

1/4 teaspoon cinnamon

Directions:

1. Clean hands, area, and equipment.
2. Add sugars and cream together, thoroughly.
3. Add eggs.
4. Add vanilla and nut meats.
5. Mix flour, baking powder, salt, and spices.
6. Shape into rolls about 1/2 in diameter.
7. Wrap in waxed paper.
8. Chill for several hours or overnight.
9. Slice rolls 1/8 inches thick.
10. Place on cookie sheets.
11. Bake in toaster oven at 425 degrees for 8 to 10 minutes or until golden brown. Make 4 dozen cookies.

A-a Games/Activities

A-a Around The World

Copy words onto flash cards. Pictures could be drawn/pasted on the back. Children could use these for games like "Around The World." All children sit down except for "It." "It" stands in the back of a student and each student gets one try to read the word. The fastest child that is correct, gets the card. "It" either sits down (if other child reads it faster) or stands behind another child. The child with the most cards wins.

Adopt-A-Letter Book

Children write an "Adopt-A-Letter Book." The first letter could be A. Students would look in magazines, catalogs, newspapers, or discarded books with pictures for pictures of items that begin with the letter "A-a" or have the /a/ sound. The student would name the item and dictate or write a sentence or paragraph about the item describing its use/purpose/function/abilities (like ape, acorn, apple, ax, apricots, anteaters, ant, antelopes, apron, airplanes, alarms, avocados, almonds, alphabet, arm, animals, ankle, arrow, and armadillo).

Apple, Almond, Apricot, Asparagus

Children form a standing circle. Children chant "Apple, Almond, Apricot, Asparagus." One child is in the middle ("it"). He says, "Tell me when your birthday comes," while pointing to a child in the circle. That child must then state the name of the month he was born in. All children who were born in that month must sit down. The game continues until only one child is standing, and that child is then chased around the circle of seated children by the child in the middle of the circle. Whoever is seated last is ... "it!" Children continue chanting "Apple, Almond, Apricot, Asparagus."

Animal Crackers

Animal crackers could be purchased and children could predict how many cookies of each animal will be found in each box. Teacher or students may chart/graph the predictions. Children classify or sort, then count each group of animals and tell teacher. Teacher or students then chart/graph findings and compare with predictions. Stories could be dictated/written about each animal.

Apples and Stuff

Children can research/ascertain all the products made from apples ... apple fritters, drink juice, roll/bar, turnover, butter, cider, or croissant. Children could learn the names like: Delicious, Granny Smith, Jonathan, Golden Delicious, and Macintosh. Teacher shows children red, green, and yellow apples. Children predict which apple they will like the best. Teacher graphs predictions. Children taste the apples to verify their predictions. Individual students then indicate their favorite apple and this information is added to the prediction chart. Children could then ascertain information from home or friends and chart it.

AUTOGRAPH BOOKS

Students can make autograph books and exchange autographs. The student with the most autographs could win the game. The teacher can encourage students to collect autographs from friends, teachers, custodians, office help, principals, vice principals, and friends that live near them.

A-A FOOD/TASTE CHART

The teacher could have on hand samples of apricots, almonds, avocados, apples, artichokes, and anchovies for students to taste. Then, have the students describe the taste to the class and place a Post-It™ (with their name) on the chart with a picture of the six foods. They can then predict which food will be the class favorite. The chart will reveal itself. It may amaze you.

APPLE SEEDS

When students are learning about apples, their names and tastes, the teacher could extract all the seeds and the students could count the seeds from each variety and a chart/graph could show which apple type yields the most seeds. The seeds could then be planted into paper cups or bowls. In the cup/bowl could be 1" or 2" of planting soil and one or two holes at the bottom for drainage. The children could then chart or graph the growth of the seeds by measuring daily. The cups/bowls may need to be taken outside daily for adequate sunlight to germinate.

APPLE, PEAR, PEACH, AND PLUM

Students can play "Apple, Pear, Peach, and Plum." The students form a circle. The students then chant, "Apple, Pear, Peach, Plum ..." "It" is in the middle and he/she points to a child and said, "What is your favorite word that starts with A-a (in 10 seconds). If that child can name a word, "it" chases the child around the circle until he/she finds his place and sits down. If "it" catches him/her before they can get to their place and sits down, he/she goes into the A-a pot. If the child sits down before "it" catches him/her, he/she is now "it."

AIR POLLUTION TRAP

Students can make an air pollution holder or trap. Use the shallow dish. Smear Vaseline™ all over the inside of the dish. Set the dish on a window sill or somewhere in the classroom. Leave the dish out for several days and observe it daily. Use a magnifying glass to see/observe what pollutes our air.

AN A-A AUTOBIOGRAPHY BOOK

Have each child talk to their parents and find out where their parents come from. Allow each child to write one page of his autobiography about his family, his parents and family, and their parents and family. Add a picture. This could be made into a class book to learn about each other. A world map could be used to point out states/countries other than ours.

APPLE STORIES

The teacher could read one or more of the following folk tales:
- *A Little Bear's Star*, by Carol Catron and Barbara Parks, found in *Cooking Up A Story*, published by T. S. Denison
- *A Little Red House With No Doors Or Windows*, by Caroline Sherwin Bailey
- *An Apple Wish* or *Evidence of Moonbean* by David Cooper and Lynn Taylor, found in Pocket Book. (It also gives patterns. The teacher tells of the Jewish custom or tradition of dipping a slice of apple into honey for a sweet new life. It is done for Jewish New Year's in September.)

AN ARBOR

Students can grow an arbor using apple seeds, avocado seeds, orange seeds, lemon seeds, or small trees that could be purchased or grown from seeds or seedlings. Each child could have their own tree to make an arbor. They could name, describe, measure, compare/contrast with others. Drawings can also be made. A rule of thumb: plants grow towards the light and need water, light, and food.

A-a INVENTIONS

The apple slicer, apple peeler, airplane, ax, apron, aquarium, arrow, and astronaut outfit are A-a inventions. Children/students could make their own inventions of recyclable materials or of scraps, Styrofoam, wood, metal, and plastic. A sentence or paragraph about what the invention is and does could be glued on the cardboard or base. This encourages creativity and writing.

ANIMAL GUESS

Teacher could list all the names of the animals in the Animal Word List. Teacher or "it" could give three to four clues. (Teacher does need to explain that all living creatures are either plant or animal and that an insect, spider, or mammal are all animals.) The students get 20 tries/guesses to guess the animal. The student who is correct becomes "it."

"A-A" FINGER GAME

The teacher states words like if, ham, hat, sad, apple, add, at, jam, pack, pad, atom, black, fast, dad, rat, cat, had, has, ate, ape, age, bake, say, race, face, jade, blade, jail, rain, way, gave, rave, shave, and cave. These words could also be put on flash cards so the children can hear and see the words. If the word has a short /a/ sound, the student puts up one finger; if the word has a long /a/ sound, the child puts up two fingers. The child with the most points wins.

A-a Word Lists

Short /a/ Words in initial position:

am	ask	after
and	animal	ax
an	apple	add
act	apricot	albatross
anaconda	address	at
arm	act	atlas
athlete	ambulance	ant
as	adjective	arrow
atom	ash	answer
attack	Africa	

Short /a/ Words in medial position:

bag	cap	bat
can	bad	cat
back	happen	dad
gap	fast	ambulance
dam	gash	dash
fan	ham	fat
hat	had	stamp
man	tack	tan
van	stand	tag
sat	sash	mat
sad	rat	has
nap	back	map
hash	jam	lag
lap	pan	pad
pack	mast	strap
trash	crash	smash
flat	jab	thank
drank	blank	tramp
began	plant	hand
stamp		

Long "A" Words in the initial position:

apron	April	Asia
ate	age	Angelfish
ape	aliens	able
able	aid	ace
away	again	acre
agent	ache	aid
aim	always	apex

Long "A" Words in the medial position:

contain	pail	way
came	game	same
cave	gave	save
shave	rave	wave
pain	sail	jail
may	rain	may
bake	take	make
say	way	pace
race	face	safe
fake	quake	stake
plane	vane	cape
gape	grape	shape
tape	escape	jade
blade	shade	wade
bare	dare	fare

Other "A" Words:

all	are	around
arrive	art	Aye-Aye
about	above	ago
alone	alike	appear
away	again	ahead
another	agree	ark
armor	arm	always
also	already	almost
although	art	author
autoheap	auction	altogether

alternate	altar	almanac
almighty	awful	area

Foods:

artichoke	asparagus	avocado
apricot	apple	almond
anchovies	Angel food	acorn
arrowroot	awn	ale
anise		

Animals:

ant	alligator	albatross
anaconda	anteater	ape
angelfish	armadillo	antelope
alpaca	Armadillo lizard	asp
auk	Aurochs	axolotl
Atlantic Puffin	Aphid	Angler fish
Aye-Aye	Apteryx	agouti
Argali	Australian Horned Frog	
Amazon terrier		

Everyday Objects:

ax	Atomizer	Aster
add	age	April
altar	almanac	autograph
ascot	August	Author
Autoharp	autumn	alarm clock
alphabet	attic	abacus
aquarium	Amethyst	ankle
ark	arm	army
aspirin	about	above
accident	across	act
add	aluminum	August
address	ago	ail
aim	air	alien
alive	all	ankle
amaryllis	ammonia	amphibian

Areas:

Amsterdam	Alps	Amapa
Alexandria	Albuquerque	Alhambra
Africa	Australia	Asia
Airdale	Albany	Alaska
Ajmer	Amazon	Amboise
America	Arizona	

Inventions/musical instruments:

autoharp	accordion	abacus
almanac	Atlas	ambulance
aquarium	aspirin	address
arrow	aluminum	

12

A-a Reading Resources

Aliens for Breakfast — Extra and Spinner: Random House

Apple Mouse — Ulrick Thomas

Apple Pigs — Ruth Orbach

Johnny Appleseed — Aliki

Johnny Appleseed — Eva Moore

Johnny Appleseed — Steven Kellogg Morrow, 1989

Johnny's Secret — Frank Lewis

Little Bear's Star — Carol Catron and Barbara Parks: Cooking up a Story — T. S. Denison

Pocket Book — David Cooper and Lynn Taylor: Pocket Book Press, Dublin Calif.

Ten Apples on Top — Dr. Seuss: Random House/Beginner Book,, 1960

Who's Got the Apple — Jan Loot: Random House

Windows — Caroline Sherwin Bailey

Apple Pie — Tracy Pearson: Dial, 1986

Amos and Boris — William Steig: Penguin, 1971

Angelina Ballerina — Katharine Holabira: Potter, 1983

Anansi the Spider — A Tale from Ashanti — Gerald McDermott: Holt, 1973

Alexander and the Terrible, Horrible, No Good, Very Bad Day — Judith Viorist: Aladdin, 1972

Annie and the Wild Animals — Jan Brett: Houghton Mifflin, 1985

About Animals — Richard Scarry: Golden Press, 1976

Ants — Diana Ferguson: Wonder Books, 1977

Apples and How They Grow — Bruce McMillan: Houghton Mifflin, 1929

Are You My Mother — P. D. Eastman: Random House, 1960

Albert's Thanksgiving — Leslie Tryon: Atheneum, 1994

Abiyoyo — Pete Seeger: Aladdin, 1986

Angelina Ballerina — Katharine Holabird: Clarkson N. Potler, 1983

Angry Arthur — Hiawyn Oram: Unicorn, 1989

Annie And the Old One — Miska Miles: Joystreet/ Little Brown, 1971

Amelia Bedelia — Peggy Parnish: Harper Trophy, 1963

Amanda Pig and Her Big Brother Oliver — Jean Van Leevwen: Pied Piper, 1982

Alpha Bugs — David A. Carter: Little Simon,, 1994

"B-b" Recipes

BUTTER 'N' BAGELS

Materials:

toaster oven
knife
4 small bagels
measuring cup

4 plastic jars with tight lids
4 clean marbles
4 cups whipping cream
pinch salt

Directions:

1. Clean hands, area, and equipment
2. Pour 1 cup of whipping cream into each container.
3. Put a clean marble into the cream and close lid tightly.
4. Shake, shake, shake, until butter forms. These are the curds—throw out the whey (watery substance). These words are from "Little Miss Muffet."
5. Salt lightly.
6. Cut bagels into 2 equal pieces and toast until golden brown.
7. Spread butter on bagels.

BUNNY BREAD

Materials:

1 cup brown sugar
1/3 cup oil
1 1/2 cups flour
1/2 teaspoon salt
1 teaspoon cinnamon
1/4 cup pineapple
muffin tins (24)
muffin liners (24)
toaster oven

3/4 cup creamy peanut butter
2 cups finely shredded carrots
1 teaspoon baking powder
1 teaspoon baking soda
1 teaspoon nutmeg
1 big mixing bowl
1 small mixing bowl
mixing spoon

Directions:

1. Clean hands, area, and equipment.
2. Combine sugar, peanut butter, oil, and eggs in big bowl.
3. Beat with spoon until creamy.
4. Add carrots, milk, raisins, pineapple, and vanilla.
5. Mix flour, baking powder, baking soda, and salt in small bowl.
6. Combine big bowl and small bowl and mix together.
7. Pour into muffin tins with paper liners.
8. Fill each liner only 3/4 full!
9. Bake at 350 degrees for 25 minutes.

Bodacious Bagels

Materials:

2 packages yeast
1 tablespoon salt
2 teaspoons salt
1-1/2 cups water
2 tablespoons water
3 tablespoons sugar
1 tablespoon sugar
paper towels
toaster oven
slotted spoon
floured board

1-1/2 cups flour
1/2 cup flour
a few drops of oil
2 tablespoons margarine
a few pinches of coarse salt
1 tablespoon sugar
1 egg white
electric skillet
electric mixer
1 baking sheet
2 mixing bowls

Directions:

1. Clean hands, area, and equipment.
2. Mix 1-1/2 cups flour and 3 tablespoons sugar.
3. Add 1 tablespoon salt and yeast.
4. Heat lukewarm water and margarine, then add to flour mixture.
5. Allow to sit for 5 minutes, then beat at medium speed for 2 minutes.
6. Add 1/2 cup flour and beat at high speed for 2 minutes.
7. On floured board, knead dough 8 to 10 minutes.
8. Place in covered, oiled bowl, and let rise in warm place.
9. After one hour, punch dough down.
10. Add 2 teaspoons salt and 1 tablespoon sugar.
11. In electric skillet, heat 1 inch of water and simmer.
12. Divide dough into 12 pieces and shape into smooth balls.
13. With floured finger, poke a 1-inch hole in each.
14. Drop bagels into simmering water.
15. Cook 3 minutes, turn and cook 2 more minutes.
16. Turn again and cook one more minute.
17. Drain on paper towels, then place on greased baking sheets.
18. Mix egg white with 2 tablespoons water.
19. Brush mixture on bagels, then sprinkle with coarse salt.
20. Bake in toaster oven at 375 degrees for 25 minutes.
21. Cool before eating.

BUSY BANANA PUDDING

Materials:

1 very ripe banana   1 teaspoon plain yogurt
mixing bowl   2 tablespoons applesauce

Directions:

1. Clean hands, area, and equipment.
2. Mash banana in mixing bowl.
3. Add applesauce to banana.
4. Stir in plain yogurt.

BEAUTIFUL BROWNIES

Materials:

1 1/4 cups flour   1/2 teaspoon baking soda
1/2 teaspoon salt   1-1/2 teaspoons vanilla
1/2 cup butter   3 tablespoons water
1 cup sugar   12 ounces of chocolate chips
1 cup chopped nuts   1 cup miniature marshmallows
3 extra large eggs   saucepan
9"x13" baking pan   2 mixing bowls
spoon   measuring cups and spoons
toaster oven   heating element

Directions:

1. Clean hands, area, and equipment.
2. Preheat oven to 325degrees.
3. Grease baking pan.
4. In small bowl, combine flour, baking soda, and salt, set aside.
5. In saucepan, combine sugar, butter, and water, bring to boil.
6. Remove from heat and put in mixing bowl.
7. Add chocolate chips and vanilla.
8. Stir until morsels are melted and mixture is smooth.
9. Add the eggs, one at a time.
10. Combine flour mixture and chocolate mixture.
11. Stir in chopped nuts and miniature marshmallows.
12. Spread into greased pan and bake at 325 degrees for 30 minutes.
13. Boy! Oh Boy!

No Bake Bonkers Banana

Materials:

4 pieces bread

1 cup chopped nuts

1/2 cup honey

4 bananas

8 tablespoons peanut butter

Directions:

1. Clean hands, area, and equipment.
2. Cut each piece of bread in half.
3. Cut each banana in slices.
4. Spread 1 tablespoon of peanut butter on each half piece of bread.
5. Place banana slices on top of peanut butter.
6. Drizzle with honey.
7. Sprinkle chopped nuts over honey.

Buttery "B" Cookies

Materials:

1 cup sugar

1 large egg

aluminum foil

oven 1/2 teaspoon ground cinnamon

refrigerator

1/2 teaspoon vanilla extract

4 1/2 cups all-purpose flour

1 1/2 cups butter, unsoftened

frosting/food coloring

bowls

Directions:

1. Clean hands, area, and equipment.
2. In big bowl, combine butter and sugar.
3. Beat until fluffy.
4. Beat in egg and vanilla.
5. Add flour, cinnamon, and mix thoroughly.
6. Chill.
7. Divide into equal balls. Give each child a ball, "B-b" cutters, piece of foil, and a bit of flour.
8. Preheat oven to 375 degrees.
9. Cut and place on foil.
10. Bake 6 to 9 minutes.
11. Cool.
12. Decorate and eat B-b's.

"B-b" Games/Activities

Beast Game

The teacher explains that a "beast" is a 4-footed animal, or any animal except a man. The teacher then writes any beast names from the "B-b" Animal List and "it" gives two to three clues. Students guess. The student who guesses correctly becomes "it".

Bear Hugs (A Center Activity)

Each student goes to the center to:
1. Trace a bear.
2. Cut out a bear.
3. Write a friend's name on the first line of the bear.
4. Write a message on the following lines.
5. Sign on the last line.
6. Deliver the bear hug to its intended recipient.

Bouncing Ball

The teacher designates first base, second, base, third base, and home. The child stands at home, reads the card or states if the word has /B-b/ sound. If she is correct, she proceeds to first base. The children are divided into equal teams. "Outs" occur when a student is incorrect.

Bingo

The children can sing Bingo; it is found in Silver Burdett Centennial Edition —1985. The game might also be played. Use a square tag board and divide it into 25 equal squares. Write "B-I-N-G-O" on the top and write 25/30/35 words on small cards. Use the cards to write the twenty-five words on. When the word is called, students place a marker on the word. The first child with markers five across, horizontal, or diagonally wins.

Bean Bag Bugaboo

The teacher sets up four cooperative or relay teams. This game can be played outdoors or indoors. The teacher uses chalk or tape to set up an equal course for each group. The teacher needs to obtain four sticks of equal length (yard sticks could be used) and four small bean bags. When teacher says "GO", each team sends two students on either side of the stick with the bean bag in the middle. The teams must walk the course with the beanbag on the stick. If the bag drops, the team must stop and put it back on before continuing. A team wins when everyone on the team has walked the course. This activity also builds up team spirit and positive interaction.

Bear Facts Book

Bears live all over the Earth. Bears are located/found in many countries. Panda bears are in China. Polar bears are in the arctic and brown and black bears are in America, Russia, and other countries. Bears are found in temperate and arctic zones and grizzly bears are found in America. They are heavy mammals, which walk on the soles of their feet, have shaggy fur, short tails, and hibernate. Have the students look into an encyclopedia and locate where the different bears are located/found, what kind they are, what they eat, and then make a class Bear Facts Book.

BOUNCING BUBBLES

Go outdoors and cover an area with butcher paper. Draw large circles. In the middle, have a large plastic bowl with: 1 cup Dawn™ liquid detergent, 2 cups warm water, 4 tablespoons glycerine (from drugstore), and bubble makers (straws or wires twisted to make a holder and circle). Each student dips and blows bubbles and a mark is made if the bubbles land in the circle. The colored circle with the most dots is the winner.

"B-B" BAG

The teacher could have items that start with a "B-b" (bat, ball, bell, boat, bus, bear, brush, book, and other items in a bag). Students must guess what the item is after hearing five clues. They have 20 guesses only!

"B-B" FLASH CARDS

The teacher could write the words on flash cards. The cards could contain pictures. Students could write sentences or paragraphs using 1-2-3 words. These paragraphs could be written using inventive spelling or dictating to another person/aide/tutor/teacher and copied.

"B-B" BASKETBALL

Construct a circle/hoop and use a foam-type ball for this game. The classroom is divided into four teams. Each team has an equal number of players. (If classroom is large, four teams can be formed.) The teams face "it." "It" shows the word (flashcard) for both teams. The team that reads it first and is correct, gets to throw the basketball through the hoop. If "it" makes the basket, the team wins a point. The team with the most points wins.

CRAZY "B-B" ANIMAL BOOK

There are many animal names that start with the /B-b/ sound. Have students research information about these "B-b" animals and write facts. The facts could then be scrambled/interchanged and a crazy book could be written about a bull that lives under water and eats carrots. Children love to read crazy books.

"B-b" Word Lists

Everyday Objects:

bag	ball	balloon
bat	barn	bus
bed	bell	bicycle
blanket	boat	blouse
button	broom	brush
bongo drums	bassoon	bulbs
book	bar	banjo
base	belt	box
bowl	bracket	buck
beak	beach	Buttercup
bubble	boy	bone
bike	bouquet	beret
bow	bill	back
bugle	bum	

Animals:

bear	buck deer	buffalo
bee	bird	beetle
bighorn sheep	bullfrog	bunny
bloodhound	Blesbok	bluefish
bumblebee	bulldog	Bactrian camel
bluejay	boar	boa
bison	bull	baboon
badger	beagle	beaver

Foods:

blueberries	beans	bell peppers
broccoli	beets	bacon
barbecue sauce	banana	basil
bagel	butter	buns
bamboo shorts	biscuit	berry
brussel sprouts	Brazilian nuts	bread
blueberry		

Descriptive Words/Action Words:

best	black	bad
bite	balance	bet
bounce	blue	bake
bit	battle	brown
beam	bump	blow
bright	beat	bunch
blew	big	beep
boil	burn	bought
beg	born	brought
brag		

Musical Instruments/Inventions:

bassoon	broom	blouse
boat	box	banjo
bicycle	balloon	bracket
belt	bell	barn
bat	ball	bongo drums
bugle		

"B-b" Reading Resources

Brown Bear, Brown Bear, What Do You See? — Bill Martin: Holt, Rinehart and Winston, 1984

Bear and Mrs. Duck — Elizabeth Winthrop: Holiday House, 1989

The Best Friends Club: A Lizzie and Harold Story — Elizabeth Winthrop: Lothrop,, 1990

Bridge to Terabithia — Katherine Paterson: Harper Trophy, 1977

The Black Stallion — Walter Farley: Knopf, 1941

Buffalo Woman — Paul Goble: Aladdin, 1984

Big Red — Jim Kjelgaara: Bantam, 1945

Babar's Anniversary Album — Jean and Laurent De Brunhoff: Knopf, 1933

Baboushka and the Three Kings — Ruth Robbins

Bananas: from Manolo To Margie — George Ancona

Beary More — Don Freeman: Puffin, 1968

Beastly Boys and Ghastly Girls — William Cole

Big Bad Bruce — Bill Peet: Houghton Mifflin, 1984

(The) Biggest Bear — Lynd Ward

Birthday Party and Other Tales — Annie Ching

Black Is Brown Is Tan — Arnold Adoff

Bobo's Dream — Martha Alexander

Bread and Jam For Francis — Russell Hoban: Harper Trophy, 1960

(The) Bremen Town Musicians — Grimm Brothers

Brian Wildsmith's A-B-C's — Brian Wildsmith

Bringing the Rain to Kapiti Plain — Verna Aardema: Pied Piper

Bunnicula: A Rabbit Tale of Mystery — Deborah and James Howe: Avon, 1979

Little Bear — Else H. Minarik: Harper Collins, 1957

(The) Three Bears — Paul Goldone

Ask Mr. Bear — Marjorie Flack: MacMillian, 1932/Puffin

Teddy Bears, 1 To 10 — Susanna Gretz: Follett, 1969

Benjamin's Book — Alan Baker, Lothrop, Lee, and Shepard, 1982

Bedtime for Frances — Russell Hoban: Harper Trophy, 1960

Best Friends — Steven Kellog: Pied Piper, 1985

Babushka — Arnold Russian Folktale & Charles Mikolaycak: Holiday, 1984

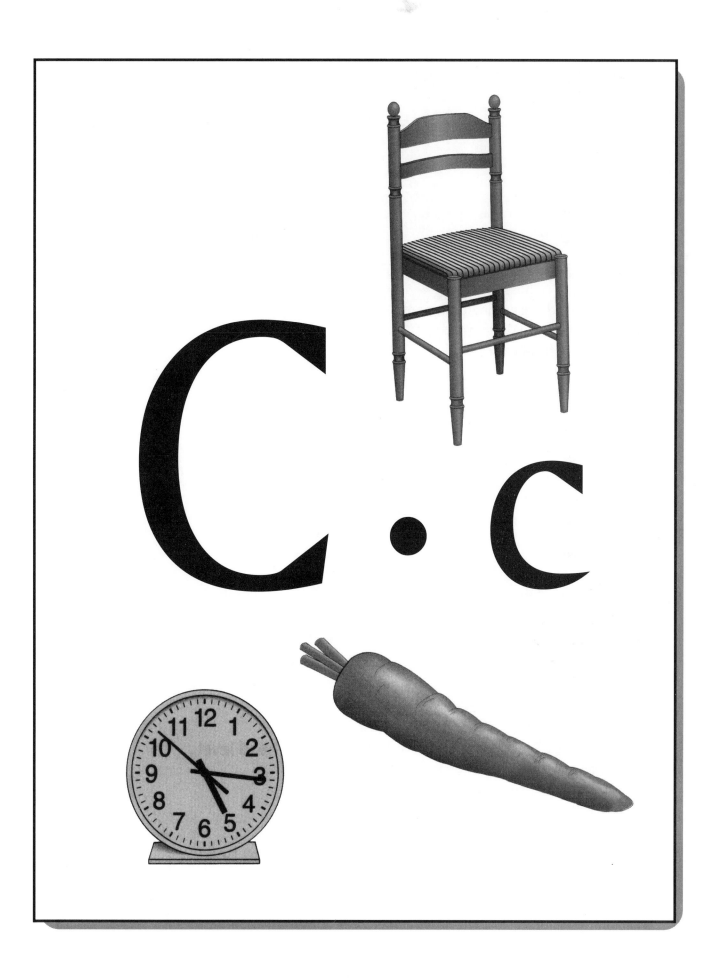

C-c Recipes

CLEVER, CAPABLE CART

Materials

spreader

knife

cutting board

cream cheese

toothpicks

celery

carrots

peeler

raisins, nuts, or trail mix

Directions:

1. Clean hands, area, and equipment.
2. Wash celery and carrots carefully.
3. Cut ends from celery stalks.
4. Peel carrots.
5. Slice carrots into disks, 4 slices per cart.
6. Spread cream cheese in the groove of the celery stalks.
7. Top with crawlers: raisins, nuts, or trail mix.
8. Attach wheels (carrots) to celery cart with toothpicks.

CRUNCHY CARAMEL CORN

Materials:

1 cup maple syrup

1 teaspoon vanilla

1 cup brown sugar

1 tablespoon butter

1/4 teaspoon salt

large bowl

wooden spoon

1/2 cup water

5 cups popped corn

2 cups peanuts/pecans

1 cup of crunchy cereal

saucepan

1-1/2 cups thin pretzel sticks

waxed paper

Directions:

1. Clean hands, area, and equipment.
2. Put sugar, syrup, salt, and water in saucepan.
3. Boil until 1/2 spoonful of mixture forms a "soft ball" when dropped into cold water.
4. Remove from heat and stir in butter and vanilla.
5. Mix popcorn, nuts, cereal, and pretzels in a large bowl.
6. Pour the syrup over the mixture.
7. Stir with a large wooden spoon until mixed completely.
8. Place clusters on waxed paper wrap and enjoy.

CAROB CANDY

Materials:

2 tablespoons butter
refrigerator
2 tablespoons honey
9" square pan
sauce pan

1 cup chopped almonds or walnuts
2 tablespoons carob powder
1 teaspoon vanilla
1/2 cup raisins

Directions:

1. Clean hands, area, and equipment.
2. Melt 2 tablespoons of butter in a saucepan.
3. Add 1 cup of chopped almonds, walnuts, and raisins.
4. Remove from heat.
5. Add 2 tablespoons of carob powder.
6. Add 2 tablespoons of honey.
7. Add 1 teaspoon of vanilla.
8. Stir well.
9. Grease a 9" square pan with butter.
10. Put into a 9" square pan.
11. Cool in the refrigerator.
12. Cut and enjoy.

COOKIE CREEPIES

Materials:

1 teaspoon cinnamon
1/4 cup granulated sugar
1/3 cup light corn syrup
raisins, nuts, trail mix

1/4 cup graham cracker crumbs
1/2 cup creamy peanut butter
Butter or margarine
refrigerator

Directions:

1. Clean hands, area, and equipment.
2. Mix graham cracker crumbs, sugar, and cinnamon.
3. Blend peanut butter and syrup.
4. Combine together.
5. Refrigerate for 20 minutes.
6. Coat hands with butter or margarine before modeling.
7. Model into creepy caterpillar or other "creepie."
8. Decorate with raisins, nuts, or trail mix to make a face.
9. Chill for several hours.

Christmas Chocolate Fudge

Materials:

3 cups sugar
1/2 cup evaporated milk
2 cups chocolate chips
1 teaspoon vanilla
pan

3/4 cup margarine
saucepan
1 jar marshmallow creme
1 cup nuts

Directions:

1. Clean hands, area, and equipment.
2. Combine sugar, margarine, and evaporated milk.
3. Place into saucepan.
4. Bring to a rolling boil, stirring constantly.
5. Boil for 5 minutes over medium heat, stirring constantly.
6. Remove from heat.
7. Add chocolate chips, marshmallow creme, vanilla, and nuts.
8. Beat until blended.
9. Pour into a greased pan.
10. Let it cool, then cut and enjoy.

Crazy Chili

Materials:

3 onions chopped
3 celery stalks
garlic salt
oregano
cumin
bay leaf
cutting board
knife
crock pot
wooden spoon

2 lbs. coarse ground beef
1 can of 6-oz tomato paste
2 cans of 16 oz stewed tomatoes
2 (#2) cans tomato sauce
3 chopped garlic cloves
2 bottles of 3 oz. chili powder
2 tablespoons salt
1 tablespoon ground pepper (unblended)
1 can green chilies (cooked, diced)
1 teaspoon chopped cilantro

Directions:

1. Clean hands, area, and equipment.
2. Brown beef and onions in fry pan (electric fry pan or at home & bring to school)
3. Put meat, onions, fat (from beef) into crock pot.
4. Chop celery, garlic, and add to pot.
5. Add all ingredients and season to taste.
6. Cook chili for about 2 1/2 to 3 hours.
7. Serve with corn bread, corn chips, or corn tortillas.

C-c Games/Activities

CHEESES

There are so many types of cheeses: Edam, Cottage, Cream, Cheddar, Monterey Jack, Swiss, Feta, Gruyere, etc. These could be cut and children could taste four or five different kinds and the results could be charted/graphed to determine the class' favorite. Other teachers/people could also give their opinion. The winners could be stated. A letter featuring the results could then be written to the cheese company.

COLORS, COLORS, COLORS

Children form a circle and then decide what their favorite color is, remember that color. One child is "it" and stands in the middle of the circle with chalkboard and eraser on the ground. "It" calls out a name of a color and that child tries to grab the eraser before he/she taps him/her. (Only one child can have the name of a color (blue, red, green, purple)). If "it" grabs the eraser first, the other child is put in the "paint can". The child that grabs the eraser before "it" is then "it."

CHILDREN CONCOCT A CLASS COOKIE.

Children read several cookie recipes. Children decide what the commonalties are in the recipe. Children then concoct/make up classroom cookie recipe and challenge other classrooms to have a cookie cook-off. Get the school to vote on most creative, colorful, crunchy, curious, comfortable cookie. Cookies could be sold for cash and other ingredients bought to concoct another type.

"CHUG-CHUG" DODGE BALL

Children form a circle. Four or five children form a "train"—Children line up one behind the other, hands on other children's waist. The first is the engineer and the last is the "caboose." Ball throwers aim for and try to hit caboose below the waist. The rest of the train says, "Chug, chug, chug, chug," and tries to protect the caboose with feet only. If the train falls apart, they may get back together. The train parts must cooperate and work together. The child in the circle that hits the caboose below the waist becomes the engineer. The engineer and all the train members move, form another train, and the game continues.

CHICK, CHICK, COW

Similar to "Duck, Duck, Goose." Children form a circle and sit. "It" has a handkerchief or eraser or object. It says, "Chick, chick, cow, chick, chick, cow," until "it" leaves the object behind a child. That child and "it" run around the circle until "it" sits in child's place or until child taps "it." If "it" is tapped he/she sits in the "chili pot" until someone replaces her/ him.

CAPTAIN SAYS

Children form into lines or assemble in front of "Captain." As on a ship or team "what the captain says goes". The captain states commands, like: "Touch your toes," and "Touch your head," and the children do it. If the Captain says "Touch your toes," without saying, "Captain says," and the child does the action, then the child sits down and is considered out. The last person up becomes the Captain.

CHICK-A-CHICK-A-CROW-CROW

This is similar to Steal the Bacon. The Chicks are in a line numbered from 1 to "?". The Crows are in one line facing the Chicks. They number one to "?" opposite of the Chicks (so that the last number is facing 1 and 1 is facing the last number). The eraser is in the middle. The chant is said by the teacher "Chick-a-Chick-a-Crow-Crow and a number, such as "3", and the 3 from the Chicks and the 3 from the Crows both try to take the eraser to their team without being tagged by the opposite team. The team with the most points wins.

CELEBRATION BOOK

Many of our students' parents, grandparents, aunts and/or uncles come from countries/cultures that celebrate holidays different/apart from the holidays that Americans celebrate. Make a class celebration book consisting of the name of the holiday and why the holiday is celebrated. A food recipe made especially for that celebration and maybe an object from that culture/area could be added. The object could be drawn on the page. Each child could get a copy of the book to share with their family. Its a total multicultural celebration.

CARROT PATCH

Carrot tops are cut, placed in glass pie plates and put in the sun. Water is added to cover 1/4 inch. Soon the carrot will grow a green stem and white roots. Carrot stems could also be planted in plastic bags with moist cotton or in potting soil or sponges.

CLEVER CLUES

Flash cards could be made and students could play 20 questions after "it" draws a word and gives three clever/good clues. Students continue to guess words or ideas until 20 questions are guessed. If they can't guess, "it" is it again. Many times after ten guesses are guessed, another clever clue could be given.

THE SOUNDS OF "C"

/C/ sounds like /K/ when followed by A-O-U. /C/ sounds like /S/ when followed by E or I or Y. Words could be written on flash cards. Students are told to point to a large /K/ card or /S/ card when they hear a C-c word and decide which sound it makes. Or older students could use a right hand or left hand to identify the sound. Teacher or "it" could read the word and the students must hear the word and determine/classify which sound the "C" makes. They receive a point if they are correct and the one that has the most points is then "it."

C-c CONTEST

Teacher could list about 20-25 words on the board. "It" could give three clues. Students then try to guess the C-c word. The student who guesses correctly is now "it." This helps with comprehension.

C-c Word Lists

car	cell	cap
can	cup	cut
cop	cart	calendar
crayon	cage	camera
candle	canoe	chair
chimney	church	comb
cause	contest	chart
cab	corduroy	cash
chapter	crown	cruise
chip	clue	cactus
coach	cage	card
carpet	cottage	cork
cow	crew	circle
clock	cart	chalk
clerk	clown	coil
coin	crane	claw
crocus		

Animals:

chameleons	cow	cub
carp	cuckoo	cockroach
cutworm	crow	crab
clam	cricket	crocodile
camel	caterpillar	cattle
cockatoo	cat	chaffinch
crane	crayfish	cougar
curlew	chinchilla	chimpanzee
cheetah	cod	crested newt
chamois	cuttle fish	cabbage worm
cabbage butterfly	cowbird	Crested Newt
Crocodile Bird	collie	civet

Foods:

cabbage	cake	candy
cantaloupe	crab	carrot
casaba melon	cashews	catfish
cauliflower	celery	cereal
cheese	cherry	chestnuts
chicken	chili	cinnamon
clams	cocoa	coconut
cookies	corn	chips
cucumber	currants	custard
cilantro	condiments	chocolate chips
cereal	corned beef	curry
cream	cider	citrus
clove	cob	cherry
chives	cod	coffee
currant	cafe-au-lait	

Descriptive Words/Verbs:

cheat	charm	chime
clear	caught	connect
cute	climb	command
cut	collect	came
come	could	call
cook	cool	carry
chew	curl	

Inventions/Musical Instruments:

castanets	crayons	candle
carpet	clock	coin
cup	crown	cage
cottage	cap	calendar
chart	cruise	chalk
canoe	church	clarinet
cymbals	coronet	concertina

Areas:

Cabinda	Caddo	Caelian
Caesarea	Caguas	Cagliari
Cairo	Caithness	Cajun
Calabria	Calais	Calcutta
Callao	Calvados	Calydon
Cambria	Cambridge	Cameroon
Campagna di Roma	Campeche	Campinas
Canaan	Canal Zone	Canary Islands
Canberra	Candia	Cannes
Cantabrigian	Cape Cod	Cape Dutch
Capua	Central America	Caracas

C-c Reading Resources

Cricket in Times Square — George Selden: Dell Yearling, 1960

Caps for Sale — Esphyr Slobodkina: Harper Trophy, 1947

Carrot Seed — Ruth Kraus (Harper and Row)1952

The Cat in the Hat — Dr. Seuss: Random House, 1956

The Very Hungry Caterpillar — Eric Carle: Philomel Publishing, 1969

Chair for My Mother — Veru B. Williams: Mulberry, 1982

Charlotte's Web — E.B. White: Harper Trophy, 1952

Charlie and the Chocolate Factory — Roald Dahl: Penguin, 1963

Chester the Wordly Pig — Bill Peet: Houghton Mifflin, 1985

Chicken Little — Steven Kellogg: Pied Piper, 1985

Child of the Owl — Laurence Yeb: Harper Trophy, 1979

Chinese Mother Goose Rhymes — Robert Wyndham

Cinderella — Charles Perrault: Aladdin, 1954

Corduroy — Don Freeman: Puffin, 1968

Corn Is Maize: The Gift of the Indians — Aliki: Mulberry, 1984

Cranberry Thanksgiving — Wende and Harry Derilin: Four Winds, 1971

Crow Boy — Taro Yashima

The Great Cheese Conspiracy — Jean Lee Uwen

If You Give a Mouse a Cookie — Laura Numeroff: Harper & Row, 1985

Millions of Cats — Wanda Gag

Curious George — H.A. Rey: Houghton Mifflin, 1942

Cleaver of the Good Luck Diner — James Duffy: Scribner's, 1990

Catwings — Ursula K. Leguin: Scholastic/Orchard, 1988

Cupid — Babette Cole: Putnam, 1991

Crazy Clothes — Niki Yektai: Bradbury, 1989

Chocolate Dreams — Arnold Adoff: Lothrop, 1990

Chicka Chicka Boom Boom — Bill Martin Jr. and John Archambault: Simon & Schuster, 1990

Changes, Changes — Pat Hutchins: Aladdin, 1971

Cloudy with a Chance of Meatballs — Judith Barrett: Aladdin, 1978

Cat Goes Fiddle-I-Fee — Paul Galdone, 1985

El Chino — Allan Say: Houghton Mufflin, 1990

The Crane Wife — Sumiko y Agawa: Mulberry, 1981

The Chocolate Touch — Patrick Skene Catling: Bantam, 1979

Cowboys of the Wild West — Russell Friedman Clarion, 1985

The Carrot Seed — Ruth Kraus: Harper and Row, 1945

Charlie Needs a Cloak — Tomie DePola Prentice: Hall, 1973

Cat Goes Fiddle-I-Fee — Paul Galdone: Clarion, 1988

Carousel — Donald Crews: Greenwillow Books, 1982

The Jolly Christmas Postman — Janet and Allan Ahlberg: Little Brown and Co., 1991

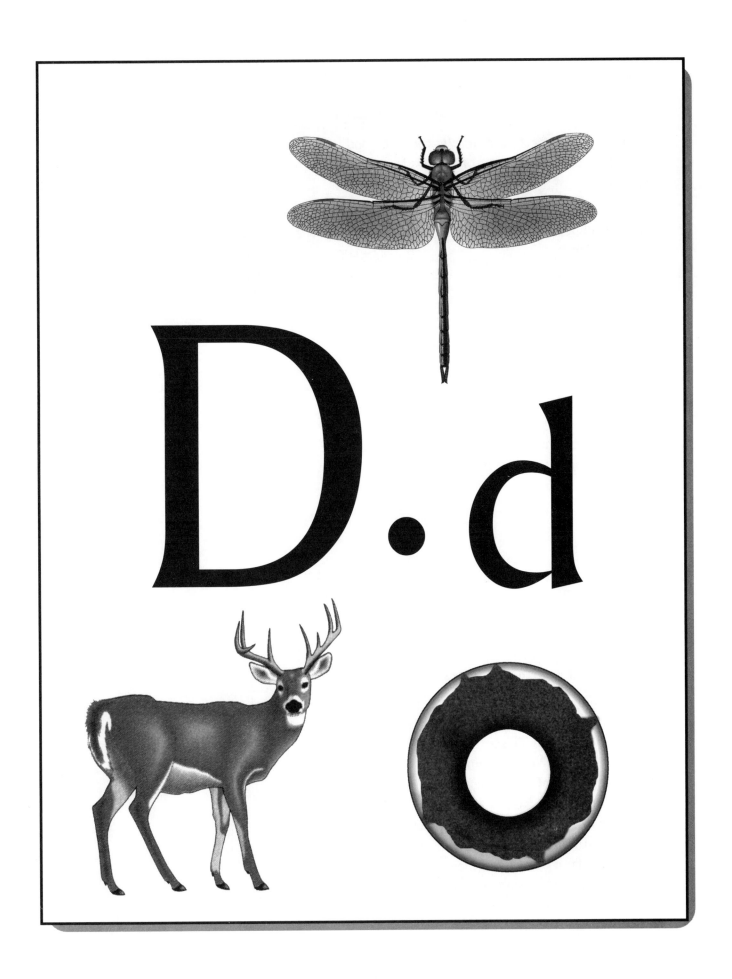

D·d

D-d Recipes

DIPS

Guacamole—be sure to use lime/lemon juice and keep covered till served. (You can also put pits in to keep from turning brown.) Refrigerate until the time comes to use it.

Materials:

ground cumin

1/4 onion-chopped

garlic powder

bowls

spoons

3 ripe avocados (peeled & pitted)

2 tablespoons cilantro (chopped)

1/4 cup lime/lemon juice

chili powder or pepper

tabasco sauce (hot sauce)

Directions:

1. Clean hands, area, and equipment.
2. Mash avocados.
3. Blend in cilantro (chopped), onion (chopped), salt/pepper, and ground cumin to taste.
4. Add fresh lime/lemon juice.
5. Stir.
6. Add seasonings to taste.
7. Serve with tortilla strips, chips, baked tortillas, or with vegetables like celery, carrots, cucumbers, and/or jicama.

DELIGHTFUL DOUGHNUTS

Materials:

plastic bag

1-2 cloth aprons

mitt pot holders

1 cup sugar

1/2 cup cinnamon

electric skillet — with high edges/sides

slotted spoon

biscuit cutter

2-3 tubes of refrigerator biscuit dough

paper towels

2 cans Crisco™

Directions:

1. Clean hands, area, and equipment.
2. Open 2 cans of Crisco™.
3. Heat Crisco™ until boiling.
4. Open tubes of refrigerator biscuits.
5. Cut holes with biscuit cutter.
6. Drop dough in hot shortening carefully.
7. Fry until golden brown.
8. Use slotted spoon to remove and place on paper towels.
9. Put delightful doughnuts in plastic bag with sugar and cinnamon.
10. Shake! Shake! Shake!

BAKER'S DOUGH #1

Materials:

4 cups of flour
1 cup of salt

1 1/2 cups of warm water
acrylic paints and varnish

Directions:

1. Clean hands, area, and equipment.
2. Mix all ingredients into a bowl.
3. Knead dough for 5 to 10 minutes.
4. Roll out dough to 1/4 inch thick.
5. Cut with cookie cutters or sculpt.
6. Make a hole at the top.
7. Bake at 250 degrees for 2 to 2 1/2 hours or until golden brown.
8. When cool, paint with acrylics and varnish.

BAKER'S DOUGH #2

Materials:

1 1/4 cups water
3 cups flour
1 cup salt

2 tablespoons corn starch
2 teaspoons cooking oil
food coloring

Directions:

1. Clean hands, area, and equipment.
2. In a large bowl, combine oil, salt, water and slowly add starch and flour.
3. Mix.
4. Knead until smooth. Flour may be added, if sticky.
5. Add food coloring if desired.
6. Sculpt.

DUCKY-DOUGH

Materials:

2 cups flour
1 cup butter
aluminum foil

a few drops of yellow food coloring
3/4 cup powdered sugar

Directions:

1. Clean hands, area, and equipment.
2. Mix flour and powdered sugar.
3. Add 1 cup butter and a few drops of yellow food color.
4. Shape dough into duck-shape on foil.
5. Bake at 325 degrees for 10 minutes.

Play Dough™

Materials:

1 cup flour

1 tablespoon oil

1 tablespoon of salt

1 cup water

1 teaspoon vanilla

2 teaspoons food coloring

2 teaspoons cream of tartar

Directions:

1. Clean hands, area, and equipment.
2. Mix flour, oil, water, salt, cream of tartar, and food coloring.
3. Heat in a saucepan over medium heat.
4. Cook until mixture forms a ball.
5. Knead until smooth.
6. Store in refrigerator.
7. Dough must be at room temperature to be used.
8. May be used repeatedly.

Double-Duty Pizza
(Mexican-Style Pizza)

Materials:

grater

cutting board

bowl

knife

pastry brush

oven/toaster oven

1/2 cup sliced olives

1 jar of pizza sauce

1/2 to 1 cup parmesan cheese

1/4 teaspoon crushed red pepper

1/2 tablespoon cilantro

1/2 can chili beans and sauce

1/2 teaspoon pizza seasoning

1/4 teaspoon dried oregano

1/4 sliced/chopped red/green bell pepper (optional)

1 1/2 cups shredded Mozzarella cheese, cheddar cheese, or both.

1 12" prepared pizza crust (select correct size if using toaster oven) or Italian Bread Shell. (Individual bread shells could also be purchased.)

1 lb. ground beef

Directions:

1. Clean hands, area, and equipment.
2. Grate Mozzarella and/or cheddar cheese.
3. Brown ground beef and drain.
4. Mix beef with chili beans & sauce.
5. Spread bean/beef sauce onto pizza crust & seasonings.
6. Sprinkle cheese(s), olives, pepper, and cilantro.
7. Bake 10-15 minutes at 350 to 400 degrees until cheese has melted and share (that's the double duty).

D-d Games/Activities

DELIGHTFUL DANDY DOLLS

Girl and boy shaped dandy dolls could be made of paper, tag board, corn husks, and/or socks. The head, hands, and feet are cotton balls. Rubber bands hold the shape at the neck, arms, and legs. These dandy dolls could then be dressed to reinforce the D-d sound. They can be used to play families and work on social skills.

DUCKS ON PARADE

Children could line up and play "Ducks On Parade." The person who is "it" leads and all of the ducklings follow. Mamma Duck could hop, waddle, walk, and the ducklings would copy it. A timer is set for 1 or 2 minutes so that several students get a chance to be Mamma Duck.

D-D TRICK

A trick or hint could be told to help students who have trouble learning D-d from B-b. Have student point thumb in the air and make a fist with the four fingers. The palms should face each other. The left hand is first and it's a "b" and the right hand is second and it's a "d."

D-D BAG

A D-d bag could consist of a dish (plastic), dominoes, doll (plastic), a dragon, dinosaur, duck (plastic), and the "teacher" who has the bag chooses one thing and gives three clues. The other students try to guess what is in the bag. After ten guesses, another clue could be given. The student that guesses the object is then the "teacher".

D-D BOOK

A D-d book can be made with cut up pictures from discarded books, catalogs, magazines, and old workbooks. A line can then be written or dictated describing the object. A disjointed picture could also be made. Several parts are cut out and glued together to make a disjointed _____ (put object's name on space) and the children could name and describe their D-d pictures.

D-D DRUMS

Drums can be made of coffee cans, oatmeal boxes, and salt boxes. Canvas or rubber from tires can then be cut to cover the top and bottom. The material or rubber must be at least 1 inch greater in diameter than the can or box. Drums can be played with wooden spoons, or sticks covered with canvas/material, or hands. In earlier days, hides would cover the containers. Indians would paint them and use them for many ceremonies.

DAD BOOKS

"Dad" books could be made with the first page stating his name. The rest of the pages might then describe what color he likes best, his favorite food, his favorite car, what his job is, if he likes it, what jobs he does around the house and anything the child wants to dictate about his dad.

DOODLEBUGS

"Doodlebugs" can be made or drawn. Each child learns that bugs, another name for insects, have three parts fused together with six legs. Their bugs can have long, short, curved antennae, furry or non-furry legs, spotted striped or crazy shaped bodies, and what they eat will differ. They may want to draw pinchers. (They could then write a sentence/ paragraph describing his/her Doodlebug.)

DAFFY DOT

"Daffy Dot" designs can be made. A glue bottle and many colored holes from a paper punch or dots are supplied to the children, and they construct their design, of dots and glue, on black construction paper. A line(s) can then be glued on for children to write what their Daffy Dot design is.

DANDY DRAGON

A "dandy dragon" is a mythical monster, which may have wings and claws. It can also breathe fire. Have students paint and draw, or color a picture of a dandy dragon. Have student write/dictate about their dragon and make a class book. Books about dragons can be made available.

DOMINOES

Dominoes can be made or purchased. Children like to match the dots (0-6). Picture dominoes can also be purchased or made of matching pictures on tag/railroad board, then laminated. Each child draws five to seven dominoes from the center pile and takes turns matching one side of the piece to the other. Each piece is divided into two pictures or dots. The first one who doesn't have any pieces left is the winner.

DEAR DOGS

Dogs are man's best friend. Children can draw pictures/paint/cutout pictures of dogs or bring pictures of their dogs from home. Those children who do not own a dog can cut one out of a magazine/catalog or discarded book. "Dear Dog" class books could be made. Each student tells: the dog's name, what they eat, like to do, their breed, and what color they are. These are each "dear-dogs".

DUCK DUCK GOOSE

"Duck, Duck, Goose" can also be played. Have the children sit in a circle. The person/child who is "it" says, "Duck, duck, duck..." and taps each student on the head, or shoulder. When he wants another student to chase him/ her around the circle he/she says "Goose." The Goose chases the duck around the circle until the duck sits down in the Goose's place. If the Goose catches the Duck, the Duck must then sit in the middle of the circle. Goose then says the "Duck, duck, duck..." words and the game goes on.

D-d Word Lists

Everyday Objects:

dandelion	door	drill
doctor	dishwasher	dump
dentist	dancer	decibel
ditch	drills	debt
dart	dirt	drum
dial	dish	day
dawn	door	disk
decanter	diamond	dome
dam	degrees	daughter
dock	door	diaper
daffodil	dwarf	dahlia
daisy	dust	diplomat
democracy		

Animals:

duck	dinosaur	dog
dragonfly	Dingo	dolphin
dachshund	Dromedary camel	deerfly
Dutch Belted	dungbeetle	devil fish
Doberman Pinscher	dollarfish	Dalmatian
deer	deer mouse	Dodo
dugong	deerhound	duckling
dogfish	Diamond-back Terrapin	

Foods/food related:

doughnuts	dates	desserts
drumsticks	deviled eggs	dumplings
decaffeinated coffee	dipping sauces	dips
duck	dandelion greens	dairy
Danish pastry	drupe	degree
digest	dine	diner

Descriptive words/things:

down	dainty	dance
double	dope	dose
doodle	dowry	dandy
danger	dark	display
draft	dash	daze
dazzle	dead	drag
deal	dear	death
debit	Dodger	decay
decide	deck	deep
disobey	dock	divine
defeat	default	dime
deficit	driven	duty
dull	dug	dry
difficult	drive	different
dreary	deadbeat	dead duck
deadlock	dirigible	diploma
didy	deed	delirious
demon	dictator	

Action words:

debate	decay	deal
decorate	declare	defend
decrease	deliver	delay
demand	die	

Inventions/Musical Instruments:

drum	diaper	ditch
dart	dial	decanter
dam	dock	door
dishwasher	drill	dish
disk	drills	decibel
debt	dome	debate

D-d Reading Resources

Dinosaur Garden — Lisa Donnelly: Scholastic, 1990

Make Way for Ducklings — Robert McCloskey

Case of the Elevator Duck — P. Berends

What Happened to Dinosaurs — Bernard Most: Voyager, 1978

What Happened to Patrick's Dinosaurs — Carol and Donald Carrick

When the Drum Sang: An African Folk Tale — Anne Rockwell

Doctor Desoto — William Steig

Dancing in the Moon: Counting Rhymes — Fritz Eichenberg: Voyager, 1955

The Day Jimmy's Boa Ate the Wash — Trinka Noble: Pied Piper, 1980

Don't Touch My Room — Patricia Larkin: Joystreet/Little, Brown, 1982

The Dancing Granny — Ashley Bryan: Aladdin, 1977

Dinosaurs Divorce: A Guide for Changing Families — Brown Marc, & Laurence Joystreet/Little, Brown.

Danny and the Dinosaur — Syd Hoff: Harper Collins (I Can Read), 1958

Digging Up Dinosaurs — Aliki: Harper Trophy, 1981

Dinnie Abbie Sister/R/R — Riki Levinson: Bradbury, 1987

Dinosaurs Are Different — Aliki: Harper Collins, 1985

Daddy-Long-Legs — Jean Webster: Bantam, 1982

Danny the Champion of the World — Ronald Dahl: Puffin, 1975

A Dark Dark Tale — Ruth Brown: Pied Piper, 1981

Dawn — Uri Shulevitz: Sunburst, 1974

Dad's Car Wash — Harry A. Sutherland: Atheneum, 1989

The Day the Dragon Came to School — Marie Tenaille: Alladin, 1989

The Dinosaur Who Lived in My Backyard — B. G. Hennessy: Viking, 1989

The Dog — John Burningham: Crowell, 1975

Dogs and Dragons, Trees and Dreams — Karla Kuskin: Harper and Row, 1980

Dinosaur Bones — Berenstein: Beginner Books, 1980

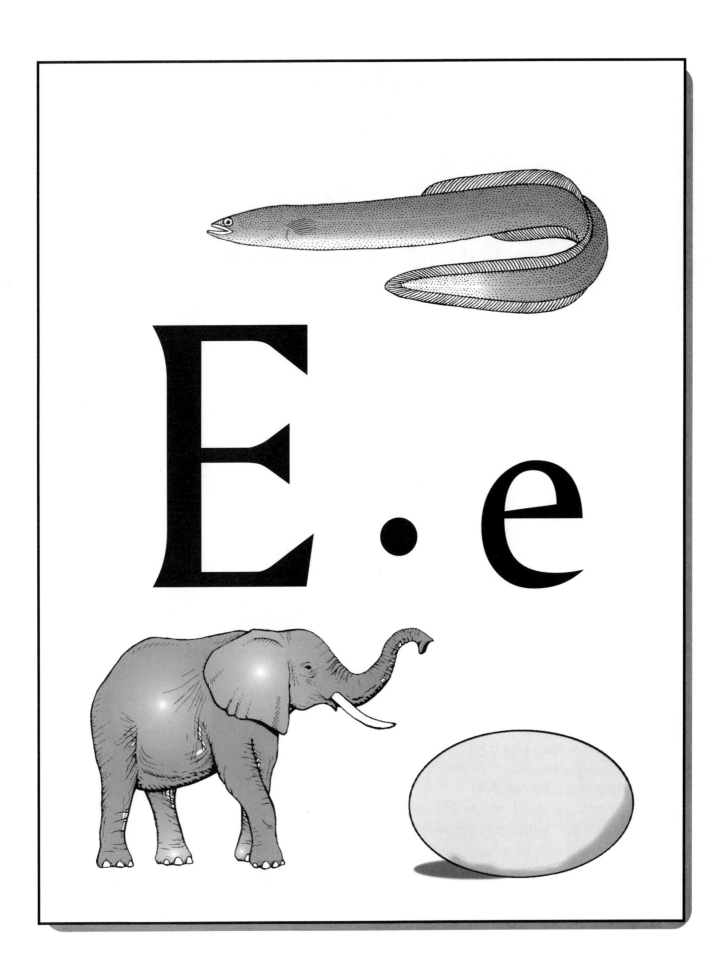

E · e

E-e Recipes

Exceptional Electric Green Eggs

Materials:

1 electric frying pan
2 tablespoons butter
1/4 cup milk
1/4 cup shredded cheese
8 large eggs

2 drops green food coloring
seasonings
1 wooden spoon
1 plastic container
plastic spoons and plates

Directions:

1. Clean hands, area, and equipment.
2. Crack each egg on the side of a bowl.
3. Put each egg into the plastic container.
4. Add green food coloring, milk, cheese and seasonings and shake.
5. Heat electric frying pan to 350 degrees and melt butter.
6. Add egg mixture to melted butter and stir with a wooden spoon.
7. Cook and stir until the eggs are fluffy, about 2-3 minutes.
8. Electric! Enjoy.

Elegant Eggs

Materials:

1 sauce pan
1/3 cup mayonnaise
1 mixing bowl
paprika or olives
stuffings (crumbled cheddar cheese, cooked chicken, chopped celery, bacon bits, and/or canned crab meat)

6 eggs
1 tablespoon of vinegar
salt

Directions:

1. Clean hands, area, and equipment.
2. medium heat.
3. When water is boiling at medium heat. Add salt and the rest of the vinegar and boil eggs the same way for 15 minutes.
4. Let eggs cool; peel and cut into two equal parts lengthwise.
5. Take out yolks carefully.
6. Combine yolks with mayonnaise and your choice of stuffings.
7. Return yolk mixture to egg whites and cool.
8. Decorate with paprika or olives.
9. Enjoy elegantly!

EASTER DOUGH

Materials:

2 drops food coloring	2 cups flour
2 cups water	1 bowl
white glue	aluminum foil
plastic bottles	yarn
acrylics or markers	glitter

Directions:

1. Clean hands, area, and equipment.
2. Place food coloring, water, and flour in a bowl and mix. This is Easter Dough.
3. Use white glue to make an oval egg shape on aluminum foil.
4. Place yarn on glue.
5. Let it dry thoroughly.
6. Pour Easter dough into plastic bottles.
7. Fill in yarn oval by squeezing Easter dough into designs.
8. Dry, then peel off.
9. Acrylics, markers, or glitter can be used to finish decorating.

ENORMOUS ELEPHANT

Materials:

1 electric frying pan	1 spatula
1 large bowl	1 banana
2 chocolate cookies	2 teaspoons baking powder
3/4 cup flour	2 teaspoons salt
1/2 cup milk	2 eggs
1/4 cooking oil	camera

Directions:

1. Clean hands, area, and equipment.
2. Mix baking powder, flour, salt, milk, and eggs in bowl.
3. Cook in heated oil in an electric frying pan.
4. Cook two circles per elephant.
5. Put largest enormous elephant circle (about 4") on plate.
6. Cut second circle in half and put on sides of whole circle for ears.
7. Use banana slice for trunk.
8. Add cookies or candy for eyes.
9. Take picture before eating.

ECSTASY SQUARES

Ingredients:

1 1/2 cups graham cracker crumbs
1 cup chopped walnuts and almonds combined
1 teaspoon cinnamon
1/4 cup brown sugar
1 cup flaked coconut
2 tablespoons milk
9"x13" pan (greased with margarine)
7 oz. jar marshmallow cream or 1 large can of sweetened condensed milk

3 cups chocolate chips
6 tablespoons melted butter
oven
1 teaspoon vanilla

Directions:

1. Clean hands, area, and equipment.
2. Preheat oven at 350 degrees.
3. Combine graham cracker crumbs, sugar, butter, and cinnamon in large bowl.
4. Press into pan.
5. Bake for 7-10 minutes. Afterwards, remove and cool.
6. Mix chocolate chips, coconut, and nuts.
7. Cover over crumb mixture.
8. Mix together marshmallow cream with milk and vanilla (or condensed milk).
9. Drizzle over chips.
10. Bake for 15 more minutes.
11. Cool and cut. Ecstasy!

ELEMENTARY EGG NOG

Materials:

blender
1 quart of milk
1/2 dozen eggs
(keep in refrigerator until ready to use)

glasses
1 teaspoon vanilla
any flavored ice cream to taste

Directions:

1. Clean hands, area, and equipment.
2. Blend cold eggs, milk, and vanilla.
3. Add ice cream to taste.
4. Pour into glasses.
5. Say, "It's Elementary."

EASY ENCHILADAS

Multicultural-Spanish flavored (4 tortillas dipped into sauce and rolled). It has a filling. It is covered with a sauce and baked.

Materials:

2-3 cans of enchilada sauce (10 oz.)
2 cups grated cheddar cheese
1 doz. corn tortillas   1 small onion, chopped
1 can diced chiles (4 oz.)   baking dish
1 can sliced black olives   grater (if necessary)
electric fry pan   spoon knife
oven bowl

Directions:

1. Clean hands, area, and equipment.
2. Heat enchilada sauce in electric fry pan until bubbly (on medium heat).
3. Turn off heat. Dip each tortilla in sauce until softened.
4. Blend grated cheese, chopped onion, sliced olives, and chiles in bowl.
5. Fill each softened tortilla and roll.
6. Cover bottom of baking dish with 1/2 sauce.
7. Place each enchilada into dish.
8. Cover with remaining 1/2 of sauce.
9. Sprinkle with remaining cheese, onion, olive, chili mixture.
10. Bake for 25-30 minutes at 350 degrees.
11. Serve with sour cream.

E-e Games/Activities

ELEPHANT PARADE

Student extends arms like a trunk of an elephant. The elephant/student moves his arms together from side to side and bends over. Slow moving music could be played. "Elephants" walk in a circle surrounded by chairs or walk on pieces of paper, swinging their trunks, and a paper tail could be taped on for tails. When the music stops, the elephant without a chair or piece of paper to stand on or sit on is out. The game continues until only 1 elephant is left. He is "it" and plays the music.

EXCITING EGGHEADS

Have each student save an egg. Remove raw egg from each shell by blowing (directions on Egg Shell trees). Break eggs in half. Allow students to draw faces on each half-shell with permanent ink. Put commercial soil into 3/4s of each half-shell. Sprinkle grass seeds into each egghead and cover with soil. Water/sprinkle carefully each day. Students can estimate the length of hair each egghead will grow. Students can take home their eggheads in egg cartons cut into halves or fourths.

EARTH GAME

Teacher lists 30-35 words from E-e list that relate to the Earth and may be found on the Earth. "It" gives 3-4 clues and students guess. They only have 20 chances to guess. The child/student who guesses the word correctly becomes "it". If no one guesses, "it" remains "it" again.

EGG YOLK PAINT

Use 2 well-mixed yolks. 1/4 teaspoon of water and 2 drops of food coloring. Also, use a new or very clean thin paint brush. Blend egg yolk into water, add food coloring. Paint a design on white bread. E-e's could be painted. (If this has been out of the refrigerator 20 minutes, or longer, DO NOT EAT!)

"E-E" BOOKS

"E-e" books can be made from pictures found in catalogs, discarded (text) books, newspapers, and old magazines. Each child must find a picture/object/thing either starting with an "E-e" or has an "E-e" sound in it. Then either dictate or write what it is and its function. A class book could be made with each child's page added to it. It could be added to the classroom library. A cover could also be made of sandpaper, cut out in the shape of capital-lower case E-e.

E-E FLASHCARDS

The teacher makes flashcards of all the E-e words with illustration. The students then sit at a center or in a reading circle. They use the words in a sentence. They can also be asked to classify them (long/short vowels — nouns/verbs).

EGG SHELL TREES

1) Get a branch. Dry it. Use Plaster of Paris to secure branch into container. Allow it to dry.
2) Blow raw eggs. (Using a fresh raw egg, poke small holes in both sides and blow). When egg is dry, rinse it carefully.
3) Dye or paint eggs.
4) Use a pipe cleaner (folded in half) and stick bent cleaner carefully inside egg — twisting shell until it holds.
5) Attach circle to the branch.

BIG-LITTLE E's

The teacher makes a pattern of a large and small "E" and the smaller children copy it. Students then glue the E's onto paper. (Use either on tag or construction paper.) They could fill it with E's found in alphabet soup, E's from alphabet cereal, or broken eggshells.

FIND THE "E-e"

Children are be given the newspaper and a felt marker or pencil. The timer is set for 2-5 minutes. The child who finds the most E-e's wins. They could then cut them out and paste them to a paper.

"E-e" GAME: ONE FINGER OR TWO

Words like: ear, eat, exit, elf, feed, seed, egg, edge, ever, else, elm, exit, echo, feet, excel, wet, met, pet, get, let, pen, ten, hem, bed, red, fed, set, bet, den, hen, keg, them, stem, fell, yell, sell, pest, rest, test, jet, vet, wet, best, vest, deck, peck, leg, meet, beet, week, peek, cheek, deep, jeep, sleep, weak, beak, leak, heat, beat, and meat could be made onto flash cards. Teacher states the word. If the word has a short /e/ sound, the student puts up one finger; if the word has a long /e/ sound, the child puts up two fingers. The child with the most points wins.

EASY EASEL BOOK

Each child is given a flashcard with a word that begins with "E-e" or has an "E-e" sound. The child then dictates or writes about that "E-e" word. He names it and name's its function. (This is totally creative—not bound by a picture.) He/she could also make up a word that starts with an "E-e" sound, tells its color, and describes it in any way that he/she wants. Then he paints a picture of it using his words. When the picture dries and is glued to a paper. A class book is made of an Easel book.

EPITOME

This is a short statement (of the main parts) of a book or a summary. The class could read one of the "E" books together, or have it read to them. Each student could write a short summary or main idea of the book and illustrate it. It could be published and kept in the class library to review or refresh the idea of the book.

E-e Word Lists

Short "E" words in the initial position:

eggs	empty	elephant
elf	edge	else
echo	egg rolls	Eskimo
elderberry	end	eggnog
every	elementary	egg plant
egg foo young	enchilada	endive

Long "E" words in the initial position:

even	eraser	equal
ear	evil	eclairs
eat	eerie	eagle
each	ease	easy
eel	emu	easily
Easter	easel	eaves
erratic	essential	eve
eke	eager	eaten
eastern	effective	efficient
east		

Short "E" Words with vowel in medial position:

when	let	set
spell	best	deck
get	jet	then
them	went	next
beg	den	hen
keg	very	help
red	bet	fell
hem	leg	left
tell	well	bell
bed	fed	met
let	peck	peg
sell	vet	west
yen	yell	pen

52

pest	set	ten
vest	well	yet
mend	lend	spend
wet	trend	chest

Long "E" in the medial position:

beep	bean	cheat
feet	jean	leap
beet	beat	deed
heel	keep	leak
beak	cheek	deep
heat	seed	lean
beam	cheap	feed
jeep	seek	sheep
seem	sheet	meet
team	peep	week
meter	female	mean
need	seep	weak
react	being	meat
teen	really	peach
peek	depot	sea
see	tea	flea
weed	three	wheat
read	given	area
least	beat	clean
legal	deal	leaf
feast		

Foods:

eclairs	egg foo young	eggnog
eggplant	egg rolls	eggs
elderberry	enchilada	endive

Animals:

eagle	eel	elephant
elk	emus	ermine
echidna	elf owl	earwig
Eskimo dog	eft	emu

Other E-e words:

Easter	ear	earth
easy	eat	echo
edge	eight	elementary
eleven	elf	elm
emerald	end	enemy
energy	engine	enter
eraser	even	every
evil	excited	exit
equipment	elastic	eerie
envelope	enjoy	Edelweiss
equal	eye	explain
epidemic	engage	extinct
evergreens	edge	

Inventions/Musical Instruments:

electric guitar	eraser	engine
elastic	envelope	equipment
endowment	English horn	engrave
ensign	entertainment	epaulets
epergne	epic	episode
epitome	epoxy	erection
escutcheon	error	escape
estate	ether	etch

Descriptive words:

enormous	enhance	euphemistic
enigma	equator	equity
excellent	exceptional	evil
exactly	evident	excitable
exclusive	excited	extended
execrable	executory	exogenous

E-e Reading Resources

The Elephant — Arnold Lobel: Scholastic, 1981

Eggs — Wonderbooks, 1971

The Enormous Egg — Butterworth: Dell Yearling, 1956

Green Eggs and Ham — Dr. Seuss: Random House, 1960

Emperor's New Clothes — Hans Christian Anderson: Harper Trophy, 1982

Elves and Shoe Maker — Grimm Brothers

Emma's Pet — David McPhail: Unicorn, 1984

Duke Ellington — King Of Jazz: Elizabeth Montgomery

Elephant's Child — Rudyard Kipling

Eloise — Kay Thompson: Simon & Schuster, 1955

The Elephant and Bad Baby — Elfrida Vipont: Coward, 1987

Ernest and Celestine — Gabrielle Vincent: Mulberry, 1982

Encyclopedia Brown — Donald Sobol: Bantam, 1963

Every Living Thing — Cynthia Rylant: Bradbury, 1985

Each Peach Pear Plum, An "I Spy" Story — Janet & Alan Ahlberg: Puffin, 1979

Eyes of the Dragon — Margaret Leaf: Lothrop, Lee & Shepard, 1987

The Little Engine that Could — Watty Piper: Scholastic, Inc., 1961

Even that Moose Won't Listen to Me — Martha Alexander: Dial, 1989

The Empty Pot — Demi, Holt, 1991

Ester's Trunk — Jez Alborough: Warner, 1989

Elbert's Bad Word — Audrey Wood: Harcourt Brace Jovanovich, 1989

Eagle-Eye Ernie Comes to Town — Susan Pearson: Simon & Schuster, 1991

Emily and the Enchanted Frog — Helen V. Griffith: Greenwillow, 1990

The Enormous Crocodile — Roald Dahl: 1978

Everybody Needs a Rock — Byrd Baylor: Scribners, 1974

The Eyes of the Amaryllis — Natalie Babbitt: Sunburst, 1977

The Egypt Game — Zilpha Keatley Snyder: Dell Yearling, 1967

Einstein Anderson: Science Sleuth — Seymour Simon, Puffin, 1980

Earth Songs — Myra Cohn Livingston: Holiday, 1985

Ella — Bill Pete: Houghton Mifflin, 1984

The Most Wonderful Egg in the World — Helme Heine: Anthenium, 1983

Emma's Christmas — An old song resung and pictures by Irene Trivas: Orchard Books, 1988

Everyone Knows What a Dragon Looks Like — Jay Williams: Four Winds, 1976

— Lois Ehlert: Trumpet Club, 1989

F·f

F-f Recipes

Fruity-Fresh Fruit Salad

Materials:

1 wooden cutting board	1 can fruit cocktail
1 can mandarin oranges	1 pear
1 bunch of grapes	1 cup miniature marshmallows
1/4 cup broken walnuts	1/2 cup mayonnaise
1 large bowl	mixing spoons
1 knife	can opener
1 cup marshmallow creme	

Directions:

1. Clean hands, area, and equipment.
2. Open can of fruit cocktail and mandarin oranges and drain.
3. Dice apple, pear, banana (quickly in the juice so it will not discolor), and grapes.
4. Place fruit in large bowl with canned fruits (drain).
5. Add walnuts and marshmallows.
6. Combine mayonnaise and marshmallow creme in small bowl.
7. Mix.
8. Blend small bowl (mayonnaise and creme) with large bowl (fruits and nuts).
9. Stir only until blended.

Fun Fondue

Materials:

cut up fruit into large chunks/pieces like: bananas, apples, pears, strawberries, and sweet cinnamon or raisin bread.

1 sauce pan	knife
1 hot plate	cutting board
1/2 stick of butter	1/4 teaspoon cinnamon added to sauce
1 pkg. (12 oz) semi-sweet chocolate chips	
1/2 can sweetened condensed milk	
1 pkg. of new bamboo sticks (skewers)	

Directions:

1. Clean hands, area, and equipment.
2. Over low heat, melt and keep butter, chocolate, and milk warm.
3. Cut up fruit and put on, 1 or 2 pieces per skewer only.
4. Dip fruit into sauce.
5. Fun, fun, fun.

Fajitas

Materials:

1 to 1-1/2 pounds flank steak or chicken breast

1 spatula	1 tablespoon vegetable oil
1 knife	1 wooden cutting board
1 medium onion	1 medium bell pepper (may omit)
1/8 teaspoon cumin	1 package fajitas seasoning mix
1 electric frying pan	1 package flour tortillas

1 teaspoon of fresh cilantro (optional)

1/8 teaspoon chili powder

toppings (guacamole, sour cream, cheese, canned or bottled salsa)

Directions:

1. Clean hands, area, and equipment.
2. Cut steak or chicken into thin strips.
3. Cut onion and green pepper into thin strips.
4. Dice tomatoes, onions, and cilantro (optional).
5. Dice avocados or mash into guacamole.
6. Warm tortillas in aluminum foil.
7. Heat oil in electric fry pan.
8. Add vegetables (peppers and onions) and stir.
9. Add meat or chicken strips.
10. Stir until just cooked—about 5 minutes.
11. Drain.
12. Add fajitas seasoning mix and, 1/2 cup water.
13. Simmer until meat is coated.
14. Serve meat and vegetables wrapped in warm tortillas.
15. Put on topping and enjoy.

Frothy Fruit Shake

Materials:

blender	1/8 teaspoon vanilla
1 tablespoon sugar	1 cup powdered non-fat dry milk
1 tablespoon cinnamon	3 cups of any fruit juice (not pineapple)
ice cubes or cracked ice	1 raw egg (cooled until used)

Directions:

1. Clean hands, area, and equipment.
2. Combine all ingredients into blender.
3. Blend until frothy.
4. Serve in glasses.
5. Flip out!

Famous Four Berry Pudding

Materials:

4 kinds of fresh or canned berries: raspberries, blueberries, strawberries, blackberries (if fresh, cook (stew) with, 1-1/2 cups water and sugar to taste)

1/2 teaspoon ground cinnamon, nutmeg, and ginger

1 deep dish (buttered)	3 cups of cream or milk
8—10 pieces of bread	4 eggs 1/2 cup sugar

dish (which will fit into toaster oven, portable oven, or regular oven)

Directions:

1. Clean hands, area, and equipment.
2. Butter dish.
3. Butter pieces of bread. Place in dish buttered side down.
4. Cover with stewed fruit or canned fruit mixed together.
5. Cover fruit with more bread.
6. Pour egg mixture onto second layer. It will saturate bread.
7. Repeat with buttered bread—butter side down—and cover with fruit and then egg mixture. Be sure no bread shows until dish is filled.
8. Mix eggs and milk/cream together with cinnamon, nutmeg, and sugar/ginger.
9. Bake at 325 degrees for 40 mins. to, 1 hr. and, 15 mins. depending on dish's size. Cover with foil if it's getting too brown.
10. Chill, cut, and flaunt with others!

Fabulous Fantastic Fudge

Materials:

4 cups marshmallows plus one handful

2/3 cups evaporated milk	margarine (to grease the pan)
1/4 cup butter	1/2 cups sugar
1/4 teaspoon salt	1/2 chopped walnuts

12 oz. package of semi-sweet chocolate chips, plus one handful.

1 sauce pan	1 bowl
1 9" square pan	1 teaspoon vanilla

Directions:

1. Clean hands, area, and equipment.
2. Put evaporated milk, butter, sugar, salt, and 4 cups of marshmallows in saucepan.
3. Cook and stir until mixture comes to an almost full boil. Must constantly stir or crystals will form and it's not creamy. Cook for five minutes and then cool.
4. Fold in vanilla and nuts.
5. Add handfuls of marshmallows and chocolate chips.
6. Pour into greased 9 inch square pan.
7. Chill and enjoy.

Fabulous Corn Fritters

A fritter is a small cake or fried batter, made by Indians before the Pilgrims. It is closely related to a doughnut.

Materials:

1 cup canned cream style corn	1/4 teaspoon salt
bowl	1/8 teaspoon nutmeg
egg beater/mixer	6 tablespoons flour
2 eggs	oil
1/2 teaspoon baking powder	1/8 teaspoon onion powder
1/8 teaspoon garlic powder	3 tablespoons butter

Directions:

1. Clean hands, area, and equipment.
2. Mix flour, baking powder, salt, nutmeg, garlic and onion powder.
3. Add corn, eggs, and mix.
4. Heat oil/butter.
5. Drop corn fritter into oil one tablespoon at a time. Brown and turn over.
6. Serve at once. It's fabulous!

Fancy French Toast

Materials:

shallow bowl	1/2 cup of milk
1/2 teaspoon of salt	1/2 teaspoon of cinnamon
1/2 teaspoon of vanilla	8 slices of bread
1/2 cup (or 2 sticks) of margarine	
1 electric frying pan	1 spatula

3 to 4 eggs (add only when ready. Keep cool until used.)

Directions:

1. Crack eggs into shallow bowl.
2. Stir in milk, salt, vanilla, and cinnamon.
3. Dip and saturate bread into egg mixture (make sure both sides are covered).
4. Melt margarine in electric frying pan.
5. Add egged bread and fry until golden brown on both sides.
6. Sprinkle with powdered sugar.
7. Cut and share with a friend. Fancy!

F-f Games/Activities

F-f Puppets

Puppets of paper bags or felt hand puppets can be made to represent a flounder, fawn, firefly, flamingo, frog, fox, fish, falcon, fly, or friend. Plays can then be written and acted out. *Frederick* or *Frog-Went-A-Courting* could also be made into reader's theater. Children can then share the plays with others—and make friends.

F-f Books

An "F-f" book could be made. Each child uses magazines, catalogs, or discarded books to find one or two items that start with the F/f sound. They are cut and then glued onto paper or cardboard, and then a sentence is added/written/dictated about the pictures. The object or item's function could also be written or dictated and parent/teacher/aide writes it. It may then be made into a class book by using brads or rings.

Fasto

A game called "Fasto" could be made. An 8"x11" tag board is divided into 25 squares. "F-A-S-T-O" is written on the top. 25 words are written on 25 spaces. A word is written on a small card. As the word is read, players match the card to their board and a chip is placed in the square. When he/she has his/her chips in a row, he/she calls out "Fasto" and has won. The cards may contain words like fad, fall, fang, follow, flit, felt, flat, or other words from the list.

Frog Game

A game board is made in the shape of a frog. A start and finish space are indicated on the board. Small pictures are then pasted or glued on, 1"x1" square tag. The student then turns over the picture and names the object or "reads the picture." If the student says the picture begins with an F and it does, he advances his marker one space. If the picture doesn't begin with an F and the child says it doesn't, he also advances. The winner moves his marker from start to finish first.

Musical Footprints

Students draw their footprint shapes on butcher paper. They can then be cut out and compared by size and shape. Teacher can put footprints on the floor in the shape of a circle. These footprints are then numbered. The children walk on the footprints until the music stops. When the child lands on/gets on four/five or fourteen/fifteen or forty, he has to name a word that begins with an F-f.

F-f Word Game

Students are given newspapers with printed words. Each child is given a marker. A timer is needed. The child that can circle the most F's in one minute wins. Then the game could be to cut out most of the F's. Then cut out the most "F-f" words.

Fractions

Fractions could be taught by measuring beans, rice, or colored water. The lesson could be modeled on how to measure. Children/student could then discover how to measure and what, 1/2,, 1/4,, 1/3, and, 1/8 means. Let them (allow them) to measure many times. Use a large plastic tub to keep rice beans or colored water available for many experiments.

FILM BOX

A film can be made. A favorite book is read and reread. Each child could have one page to illustrate. The pages could be glued on a strip of 5 inches x, 1-1/2 inches. A tag board box/holder could be made. Cut 2 inches from each edge. The film could then be pulled through the box or holder to allow the students to see the film. A dictated sentence or written sentence(s) is then written on the bottom. Children/students then read the film.

FUN FISH DISH

Each child is given a paper plate. Each student is given construction paper and glue. The teacher models how to cut an eye, fins, and a tail—the parts are glued to a form of fish. When the project is completed, the teacher distributes Pepperidge Farm Goldfish™ on each plate. Note: each handful will contain a different number and children count the fish and chart the amount in a handful.

FAMILY BOOK

A family book can easily be made with one page per family member allowed. Children dictate the name of the parent and each member of the family. (It could also be someone else who lives with the child.) The book can then be shared with the family for "Back To School" Night or "Parent's Day."

FOAMY FINGERPAINTING

"Foamy Fingerpainting" could be done. Use whipping cream shook up with food coloring. A bottle or jar for each color. The student could then paint with his/her fingers onto laminated paper, oilcloth, or toast. He/she can eat their fantastic forest or funny fish.

FARMER IN THE DELL

Each child could sing the song and illustrate it. It could be made into a film. This will help the children learn sequencing (order). The children could make their own books titled: "Fireman. Fireman, what do you see?" "I see a _____ looking at me." It could also be "Farmer. Farmer, what do you see?" "I see a donkey looking at me." "Donkey, donkey, what do you see?" "I see a cow looking at me."

FRIENDS BOOK

All children draw a picture of each of their classmates on a separate piece of paper. Then write/dictate a positive reason why he/she is his/her friend. (The teacher or helper may need to suggest reasons.) This then becomes a real self-esteem booster and helps the room build friendships. (Many times this activity helps behavior problems by telling that student he/she can be a friend).

FRUIT BOOK

A fruit book could be made with one-line descriptions. Children/students could look for pictures in discarded books, catalogs, and newspapers for fruits. Fruits could be tasted. A

F-f Word Lists

Animals:

falcon	fawn	fish
flamingo	fleas	finch
flounder	fly	fox
frog	foul	fiddler crab
fire-bellied toad	firefly	flying squirrel
frilled lizard	fang	ferret
feline	flying fox	flying gurnard
flying lemur	flying phalanger	fire-ant
fire-bird	firefly	flying fish
flying frog	fennec	fly-catcher

Everyday Objects:

face	fairy	fan
farm	farmer	flag
feather	feet	film
fin	finger	fir
fire	fist	fool
football	fork	friend
furniture	February	family
fable	factory	fur
fork	fossil	fern
fetus	factor	freedom
factory	fog	faculty
foil	fairy	flower
fluff	favorite	fraud
fictional book	flu	flake
fact	fiddle	fluoride
folk	fame	flesh
foam	fancy	fabric
fate	fact	fee
field	felt	fund
fern	flap	festival
floss	father	flight
fathom	Friday	fault

Everyday Objects cont'd.:

flute	fence	flame
food	fiction	fool
fear	funnel	fuss
fluke	fiber	fever
fruit trees	flute	fish nots
fender	fib	fiord
fit	forest	

Descriptive Words:

fancy	far	favorite
fine	first	flair
focus	foolish	fresh
funny	fright	fake
fix	felt	feel
fall	feather bed	feasible
furry	furious	funeral
fifteen	fifth	fourteen
first	fit	fire
final	facial	facetious
far	feeling	federal
fertile	flaunty	facile
faint	fine	flabby
farther	fast	fatal
feverish	firm	flat
frigidly	fat	famous
female	fantastic	fluent
flat	flax	fragrant
fallen	false	familial
fanatical	fanciful	flimsy
full	fierce	faith
fallacy	fantasy	farce

Food Words:

fennel	fettuccini	fig
fish sticks	flour	French fries

French toast	fritters	frosting
fruit	fruitcake	fruity
fudge	fat	filbert
filet mignon	fish	flavor

Verbs/action words:

fire	facing	frame
force	fade	fail
fake	float	flop
fall	fan	famish
fancy	fare	flout
fly	fashion	fast
favor	fear	flow
fell	feel	feed
felt	ferry	find
furnish	field	fight
figure	finish	fold
filch	file	fill
film	finesse	follow
fire-cure	fix	fizzle
flake	focus	fletch
freeze	flapped	flash
flatter	flaunt	flirt
flex	flip	flop
flog	flee	flit
flush	function	

Areas:

Fiji	Finger Lakes	Finland
Flanders	Florida	Fonddulac
French India	Fontainebleau	Foochow
Frisian Islands	Fredericksburg	Frigid zone
Friesland	Fribourg	Fresno
French Indochina	French Somaliland	French Sudan
French West Africa	French West Indies	

F-f Reading Resources

Flossie and the Fox — Patricia McKissack: Pied Piper, 1986

Frederick — Leo Lionni: Random House, 1967

Frog and Toad Are Friends — Arnold Lobel: Harper Trophy, 1972

Fox at School — Edward & James Marshall: Pied Piper, 1987

Freight Train — Donald Crews: Puffin, 1978

Fables — Arnold Lobel: Harper Trophy, 1980

Fisherman and His Wife — The Grimm Brothers

How to Eat Fried Worms — Thomas Rockwell: Dell Yearling, 1973

Father Fox's Penny Rhymes — Clyde Watson: Harper Collins, 1971

Finger Rhymes — Marc Brown: Dutton, 1980

Friends — Helme Heine: Aladdin, 1982

Freaky Friday — Mary Rogers: Harper Trophy, 1972

Frannie's Fruits — Leslie Kimmelman: Harper & Row, 1989

Fireflies — Julie Brinckloe: Aladdin, 1985

Frog Went—A Courtin' — John Langstaff: Voyager, 1955

Frog, Where Are You? — Mercer Mayer: Pied Piper, 1967

A Farmer's Alphabet — Mary Azarian: Godine, 1981

Feelings — Aliki: Mulberry, 1984

Fix It — David McPhail: Unicorn, 1984

Fox's Dream — Tejima: Philomel, 1987

The Flunking of Joshua T. Bates — Susan Richards Shrieve: Scholastic, 1984

The Finding — Nina Bawden: Dell, 1985

The Fledgling — Jane Langton: Harper Trophy, 1980

Fudge-A-Mania — Judy Blume: Dell Yearling, 1972

Frog, Toads, Lizards, and Salamanders — Nancy Winslow Parker and Joan Richards Wright — Mulberry, 1987

For Rent — Charles Martin: Green Willow, 1983

The Frog Prince Continued — Jon Scieszka: Viking, 1991

Fish Face — Patricia Reilly Giff: Dell Yearling, 1984

The Frog — Pat Paris: Simon and Schuster, 1990

Five Little Monkeys Jumping on the Bed — Eileen Christeloe: Clarion, 1990

G · g

G-g Recipes

GLORIOUS GINGERBREAD

Materials:

3-1/2 cups flour
1/2 cup dark molasses
1/2 teaspoon salt
3/4 teaspoon cinnamon
aluminum foil
gumdrops, raisins, cinnamon candies
1/2 cup water — add a few more drops as needed
Royal Icing: which is 1 lb. powdered sugar, 1/2 teaspoon cream of tartar, 1 teaspoon vanilla, 5-6 tablespoons of water.

1 tablespoon baking soda
1/4 teaspoon ground cloves
1 teaspoon ground ginger
1/4 cup margarine
baking sheet

Directions:

1. Clean hands, area, and equipment.
2. Combine flour, baking soda, cloves, cinnamon, ginger, and salt in small bowl.
3. Blend margarine and sugar in large bowl.
4. Add molasses to large bowl.
5. Add half of small bowl to large bowl.
6. Add water and mix.
7. Add other half of small bowl.
8. Mix.
9. Chill for 1 hour overnight.
10. Roll out dough and cut evenly.
11. Bake at 350 degrees for 10-12 minutes, or golden brown.
12. Cool and decorate.
13. Use Royal Icing to glue on decorations.

GEORGEOUS GARDEN GUACAMOLE (No Cooking)

Materials:

celery
1 ripe tomato, diced
tortilla chips
knife
fork or masher

2 or 3 ripe avocados (mashed)
1/2 teaspoon lemon juice
1/4 cup chopped onion
carrots, zucchini, jicama
salt, pepper, chili powder, or Tabasco sauce

Directions:

1. Clean hands, area, and equipment.
2. Cut avocados into two pieces and remove the skins and pits.
3. Put in bowl.
4. Mash with fork or masher.
5. Dice tomato and chop onion.
6. Add tomato and onion to avocados.
7. Add salt, pepper, lemon juice, chili powder, Tabasco sauce to taste, and cilantro.
8. Dip carrots, celery, zucchini, jicama, and/or tortilla chips into guacamole.

GRACIE/GERARDO GOURMET GIRAFFE (No Cooking-Assembly Only)

Materials:

1/2 banana   toothpicks
1/2 canned pear (cut lengthwise only if whole).
2 dried apricots or dried peaches or dried pears.
2 raisins for eyes, a red hot or M&M™ for a nose.
2 pieces of cashew nuts or date clusters for horns.
1/2 cup of toasted coconut for fur.
a spoonful of peanut butter.
1 paper plate per Giraffe.

Directions:

1. Clean hands, area, and equipment.
2. Give each group of two, two plates, one whole pear and 1 banana. They must peel and/or slice both fruits lengthwise. (If the pears come halved use one half per student)
3. Secure the pear to the banana with toothpicks.
4. Secure 2 dried fruits (same) for the ears.
5. Add 2 raisins, Red Hots™, or M&M's™ for the nose.
6. Secure date clusters or cashew nuts on head with peanut butter.
7. Use peanut butter to simulate spots on the giraffe.
8. Sprinkle toasted coconut for fur on the banana and the pear.
9. Gobble, gobble. (Take pictures.)

GRANDIOSE GOLDEN PUDDING

It was served about 1875. It was eaten in Thomas Jefferson's House (but it wasn't by Thomas Jefferson, himself; he was dead by then).

Materials:

1 cup milk   1/4 cup butter or margarine
1 apple sliced   1/2 teaspoon nutmeg
4 eggs   8-10 slices of bread (not rye)
oven or toaster oven   1/2 teaspoon cinnamon
1 teaspoon lemon zest (grated lemon skin)
baking dish or toaster oven baking plate

Directions:

1. Clean hands, area, and equipment.
2. Beat eggs with milk.
3. Soak bread into egg-milk mixture.
4. Grease pan with margarine or butter.
5. Line baking pan/dish with slices of soaked bread.
6. Fill the dish with sliced apples.
7. Sprinkle with sugar, cinnamon, nutmeg, and lemon jest.
8. Cover slices with the rest of the soaked bread. Pour in any remaining egg and milk mixture.
9. Cover and bake for one hour in 325 degrees oven or until golden brown.

GREEN GROUCH SNACKS

Materials:

1 popcorn or rice cakes per student   3 knives
1/2 to 1 cup flaked coconut (food colored green)
1/4 to 1/2 cup peanut butter
raisins or mini-marshmallows for eyes
red/black licorice whip for mouth
green food coloring bowl or jar to dye in

Directions:

1. Clean hands, area, and equipment.
2. Each child is given one round popcorn or rice cake.
3. Children/student share a knife.
4. Spread peanut butter on cake.
5. Green coconut is sprinkled over peanut butter.
6. Faces are made by using raisins, marshmallows, and licorice whip and attaching with peanut butter.

(Students could have Popsicle™ sticks stuck into each cookie and the Green Grouches could talk to each other.)

GREAT GOGOL - MONGOL
A Russian Dessert for good children.

Materials:

12 egg yolks   4-5 cups of fresh strawberries
refrigerator   9 tablespoons of sugar
electric mixer   18 lady fingers or soft cookies
paper   dessert or soup bowls

Directions:

1. Clean hands, area, and equipment.
2. Puree the berries and set aside.
3. Beat egg yolks and sugar using electric mixer on low speed for 1 minute.
4. Scrape the side of the bowl.
5. Turn electric mixer to high and beat for 3 more minutes until mixture is pale yellow and thick.
6. Add pureed strawberries and beat for 3 or 4 minutes until mixture is very thick.
7. Refrigerate for 15 minutes.
8. Serve in dessert bowls with cookies.

G-g Games/Activities

GO IN AND OUT THE WINDOW

Children form a circle holding hands. A tape of "Go In And Out The Window" or another song could be sung. The song is found in the Silver Burdett Music Book. The children join arms to make a circle. Arms are raised to make windows. The child that is "it" goes in and out with the arms around the circle till the song stops and that next person is "it." An alternate way could be one is "it" and another child weaves his way before "it" can catch him.

G-G FLASHCARDS

A teacher reads off list of words on flash cards. As each child hears the hard /g/ sound, they put up one finger. The "g" sounds like /g/ when followed by a, o, or u. If they hear /j/ sound, when "g" is followed by e, i, y, they put up two fingers.

G-G WORDS

Students can cut out large upper case and lower case letters and glue dried garbanzo beans or granola mix to "feel" the letter. Another way to help cement the letter, shape, and name is to glue/sprinkle ground ginger onto the cut out letter.

G-G ANIMALS

Student could draw pictures of a G "zoo", with a gibbon, gila monster, gnu, gopher, grass hopper, greyhound, guinea pig, gull, giraffe, gorilla, goldfish, guppy, goose, gander, goat, and write about it. They could write/ dictate at least 3-4 facts they learned about this /"G"/ animal.

G-G BAG

Students can research or "guess" the names of items in the "G-g" Bag (gadget, game, gear, gift, globe, glass, gem, or plastic replicas of a goat, gorilla, etc. Each item could be described by 3 facts. Students have 15-20 guesses to guess the G-g item.

My Green Garden

A garden of grass and flower seeds could be planted. Children/students could water by sprinkling water with their fingers like rain. Make sure containers have a hole (use nail) to drain overflow of water. Children can then water, measure, and put it in the sun. "My Green Garden" could be a book title about what they did to plant a garden. A hint—I use potting soil purchased in gardening supplies. Make sure each plant gets sun, water, and air. Without these 3 things, plants will not be green.

Gizmo

Great "Gizmo" Game/Activity could be used.

1. Divide creative learners into groups, 4-5 per group. Divide into Cooperative Learning Groups.
2. Give each group; scraps, clay, paper, pipe cleaners, pencils, paper, glue, paper clips, and whatever is handy.
3. Discuss the rules—
    1. They must all work together.
    2. They must all work to build one thing.
    3. They must all name it.
    4. They must decide what it can/will do.

They share their gizmo with other groups. This could be in an oral or written presentation. These could be written as a project to make at home also, as a family Gizmo.

G-G Pictures

The teacher collects pictures and makes match-ups (or buys cards with pictures) and the initial letter with "g" could be pulled (goat, gorilla). The children then draw a picture of what is on the card or picture and write/dictate on to several lines about it.

Goofy Class Book

A "Goofy Class" book is made of goofy words. The child must tell the function/definition of the words with an illustration. Each class could enter that "Goofy Class Book" to the office or nurse to judge. (This allows for problem-solving as well as oral language.)

G-G Goldfish

Pepperidge Farm Goldfish crackers are used to fill containers of several sizes. Each child then writes a prediction on a piece of paper with their name on the back. The predictions could be graphed; then the children can help count all the goldfish in each container. A circle could also be drawn around the closest prediction.

G-G Ghosts

Place wax or aluminum foil down. Use white glue (in squeeze bottle) and make a ghost shape. When it dries, peel it off. Use a permanent black pen to make eyes. A hole could be made with a paper punch or ice pick and these can be hung about the class. A story could then be

G-g Word Lists

Nouns - Everyday objects/thing:

golf clubs	Gamopetalous flower	gargoyle
gondola	gold	gimmick
goo	glue	gargoyle
garland	garnet	garter
gauntlet	gear	Grandma
gap	gaff	gang
gangrene	gang plank	gad
gabardine	gabelle	gavel
gantlet	gas	gym
gem	gabbro	gab
gad-a-bout	gadget	gauze
gaslight	gusset	gypsy
gazabo	game	golf
gum	ghost	gutter
gift	gauge	gear
gusto	gut	guest
garden	gain	ghetto
gait	girder	girl
guillotine	guess	guerrilla
grief	galaxy	gale
gall	galleon	geode
germ	gig	geyser
grip	gallery	galley
gambit	gamut	garage
garb	gardener	gate

Verbs - Action:

gnash	give	gab
gallop	gobble	gad
gag	go	glide
glint	glut	glow
get	got	gain
gall	galvanize	grin
gamble	gape	garble

75

Verbs – Action cont'd.:

gasp	grip	gargle
garnish	grasp	gather
gaze	gush	gurgle
gulp	guard	grunt
grump	grudge	giggle
glance	glare	glaze
glean		

Areas:

Gretna	Geneva	Germany
Genoa	Gorki	Gabon
Gaborone	Galapagos	Galicia
Galilee	Galveston	Galway
Gambia	Gandes	Garda
Garland	Garonne	Gascony
Gateshead	Gaturn	Gaul
Gwent	Guinea Bissau	Gibraltar
Gulfport	Gujranwala	Guantanamo
Guantanamo Bay	Guarani	Guadalajara
Guadeloupe		

Descriptive Words:

gabby	gentle	goofy
gory	golden	glorious
green	good	gogo
goosey	gaga	gaily
gainful	gallant	glossy
grouchy	grotesque	galling
game	gangling	gaudy
gassed	grim	garnish
gauche	gaunt	gay
gutsy	grumpy	grubby
gentle	genuine	ghastly
giddy	ginger	glad
glitzy		

food - food related:

galantine	ginkgo	griddle cake
goober	gooseberry	gum
gel	granola	gumdrops
grain	guacamole	grapefruit
guava	gumbo	grapes
garlic	garbanzos	gelatin
ginger	gumdrops	garlic bread
gruel		

Animals - Animal related:

gamecock	gamefish	gapeworm
guppy	gull	goldfish
gnu	giraffe	giant panda
gibbon	gander	grasshopper
guinea pig	gorilla	greyhound
gopher	goat	Gila Monster
gizzard	goose	gadfly
gadwall	galah	gallinipper
gill	Gall wasp	gudgeon
Guernsey	guanaco	globefish
ground fish	ground squirrel	

G-g Reading Resources

The Gift of the Sacred Dog — Paul Goble: Aladdin, 1978

Gung Hay Fat Choy — Diane Yee

Gentle Ben — Walt Morey: Puffin, 1965

The Lady of Guadalupeu — Tomie DePaola

Good-bye, Hello — Robert Welber

Good Night Moon — Margaret Wise Brown: Harper Trophy, 1947

Grasshopper on the Road — Arnold Lobel: Harper Trophy, 1972

Gilberto and the Wind — Marie Hall Ets

The Girl Who Liked Wild Horses — Paul Goble: Aladdin, 1978

Gingerbread Boy — Paul Goldone: Clarion Books, 1975

The Goldfish — Dorothy Aldis (poem)

The Drinking Gourd — F.M. Monjo

George's Marvelous Medicine — Roald Dahl: Puffin, 1985

The Giraffe and the Pelly & Me — Roald Dahl: Puffin, 1985

The Great Wall of China — Lenard Everett Fisher: Four Winds, 1986

Gingham Dog and Calico Cat — Eugene Field: Philomel Books, 1990

Go Tell Aunt Rhody — Aliki

Goldilocks and the Three Bears — Paul Galdone: Clarion, 1973

George Shrinks — William Joyce: Harper Trophy, 1985

Grandpa — John Burningham: Crown, 1985

The Growing-up Feet — Beverly Cleary: Dell Yearling, 1987

Guinnea Pig ABC — Kate Duke: Unicorn, 1983

Geraldine's Blanket — Holly Keller: Bulberry, 1984

Gila Monsters Meet You at the Airport — Marjorie Sharmat: Penguin, 1980

Gone Fishing — Earlene Long: Sandpiper: Houghton Mifflin, 1984

George and Martha — James Marshall: Houghton-Mifflin, 1972

Gorky Rises — William Steig: Sunburst, 1980

Goldie the Doll Maker — M.B. Goffstein: Sunburst, 1969

The Girl Who Loved the Wind — Jane Yolen: Harper Trophy, 1972

The Gingerbread Rabbit — Randall Jarrel: Aladdin, 1964

The Giving Tree — Shel Silverstein: Harper Collins, 1964

Galimoto — Karen Lynn Williams: Mullberry, 1990

Green Eggs and Ham — Dr. Seuss: Beginner Books, 1960

Gideon Ahoy — William Mayne: Dell Yearling, 1989

Getting Something on Maggie Marmelstein — Marjorie Weinman Sharmat — Harper Collins, 1971

The Gold Cadillac — Mildred Taylor: Bantam, 1987

The Golden Key — George MacDonald: Sunburst, 1967

Grover Learns to Read — Dan Elliot: Random House, 1985

H.h

H-h Recipes

HIGHLY HAPPY HEAD SANDWICH

Materials:

paper plates

toaster oven

cutting board

1 slice of bread per student

1/3 cup of refried beans

1/2 slice of tomato

foil

plastic forks

can opener

1 can of olives, drained

1 slice of cheese

Directions:

1. Clean hands, area, and equipment.
2. Place slice of bread on foil-lined baking sheet of toaster oven.
3. Spread beans on bread slice.
4. Cover slice completely.
5. Cut cheese diagonally or make four triangles to place on top of beans.
6. Cut olives for eyes so it can be happy. Add, 1/2 slice of tomato to make it smile.
7. Bake at 425 degrees for 6 to 7 minutes in toaster oven.
8. Serve happily.

HEAVENLY HOLIDAY HEARTS

Materials:

2 slices of bread

knife

1 bottle red food coloring

1 package of trail mix (or mixture of dried fruits, nuts and cereal)

1 jar of peanut butter or cream cheese

1/4 cup flaked coconut, colored red

Directions:

1. Clean hands, area, and equipment.
2. Cut the crust off one piece of bread.
3. Cut a circle out of the other piece of bread, then cut the circle in half.
4. Tape it at one end to look more "heart-like."
5. Place half-circles around the square piece of bread.
6. Spread peanut butter/cream cheese, trail mix and/or red colored coconut flakes.

(You can add any colored food coloring to flakes or peanut butter/cream cheese for holidays.)

HALLOO HASHBROWNS

Materials:

toaster oven
baking pan
garlic powder
1 can of Pam or no-stick cooking spray

frozen hashbrowns
apple sauce, sour cream, or ketchup
salt/pepper to taste

Directions:

1. Clean hands, area, and equipment.
2. Preheat toaster oven to 475 degrees.
3. Spray non-stick cooking spray.
4. Arrange frozen hashbrowns on shallow baking pan and place in oven.
5. Heat until lightly browned and crisp (20 to 25 minutes).
6. Season to taste.
7. Serve with applesauce or sour cream and/or ketchup.

(You can also fry with electric fry pan with 2 tablespoons of oil. Heat until golden brown. Make sure students are away from fry pan if you do.)

HUMBLE HERMAN, THE BEAR

Materials:

Electric fry pan
grater
lemon
2 small potatoes
1/4 cup flour
olives
seasonings (salt, pepper, garlic, seasoning salt)
knifepeeler

spatula
1/4 cup oil
small bowl
2 eggs
paper towels
jicama sticks

Directions:

1. Clean hands, area, and equipment.
2. Peel potatoes and place in a small bowl with several drops of lemon. (It helps keep potatoes from turning brown quickly.)
3. Grate potatoes, add eggs, flour, and seasonings.
4. Fry 1 big circle and 1 smaller circle for each Herman.
5. Fry until golden brown on both sides.
6. Cut the smaller circles in half. Place circles on paper toweling which lines paper plate. (This will drain it.)
7. Arrange on the plate so that the larger circle is the head and two half circles are the ears. The olives can be the eyes and nose. The jicama becomes the whiskers.
8. Students enjoy eating this Humble Herman.

Happy Halloween Healthy Treat

Materials:

knife
apple for 2 goblins
1 bag of raisins
1 can or natural peanut butter or orange colored cream cheese

1 date cluster or nut
1 can pineapple (chunks)
1 paper plate

Directions:

1. Clean hands, area, and equipment.
2. Cut each apple in half (also cut a slice on the bottom/side so the apple doesn't roll).
3. Spread peanut butter or orange colored cream cheese.
4. Add 2 chunks of pineapples for eyes.
5. Add one date cluster or nut for nose.
6. Add 6 or 8 raisins for a mouth.
7. Have a happy, healthy Halloween or healthy treat.
8. The face can also be made to show unhappy Halloween Healthy Treat ... to do so, place raisins so that the smile is turned down to show sadness. (Each child can make a happy and unhappy treat and then explain what makes them happy and unhappy; an extra activity.)

Hush Puppies

Many fishermen used this recipe to use up the fat after they fried the fish.

Materials:

1 or 2 cups corn meal
1 cup flour (all purpose)
1 teaspoon baking powder
1/2 teaspoon baking soda
1 roll of paper towels
1 electric fry pan
1 cup oil

1 knife
1 cutting bowl
1/2 teaspoon salt
1/2 cup milk
1/4 cup chopped onion
1 egg, well beaten

Directions:

1. Clean hands, area, and equipment.
2. Mix dry ingredients together.
3. Add onion, beaten egg, and milk.
4. Heat oil in electric fry pan.
5. Fry until golden brown.
6. Drain on absorbent paper.
7. This can be served with butter/margarine and syrup.

Horrible Hominy Grits

Materials:

1 electric fry pan
1 cup hominy grits
3 cups water
1-1/2 teaspoons salt
syrup/honey/jam
3 tablespoons cornmeal

1 qt. loaf pan
1/2 teaspoon sugar
1/4 teaspoon ground cinnamon
saucepan
hot plate

Directions:

1. Clean hands, area, and equipment.
2. Place sauce pan and water on hot plate until boiling. Gradually stir in hominy grits.
3. Cook about 1 hour, stirring occasionally.
4. Pour into a greased 1 qt buttered loaf pan.
5. Chill until firm.
6. Cut into slices & dip into corn meal with sugar & cinnamon.
7. Saute slices until browned on both sides.
8. Serve hot with syrup, honey, or jam.

Homely Houses

Materials:

peanut butter or frosting
2 graham crackers
food coloring
raisins
licorice whips
1/8 teaspoon salt
4 tablespoons milk
Royal Icing listed in "Gingerbread"

nuts
plastic knife
paper plates
date clusters
icing: tubes, cans or homemade
4 cups powered sugar
1/2 teaspoon vanilla

Directions:

1. Clean hands, area, and equipment.
2. Give each child a plate. Have adult supervise the cutting of the graham cracker square, using a plastic knife, cut on the diagonal, making 2 triangles.
3. Graham crackers can be glued (using frosting) to milk cartons to make 3-D houses.
4. The child now cements the roof (triangle) with frosting to the graham cracker square house.
5. Each child then decorates his/her house. The remains of the triangle can be cut into windows, doors, chimneys, etc.
6. Decorate with candy, raisins, licorice whips, nuts, and/or date clusters. Use Royal Frosting as glue.
7. These make beautiful gifts for Christmas presents. Use colored plastic wrap and pretty ribbons.
8. "Each child will say that his/her house is pretty, not homely."

H-h Games/Activities

H-H FLASHCARDS

The teacher makes flashcards with the words from the word list. Children/students then write the words from the cards that they can read, and illustrate it for their own alphabet book. Before putting the cards at the center, the teacher needs to go through the sounds and the words using ESL techniques or pictures. Each student could then draw a picture and write the word or dictate a sentence with an illustration to go into his or her own alphabet book.

H-H FOOD DIAGRAM

Students taste food items like honeydews, hot sauce, ham, hushpuppies, hamburgers, hickory nuts, and honey and compare the tastes, writing about their feelings about them. A diagram can also be used. Chart and graph the favorite H-h tastes.

HANSEL & GRETEL

The book *Hansel And Gretel* could be read. It could be written as a Reader's Theater; the characters could be Hansel, Gretel, Witch, Narrator, Other Children, Teacher, Father, and Step-Mother. The characters could be illustrated and glued on popsicle sticks. Another suggestion is to have scripts that are covered, then drawn on and used as a cover with illustrations of that character. The scripts could then be changed/ traded and all who want could be Hansel or Gretel or the Witch or whatever.

H-H ANIMAL BOOK

A hippopotamus, honeybee, hen, heron, hawk, hedgehog, herring, hamster, hammerhead shark, horse, haddock, halibut, hyla, hummingbird, housefly, hyenas, and howling monkey book could be made. These are animals whose names start with H-h. The animals could be compared/contrasted.

H-H SONGS

Have the children/students sing songs such as "Hush Little Baby" or "Hey Liley Liley": found in the Silver Burdett - Centennial Edition 1985.

H-H WORDS

Students look through discarded magazines, books, or catalogs for pictures of items that start with the H sound, or have an /h/ sound in it. Students could dictate or write about this item. They could name it and describe its function, whether they want one, who would want it, how much they think it should cost.

H-H PUPPETS

Paper bag puppets are made to dramatize the Nursery Rhyme Stories of *Henny Penny*, *The Little Red Hen*, *Humpty Dumpty*, and *The House That Jack Built*. The stories could be changed to fit the class. After the puppets are made, characters could be interchanged to write their own stories. Great for cooperative learning groups.

HOKEY POKEY

The "Hokey Pokey" dance could danced. The song actions to "Head, Shoulders, Knees, and Toes" could be dramatized for rhythms and E.S.L. Vocabulary.

HIPPO HUGS

The students in your room could collect Hippo hugs. (A big Hippo could be placed on the bulletin board and an envelope is given to each student to collect their hugs in.) A Hippo pattern could be copied with a line for each student's name and the date and what the child did to earn the Hip- po hug. When children earn positive rewards, their behavior changes to positive. The rules are:
1. Follow the rules.
2. Completes assignments.
3. Make another happy.
4. Being a friend to another.
5. Help someone.
The child with the most hugs wins. This could extend beyond the classroom.

HAT DAY

Hat Day is a special day in which each child wears a hat all day long. Hats are judged as prettiest, funniest, most practical, best looking, or ugliest. (The office staff or PTA could judge.) Paper ribbons could be given. Remember, a hard hat or helmet can be worn.

HIKE

Students and teacher could take a "Hike." This can be done using descriptive/directional words/concepts. A student may have to go: around the table, under a chair, jump over the river (made a colored/painted: paper), and over the rocks (made of boxes). This teaches children/students to listen/process and learn vocabulary. Teacher needs to change the script so each student must listen and proceed on the Hike.

HIDE & SEEK

Hide And Seek could be played. One student is "it." He/she closes his/her eyes and counts to 10. Others hide. "It" tries to find all the players that are hiding. It could be blindfolded. Whoever stays hidden the longest or is not found by "it" becomes it.

H-H INVENTIONS

Some inventions made that start with /H-h/ are hampers, hoes, hula, hats, hammers, heaters, helicopters, hoops, hydrants, etc. Talk about items and functions. Have each student draw/illustrate one item and describe its function. Use an illustrated dictionary: this then becomes a page/pages of your own class dictionary.

HOUSE PICTURES

Students are encouraged to draw pictures of their own houses. Their addresses could be written on the front. Inside could be a picture of each member in that house. A page per member can be written about each member. It is important that each child in your class knows his/her own address,

H-h Word Lists

Verb/Action Words:

had	harm	has
hash	have	hear
hide	hit	hold
honk	hop	hurry
hurt	hover	haggle
hail	halloo	hoard
hamper	happen	heat
haunt	hate	haul
heave	help	hurdle
hunch	hang	heal
hibernate	hug	

Noun/thing:

habit	half	Halloween
ham	Hanukkah	hat
hatchet	head	heart
heel	her	hill
him	hip	his
hit	holiday	home
horn	house	hour
hospital	horror	hope
hoop	hoe	hockey
habanera	halter	hacksaw
hail	half track	hammer
hag	hair	halo
hoop	hook	hood
honor	hoof	honeyman
homework	hole	himself
herself	hammerlock	hammock
hamper	hand	handbag
handcuff	havelock	head
heater	Heather	height
helmet	hydrogen	hue
handsome	hap	handle

86

haste	hay	hearth
heaven	helicon	heliport
humor	harmonica	harness
harvest	hazard	heap
heat	heel	helicopter
hymn		

Food/food related:

ham	hamburger	hash
hashbrowns	hazel nuts	hickory nuts
hollandaise sauce	honey	honeydew
horseradish	hot dogs	hot sauce
huckleberry	hushpuppies	Hickory nuts

Descriptive Words:

handy	happy	hazardous
heel	high	horrible
hot	horror	haggard
hairy	holy	hollow
handwritten	handsome	harsh
huge	hectic	heavy
hard	happy	heavenly
heavy duty	humble	human
he		

Animal:

haddock	halibut	hamster
hawk	hedgehog	hen
heron	herring	hippopotamus
honeybee	horse	hagfish
hare	housefly	hummingbird
hyena	Hartebeest	hyla
Howling Monkey	Hammerhead Shark	
hydrax		

Areas:

Houston	Haiti	Hamilton
Hackensack	Hague	Hainan
Hainaut	Haiphong	Hong Kong
Hollywood	Himalayas	Hampshire
Hannover	Hatteras Cape	Havel
Huntington Beach	Hattiesburg	Hawthorne
Hungary		

Musical instruments/inventions:

hatchet	horn	hammock
handcuff	heater	harp
harmonica	helicopter	hymn

H-h Reading Resources

The House that Jack Built — Rodney Peppe: Deletorte, 1970

Harry the Dirty Dog — Gene Zion

Hailstones and Halibut Bones — Mary O'Neill

Henry — Nina Bawden: Lothrop, 1988

Henny Penny — Paul Galdone: Glarion, 1978

Home for a Bunny — Margaret Wise Brown

Humpty Dumpty — Stephan Weatherhill: Green Willow Books, 1982

How to Eat Fried Worms — Thomas Rockwell: Watts, 1973

Hug Me — Patti Stren

Hugo and the Space Dog — Lee Lorenz

John Henry: The Steel Drivin' Man — Adele DeLeuw

Little Red Hen — Paul Galdone: Scholastic, 1973

Happy Birthday Moon — Frank Asch: Simon & Schuster, 1982

Harold and the Purple Crayon — Crockett Johnson: Harper Trophy, 1955

The Hating Book — Charlotte Zolotow: Harper Trophy, 1969

Holes and Peeks — Ann Jonas: Greenwillow, 1984

Hooray for Snail — John Staddler: Harper Trophy, 1984

Halloween ABC — Eve Merrian: Macmillian, 1987

Humphrey's Bear — Jan Wahl: Henry Holt, 1987

Hansel and Gretel — Rika Lesser: Sand Castle, 1984

Hershel and the Hanukkah Goblins — Eric Kimmel: Holiday, 1989

How Many Days to America? — Eve Bunting: Clarion, 1988

Horton Hatches the Egg — Dr. Seuss: Random House, 1940

How Much Is a Million — David Schwartz: Scholastic, 1985

How My Parents Learned to Eat — Ina Friedman: Houghton Mifflin Puffin, 1984

Hugh Pine — Janwillem Van de Wetering: Houghton Mifflin — Bantam, 1980

How the Grinch Stole Christmas — Dr. Seuss: Random House, 1957

A House Is a House for Me — Mary Ann Hoberman: Viking, 1978

Have You Seen My Ducklings? — Nancy Tafuri: Mulberry, 1984

A Hole Is to Dig: A First Book of Definitions — Ruth Krauss: Harper Trophy, 1952

Henry Huggins — Beverly Cleary: Avon, 1950

I-i Recipes

ICE CREAM WITH INVITING INGREDIENTS

Materials:

electric mixer
large bowl
1/2 teaspoon vanilla
8"x8"x2" pan
14 oz can Borden's brand Sweetened Condensed Milk
1/2 cup of crushed nuts shredded coconut (if desired)

1/2 cup chopped berries or fruit
2 cups whipping cream
1 cup chocolate chips
12 chocolate sandwich cookies

Directions:

1. Clean hands, area, and equipment.
2. In large bowl, combine 2 cups whipping cream, 2/3 cups condensed milk, and vanilla.
3. Chill for 30 minutes.
4. Beat with electric mixer on high speed until soft peaks form.
5. Coarsely crush 12 chocolate sandwich cookies (put in plastic bag and use hand to crush).
6. Add to cream mixture.
7. Pour into pan.
8. Sprinkle chocolate chips, nuts, berries/fruit,and coconut.
9. Cover and freeze for 4 hours.
1 0. Indulge. Invite others.

IMMEDIATE ICE CREAM IN A CAN

Materials:

1-lb. coffee can
flavoring extracts
3-lb. coffee can
(frozen berries, chocolate chips, nuts, banana can be added)

1 cup milk or cream
1/2 cup sugar
rock salt / ice

Directions:

1. Clean hands, area, and equipment.
2. Place milk or cream into 1-lb. coffee can.
3. Add 1/2 cup of sugar.
4. Add any flavoring extracts.
5. Place one pound can inside 3-lb. coffee can.
6. Pack ice & rock salt around 1-lb. coffee can and cover it.
7. Roll can back and forth for ten minutes.
8. Drain water and salt before repacking.
9. Repack and roll can for 5 more minutes.
10. Just before serving, add chopped or frozen strawberries, chocolate chips, nuts,

INCREDIBLE INDIAN FRY BREAD

This is an indian recipe to go with a Cherokee legend.

Materials:

1 electric fry pan	spatula
paper towels	1 large bowl
measuring spoon	honey or jelly
2 cups flour-preferably corn	1/4 cup oil
1 teaspoon baking powder	2/3 cups of milk
1 tablespoon sugar/cinnamon	1/2 cup frying oil

Directions:

1. Clean hands, area, and equipment.
2. Combine flour, salt, baking powder in a big bowl.
3. Add oil and water. It will make a thick mixture.
4. Flour/dust hands and board. Knead each ball. Roll into thin circle. Then heat oil.
5. Drop mixture, a teaspoon at a time, into heated oil. Cook 2 or 3 breads at a time. Fry until golden brown. Turn 1 time.
6. Fry. After that, serve with sugar/cinnamon.

(Many years ago, the Great Kahka Wonty told how the Great Spirit appeared to a wise forefather and showed him how to plant corn. The Great Spirit told him to preserve the two ears on the plant until the next spring and to plant the kernels. He should preserve the whole crop and send the two ears to each of the surrounding nations with the injunction that they were not to eat any of it until their third crop. The wise Indian did as he was commanded. By this means, the corn was distributed among the American Indians).

IOLKA IZ RISA I IZIUMA

This is a necessary part of the Russian Christmas Eve table. Iolka is a fir tree party. This is a ritual Christmas Cereal.

Materials:

3 tablespoons chopped toasted almonds or any nut

1/4 cup sugar	sauce pan on hot plate
1 1/2 cup cold milk	1 cup long-grain rice
bowls & spoons	3 tablespoons raisins
fork (Any fruit may be added)	

Directions:

1. Clean hands, area, and equipment.
2. Cook rice in 2 2/3 cup of boiling water. Follow directions on the box.
3. Allow rice to cool.
4. Add almonds, raisins, sugar, and toss with a fork.
5. Shape the mixture into a neat mound in a bowl and sprinkle with any fresh fruit.

INCY WEENCY SPIDERS

Materials:

1/4 cup shortening
2 cups flour
1 teaspoon salt
1 beaten egg
honey/syrup
10 raisins
spoons

electric fry pan
3 teaspoons baking powder
1 drop of yellow, red, blue food coloring
2 tablespoons milk
8 stick pretzels
paper plates
spatula

Coloring for brown spider: 1 drop of yellow, red, and blue food coloring

Directions:

1. Clean hands, area, and equipment.
2. Combine flour, baking powder, and salt in large bowl.
3. Combine shortening, milk, and egg in small bowl.
4. Combine large bowl into small bowl.
5. Pour a little shortening in electric fry pan or non-stick cooking spray.
6. Pour spider batter and cook until golden brown. Flip or turn over (bubbles on under side and golden brown on the side means to turn over).
7. Put in paper plate.
8. Use 8-stick pretzels on plate, 4 on each side. Put raisins for feet and 2 for eyes.

ICKY INCHWORM GARDEN
(This is a great dessert.)

Materials:

2 small packages of instant vanilla pudding
8 oz cool whip
2-3/4 cups milk
bowls
clear plastic cups
gummy worms

8 oz. package of cream cheese.
1 package of Oreo™ cookies
measuring cups/spoons
plastic flowers

Directions

1. Clean hands, area, and equipment.
2. Mix together cream cheese, pudding, cool whip, and milk.
3. Chill for 1/2 to 1 hour.
4. Remove centers of cookies (cream) and crush chocolate cookies into fine crumbs (put cookies in plastic bag and crush with book/block).
5. Fill clear plastic cups 3/4 full with chilled mixture.
6. Sprinkle cookie dust like top onto the soil in the garden.
7. Place plastic flower in the center.
8. Put Icky Inchworms in each planter.

I-i Games/Activities

I-I SOUNDS

All English vowels have two sounds: long and short. The long vowel says its name. It usually becomes a long "I", if there are two vowels together or if the word has a silent e. (Vowels change sounds depending on position or in a word with a silent e.) If the vowel is in the beginning or between two consonants, it is usually short. The words in the list could be stated/read and students put up one finger if it is short and two fingers if it is long. The points are registered and the child with the most points wins and reads the words.

I-I (PLAY DOUGH™) INITIAL COOKIES

"I-i" Initial Cookies is a recipe using Play Dough™ and/or cookie dough. Peanut Butter play dough and cookie recipes are in many chapters. Please use and eat; you can also make I-i shaped cookies with several other doughs featured in "C", "D", "E", and "S" Chapters. Shape capital and lowercase letters.

I-I LETTERS

Large construction paper letters could be traced and glue could be painted or squirted on it. Then rice could be placed on the letter. Children could then feel the configuration of the capital "I" and lowercase "i".

INCH WORMS

Each child is given an "inch worm" — a ruler that is measured or marked into six inches. The students can then measure objects (i.e. books, chairs, tables, blackboards) and before they measure they could predict how long they think items are. They could then measure many items both big and small, and compare and contrast sizes and numbers. All answers would be given in inches. They could measure the length (in inches) from his/her classroom to: office, nurse's office, cafeteria, and library.

I-I ANIMALS

Students can make an animal book of animals that names start with /I-i/ like iguanas, insects, inchworms, ibex, ibis, ivory-billed woodpecker, Irish Wolfhound, Irish Setter, Irish Bulldog, Io Moth, and Irish Terrier.

I-I FLASHCARDS

Students could be read and shown some of the flashcards made from words on word list. Using ESL techniques and strategies, pictures media, teachers could assist the /I-i/ word/sound comprehension. The flashcards could then be placed at center and students could illustrate pages of in class /I-i/ book or they could illustrate papers for their own individual A-B-C book. Children can dictate sentences about each object that they have drawn and its function.

ICE FLAVOR

Students could taste ice (ice cubes could be grinded/chopped by blenders or food processor). The ice could be flavored by flavored syrup.

IGLOOS

Students use blocks to make an igloo, which is a house for Eskimos. Blocks could also be made by boxes. Also, sugar cubes could be glued to illustrate how to make igloos.

ICE CREAM FLAVORS

Children visit an ice cream store, or place where ice cream is sold, and write down all the flavors of ice cream. They can then select five to ten people to state what their favorite flavors are. Predictions could be made and graphs/charts created. The results could be illustrated in the school newspaper or bulletin board and then given to the ice cream store.

I-I MAPS

Since so many states/countries begin with the letter /I-i/, the teacher could get a map and students could find many of the states/countries that names begin with the /I-i/ sound.

INSTANT FRIEND

Each child's name is written on a heart. All hearts are put in a box and a drawing can be held each week. Before hearts are drawn, each child's name needs to be written on the heart. Every week, students draw a name from the box. They become an instant friend for that week. The student is offered an "invitation as an instant friend." They play, line up, and eat together. This helps students learn about being irrational (unreasonable), irksome (annoying), irate (angry), to become involved in a game, ideal (model), identify (if they can be a friend-treat the same), image (person much like another) so that after the students invites and work towards becoming "instant friends" they can learn to improve their social skills and this activity will have made an impression on them and they learn about others and improve their self-esteem. Class books about their "instant friend" could be written about these people (students could then write about his/her instant friend. They could also write about the instant friend of the week. They must only write positive things). Hopefully each child will learn about three to four classmates per class. They could compare/contrast activities, personalities, after school activities, hobbies, and act.

I-I BOOKS

Books listed on Resource List could be chosen by "it" for the day. Each time the /I-i/ book is read, it is decided if it is liked. Votes are listed to determine which book is the favorite and then students can illustrate his/ her own "I-i" book or rewrite it.

INTERVIEWER

Each student is given the opportunity to learn to be an interviewer. Two to three students could cooperatively come up with four to five questions to interview parents, school staff, neighbors, friends, and family. The answers could be charted, graphed, and talked. The results could go into school newspapers or a note telling parents the results. Some of the questions may be:

1. What is your favorite food?
2. What is your favorite TV program?
3. What is your favorite snack?
4. What is your favorite sport?
5. What is your favorite book?
6. Do you have a favorite pet?
7. What is your favorite subject?
8. What is your favorite restaurant?

INVENTORS

Inventions/inventors/ideas: Children/students can learn about: Benjamin Franklin, Thomas Edison, Alexander Bell, Orville & Wilbur Wright, Whitcomb Jusdon, and inventions (to think up, produce), experiment for the first time: igloos, idle wheel, inclined plane, Indian club, inlaid wood, insole, insulators, ice skates, instruments, irons, ink, illustrations, inner tube, etc.

NEEDLE-NOSE IVY PLANTS

Needle-nose Ivy can be planted into used milk cartons. (Hint: make sure you use potting soil and poke three holes in the bottom of the carton.) The ivy could be measured charted/graphed. Children need to know that plants require sun, water, & soil to grow. Other ivy could be compared/ contrasted. (Ivy is not very expensive.)

I-I Word Lists

Short "I" in the initial position:

ill	in	inchworms
instruments	invite	Indian
idiot	is	it
into	inch	invent
igloo	insect	instead
isn't	inside	indent
important	indeed	imagination
if	infant	include

Short "I" in the medial position:

dig	pig	wig
fin	win	chin
bit	fit	hit
lit	pit	sit
inch	did	hid
lid	rid	pill
kill	fill	sick
pick	wick	mill
will	bill	thick
chick	tick	dim
him	rim	dip
hip	lip	tip
ship	chip	fish
dish	wish	city
hill	wick	Rick
will	did	this
little	which	him
big	still	give
his	different	until
begin		

Long "I" in the initial position:

iceberg	I	idea
Iris	I'm	item
icing	icy	ice
iodine	ivory	idle
isle	I've	I'll

Long "I" in the medial position:

hide	ride	side
wide	bike	nice
like	pike	tide
chime	dike	die
dice	dime	dine
dive	fight	file
fine	five	hide
hike	hive	light
lie	lice	lime
line	live	might
mice	mile	mine
night		

Inventions/Musical Instrument:

inclined plane	iron tools	insulators
inlaid	idle wheel	Indian club

Descriptive words:

individual	initial	ingenious
inflammable	indefinite	ivory
itty-bitty	isosceles	irritative
irritable	irresistible	irregular
irrational	irksome	ironic
irate	ionic	inviting
invisible	invalid	intuitive
intrusive	intricate	internal
intermediate	interior	intentional
indecent	intelligent	instrumental

instead	insincere	innocent
initiative	icy	icky
illegal	illogical	immediate
impatient	imperial	impersonal
impetuous	important	impressionable
improper	impulsive	inaccurate
incident	injustice	

Nouns:

itinerary	issue	isopod
isolation	index	isobar
Islam	Iroquois	iron worker
iodine	investigation	inventory
introduction	intimidation	intervention
interpretation	interest	intention
intellect	insurance	insult
instrument	instructor	institute
instinct	inside	inquiry
inquisition	input	impatient
ink	injustice	initiation
icicle	idol	identity
idealist	idea	ignition
illustration	image	importance
imprint	improvement	impulse
income	indicator	

Action Words or Verbs:

itemize	itch	irritate
invite	irrigate	involve
invest	invade	intrude
introvert	intimidate	interrupt
intend	integrate	inspect
inspire	inscribe	inoculate
inherit	ignore	imitate
impact	improve	include
increase	incriminate	incur
indent	inhale	inject

| infuse | inform | infatuate |
| infect | interview | |

Areas:

IndoChina	India	Illinois
Israel	Iraq	Indiana
Ireland	Iowa	Idaho
Iran	Irish Sea	Isle Royal
Italy	Ipswich	Izhevsk
Iwo Jima	Ivory Coast	Ithaca
Istria	Istanbul	

Food/food related:

ice cream	iceberg lettuce	Irish Stew
ice	ice bars	ice cream mix
ice cream bars	ice cream cups	icing
ice cream cones	inconnu	Irish Coffee
invert sugar	Indian Pudding	Indian Bread
indigestive	Indian Corn	

Animals/animal related:

inchworm	insect	ibex
ibis	iguana	Irish Setter
Irish Bulldog	Ichthyosaur	Iguanodon
imago	Indigo bunting	Indigo Snake
Io Moth	Irish Wolfhound	Irish Terrier
Ivory Billed woodpecker		

I-I Reading Resources

I Like Books — Anthony Browne: Knolph 1987

In a Dark Dark Wood — June Melser & Joy Cowley: Shortland Publications 1980

Is Your Mama a Llama? — Deborah Guarino: Scholastic 1989

Let's Look at Insects — Deborah Manley: Derrydale 1977

I Know a Lady — Charlotte Zolotow: Greenwillow 1984

I Like Music — Leah Komaiko: Harper Trophy 1987

It Could Always Be Worse — Margot Zemach: Sunburst 1977

I'm Terrific — Marjorie Weinman Sharmat: Scholastic 1977

I'll Fix Anthony — Judith Viorst: Aladdin 1969

I am Not Going to Get Up Today — Dr. Seuss: Random House 1987

I Wish I Was Sick Too — Franz Brandenberg

If You Take a Paintbrush — Fulvio Testa

I'll Always Love You — Hans Wilham: Crown, 1985

Imo's Discovery — Sheilagh S. Ogilivie

In One Day — Tom Parker

Indian Children Long Ago — Nancy Bird Taylor

Indian in the Cupboard — Lynne Reid Banks: Doubleday/Avon, 1987

Ira Sleeps Over — Bernard Waber: Houghton Mifflin, 1972

Ishi — Last of His Tribe: Theodora Kroeber

It Wasn't My Fault — Helen Lester

I Know an Old Lady Who Swallowed a Fly — Nadine Bernard — Westcott, Little Brown & Co., 1980

It Looked Like Spilt Milk — Charles G. Shaw: Harper & Row, 1947

I Am a Bunny — Ole Risom: Golden/Western, 1967

If You Give a Mouse a Cookie — Laura Joffe Numeroff: Harper & Row, 1985

I'll Meet You at the Cucumbers — Lilian Moore: Atheneum, 1988

J-j Recipes

JOLLY JUICY JELL-O™

Materials:

1/2 cup cold water

3/4 cup boiling water

3 oz. package lemon flavored Jell-O™ gelatin

ice1 cup milk

3/4 cup boiling water

1/2 cup seedless grapes cut in half

Directions:

1. Clean hands, area, and equipment.
2. Dissolve Jell-O™ in boiling water.
3. Combine cold water and ice to make one cup.
4. Add cold water to gelatin and stir until ice is melted.
5. Add one cup of milk.
6. Chill about ten minutes.
7. Add 1/2 cup of seedless grapes.
8. Pour into cups or glasses.
9. Chill about 30 minutes.

JOYFUL JUICE JULIUS

Materials:

3 cups water

1 cup milk

electric blender

2 teaspoons vanilla extract

2 teaspoons lemon extract

6 oz. can frozen lemonade

6 oz. can frozen orange juice

1 raw egg (kept cold until used)

Directions:

1. Clean hands, area, and equipment.
2. Pour cans of lemonade and orange juice into blender.
3. Add water, egg, flavorings.
4. Blend until completely mixed and bubbly.
5. Frothy.

JAMBO JELLY SANDWICH

Materials:

2 slices of bread

peanut butter

banana chips, nuts, raisins, M&M's™

butter/margarine for jam

fruit/fresh or dried

knife

Directions:

1. Clean hands, area, and equipment.
2. Two slices of bread with crust cut off — almost like circles.
3. Spread butter/margarine on side #1.
4. Spread fruit jam on side #2.
5. Put side 1 & 2 together.
6. On side #3 which is the top, spread peanut butter.
7. Add raisins, nuts, date clusters, banana chips, and dried or fresh fruit as well as M&M's™ to make a happy "Jambo" face.

JUNKET OR RENNET PUDDING
(Brand Name)

This is an English pudding. It is sweetened milk or milk sweetened, flavored and thickened into curd with rennet. It is found in a box. The directions are on the box.

Materials:

1 box of junket or 1 teaspoon prepared rennet

2 cups of milk

heavy cream

powder sugar

2 teaspoons of sugar

cinnamon or nutmeg

candy thermometer

Directions:

1. Clean hands, area, and equipment.
2. Heat 2 cups of milk to exactly 98 degrees using a candy thermometer.
3. Add two teaspoons of sugar.
4. Stir in 2 teaspoons essence of rennet or 1 teaspoon prepared rennet.
5. Let the pudding stand about 1-1/2 hours until it "gels."
6. Whip heavy cream with powder sugar.
7. Add whipped cream to pudding.
8. Sprinkle with cinnamon or/and nutmeg.

Johnny Cake #1

A Kind of Corn Bread Baked On A Griddle.

Three recipes – First is from Rhode Island, the second from the southern part of the Plymouth Colony, and the Third is for "Jogging" and/or busy people. It is baked rather than fried. Take a quantity of cornmeal, scald it with boiling water, then with cold milk, and salt it to taste. This is the recipe. Each home differed in their interpretation.

Materials:

2 cups corn meal — covered with 1-1/2 cups boiling water
1/2 cup milk   electric fry pan
1/2 teaspoon salt   spatula
oilhoney or jam or maple syrup

Directions:

1. Clean hands, area, and equipment.
2. Put corn meal in bowl and cover with 1 cup of boiling water.
3. Allow it to stand for 10 minutes or until meal is 2 times it's size.
4. Add milk to make your favorite consistency or about 1/2 cup of milk.
5. Add salt/pepper to taste.
6. Fry in oil until golden brown.
7. Serve with maple syrup or honey/jam.

Recipe #2 Southern Part of Plymouth Colony.

Materials:

1 cup of corn meal   pinch of salt
oil   1 cup of milk
electric fry pan   spatula
1 eggpinch of baking soda

Directions:

1. Clean hands, area, and equipment.
2. Make a well in corn meal.
3. Drop in an egg.
4. Drop in a cup of milk.
5. Add a pinch of salt and soda.
6. Mix and gather to form balls.
7. Add either milk or cornmeal to make balls.
8. Fry in oil until golden brown — turning once.
9. Serve with maple syrup, honey, or jam.

JOGGING JOHNNY CAKES

An easier modern/western style for busy people.

Materials:

powdered sugar
1 beaten egg
2 tablespoons sugar
2 teaspoons salt
8" square pan

2 tablespoons of butter
1 cup of milk oven
2 teaspoon baking powder
2 cups yellow corn meal
1/2 cup all purpose flour

Directions:

1. Clean hands, area, and equipment.
2. Mix dry ingredients into large bowl.
3. Mix egg, milk, and melted butter into small bowl.
4. Combine large bowl with small bowl.
5. Grease 8" saucepan.
6. Bake in 425 degrees oven for about 25 minutes or golden brown.
7. Slice and serve with powdered sugar sprinkled over it.

JIGGLING JELL-O™

Materials:

4 packages of Knox flavored gelatin
1/2 cup sugar
frosting
whipped cream
flat pan
knife
pan

4 cups boiling water
1 cup cold water
A-B-C Cutters or Cookie Cutters
8" x 13" dish
M&M's™
hot plate to make boiling water

Directions:

1. Clean hands, area, and equipment.
2. In a mixing bowl, put unflavored gelatin Jell-O™, sugar, and cold water.
3. Pour in boiling water.
4. Stir until dissolved.
5. Pour into 8"x13" dish
6. Put into refrigerator to cool.
7. Cut with knife into squares or alphabet cookie cutters.
8. Use frosting or whipped cream to have M&M's™ stick on jigglers.
9. Use hands to eat.

JUDGING JAR JAM

This jam needs only 1 cooking step and uses fruit pulp. I suggest strawberry for it's a favorite, and during the season, it's the cheapest.

Materials:

1—2 lbs. strawberries

hot plate

spoon

glass jars

3/4 pound of sugar to every pan of fruit

shallow enameled pens

sunny glass window

jars/bread

glass pans 8"x13"

Directions:

1. Clean hands, area, and equipment.
2. Hull and wash strawberries well.
3. Weigh and put in a pan, 1-2 pounds of fruit.
4. Spread 3/4 pound of sugar for every pan of fruit.
5. Cover and set aside overnight.
6. Put pans over hot plate until sugar is dissolved.
7. Boil for one minute, then stir.
8. Cool.
9. Pour into glass pans.
10. Put in sunny window or in sun.
11. Allow to stand for 2-3 days.
12. Stir seven times per day.
13. Spread on bread or it can be put into glass jars and processed.

J-j Games/Activities

J-J WORDS

Teacher could read all words in word list. Teacher could use English as a Second Language techniques & strategies to help student comprehend word. Pictures, realia could be used. Words could be placed on/in a center and student could select words to write, illustrate, and dictate a sentence about. This makes these words his or hers so they can use them in stories, writing, and reading.

J-J MAPS

Students/teacher can use map/globe to find/locate places like: Jackson Mo., Java, Jutland, Japan, Jurua, Julian Alps, Jerusalem, Juden, Juba, Joplin Mo., Jordan, and Jericho. Student could compare/contrast areas by the color of the area (arid, wet) and by rain and location. A world map could then be located and these areas drawn in.

JAMS/JELLIES COMPARISON

Students can be encouraged to compare/contrast different jams/jellies (i.e. for taste, color, texture, and sweetened/unsweetened pectin/no pectin). Jellies are made by cooking the juices and sugar. It is transparent and holds its shape. Jams are made from crushed fruits cooked with sugar until thick. Have them taste with a spoon or wooden Popsicle™ stick.

JENNY'S JUNK BOX

Jenny's Junk Box is an activity that involves children in recycling. Collect items donated by parents or from other sources. Put them in Jenny's Junk Box and give the students a time to use whatever they want for their "joy item." (They can use anything that sticks together with white glue.) Allow to dry and then the students can paint on it. They can also name it and its function and write this information on a 3"x5" card, attaching it with glue. A display can also be set up for other classes to join and observe their joyous items.

JUNGLE ANIMALS

Students can draw animals in their jungle: animals like a jaguar, jack rabbit, jackal, jackimar, jackdaw, jay, and even jellyfish. These animals are to be labeled and three or four students could join to be a judge and jury and put awards for each participant. (Animals could be made up also as long as their names started with "j.")

J-J INVENTIONS

Students could compare/contrast, learn about inventions that start with "J-j" like jack, jack boot, jacket, jack-o-lantern, jigsaw, jocks, jock strap, jawbreaker, jeep, jelly, and jam.

JETS

Children could look at pictures of jets. They could learn the names and fold paper into jets or use blocks, Legos™, or Tinker Toys™ to construct jets. Jets are jet-propelled airplanes and children can "see" the difference.

JOHNNY JUMP UP

Children can play "Johnny Jump Up." "It" is placed facing the line of children or jumpers. The birds are in front of "it" flapping their arms. There are only two birds. When "it" says, "Johnny, Jump Up" — the frogs jump towards it. If a bird using his/her arms tries to catch a frog, then the frog becomes a bird. This continues until the last frog is left and he or she is it.

JANUARY JUMP

"January Jump" can also be played. There are four teams and they crouch down. The teams must be of an equal/same number. When the bell/ whistle is blown, the last student puts hands on student crouched on the ground and jumps over him/her and then each person in the line then crouches. The next person leap frogs (or jumps) over all in line. The team that reaches the final line first is the winner.

JACK-O-LANTERN

Jack-o-Lanterns are designated as a Halloween item, but it doesn't need to be. Faces on round pumpkin circles using triangles and circles could be constructed all year long. A sentence written about the Jack-O-Lantern could be written/dictated.

JAZZ IDENTIFICATION

The teacher can play records, tapes of waltzes, classical, western, and jazz so children/students can identify and understand the difference.

HAND MADE JACKETS

Jackets are made of paper bags. A circle cut in the bottom of the bag allows the head to come out. Then cut the line from the circle to the bottom. Two other bags can be taped to make sleeves. These can then be decorated or a drawing of the outline of a jacket can be drawn and each child can design his/her own jacket. It might be decorated with prints from wallpaper books or discarded books, magazines or catalogs.

JUMPING JACKS

Children could be shown picture words and discuss what they are. Children look at the letters and sequence letters. All children sit in a circle. When the child recognizes the word, he/she jumps up and continues to jump around until the teacher calls on him/her. if the child is right, he/she gets a point. The child with the most points shows the "J-j" word cards.

J-j Word Lists

jackal	jackamar	jugum
jackdaw	jack rabbit	jaguar
jellyfish	jerboa	jumping mouse
joint worm	Japanese beetle	Jurl
jurel	Jackfish	Jungle fowl
jacksmelt	Jaeger	June Bug
Japanese oyster	Jerusalem cricket	

Everyday Objects/Nouns:

Jade	jackboot	jacket
Jack-O-Lantern	jackpot	jacks
jail	jar	jaw
jawbreaker	jeans	jeep
jet	jewelry	jigsaw puzzle
job	jockey	judge
jungle	junk	jury
journal	jag	jewel
jujitsu	Juju	journey
joy	jubilee	jug
jot	joist	jute
junction	jogging	jargon
joke	jack	javelin
joint	jacquard	jellybean
Jamboree	Jew's harp	jig juror
jazz		

Descriptive/action words:

jade	jag	joggle
Jazz	jerky	jig
jog	join	joke
juggle	joy	jump
just	juice	jerk
jolly	jingle	junior

juvenile	justify	jealous
jolt	jostle	jumble
joyous	jovial	job
Jant	joggling	jink
jangle	jeer	jar

Foods:

jam	Jell-O™	jelly
jellybeans	juice	junket
jellyroll	Jackfruit	Japanese Oyster
Jalapeno pepper	Jambalaya	jerky
Jerusalem artichoke		jujube
Japanese Persimmon		

Areas:

Jamaica	Japan	Java
Jericho	Jerusalem	Joplin
Juba	Judea	Julian Alps
Jordan	Jupiter	Jura Mountains
Jurua	Jutland	Jaffa

Names (of people, days, months, years):

Joseph	Jackson	January
Jay	John	Josh

J-j Reading Resources

Jack and the Beanstalk — Jacob Grimm

Jambo Means Hello: Swahili Alphabet Book — Muriel Feelings: Pied Piper, 1974

Jam Berry — Bruce Degan

James and the Giant Peach — Roald Dahl: Knoph/Penguin, 1961

Ji-Nongo Means Riddles — Verna Aardema

John Henry: The Steel Drivin' Man — Adele de Leeuw

Josefina February — Evaline Ness

A Jar of Dreams — Yoshiko Uchida: Aladdin, 1981

Jumanji — Chris Van Allsburg: Houghton Mifflin, 1981

Jump! The Adventures of Brer Rabbit — Van Dyke Parks, Malcolm Jones: HBJ, 1986

Jesse Bear, What Will You Wear — Nancy White Carlstrom: Macmillian, 1986

Julius, The Baby of the World — Kevin Henkes: Greenwillow, 1990

Just Plain Fancy — Patricia Polacco: Bantam, 1990

Jane Martin, Dog Detective — Eve Bunting: Voyager, 1984

The Jungle Book — Rudyart Kipling: Viking/Pufflin, 1896

Juniper Tree — Jacob and Wilhelm Grimm: Sunburst, 1973

Journey to America — Sonia Levitin: Atheneum, 1970

Jelly Belly — Robert Kimmel Smith: Dell/Yearling/Delacorte, 1981

Joshua James Likes Trucks — Catherine Petrie: Children's Press, 1988

Just Like Daddy — Frank Asch: Simon & Schuster, 1981

Jim on the Corner — Eleanor Farjeon: Knopf/Bullseye, 1958

Jacob Two-Two and the Dinosaur — Mordecai Richler: Knoph/Bantam, 1987

Giant Jam Sandwich — John Vernon Lord: Houghton Mifflin, 1973

This Is the House that Jack Built — Iris Simon: Dandelion Press, 1979

The Jet Age: From the First Jet Fighters to Swing-Wing Bombers — David Jefferies: Watts, 1989

James Marshall's Mother Goose — James Marshall: Sunburst, 1979

Jerusalem, Shining Still — Karla Kuskin: Harper Trophy, 1987

Jonah and the Great Fish — Warwick Hutton, McElderry, 1984

Joseph Who Loved the Sabbath — Marilyn Hirsh: Puffin, 1986

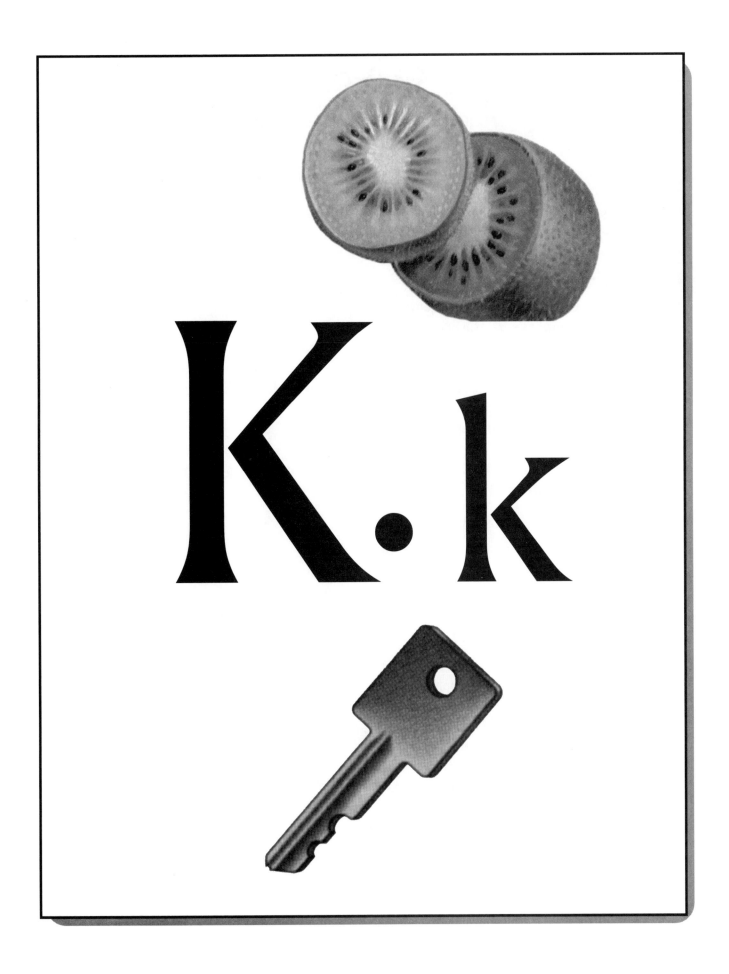

K.k

K-k Recipes

KING KUDO'S A-B-C BLOX

Materials:

small bowl
1 cup cold water
1/2 cup sugar
2 cups boiling water
1 can of non-stick cooking spray.

3 envelopes unflavored gelatin
large bowl
1 large package lemon Jell-O™
glass baking dish

Directions:

1. Clean hands, area, and equipment.
2. In small bowl mix gelatin and cold water together.
3. In large bowl, combine lemon Jell-O™, sugar, and boiling water.
4. Combine contents of large and small bowls.
5. Use spray-on cooking spray to cover dish. Pour into glass baking dish.
6. Chill in refrigerator for about 30 minutes.
7. Cut into squares or alphabet letters (cookie cutters).

(Hint: if letters/shapes are difficult to remove, dip bottom of pan in warm water for 15 seconds to loosen gelatin.)

KANGAROO KIDNEY BEAN CASSEROLE

Materials:

1 lb. ground beef
1 teaspoon salt
1 cup cheddar cheese
electric fry pan

1 small onion, chopped
16 oz. can kidney beans
1 can cream of chicken soup
toaster oven

Directions:

1. Clean hands, area, and equipment.
2. Brown beef and onion in electric fry pan and drain.
3. Stir in rinsed and drained kidney beans, soup, and salt.
4. Pour into greased toaster-oven pan.
5. Grate cheese and place on top.
6. Bake at 350 degrees for 45 minutes.

KREPLACH SOUP-A STUFFED NOODLE

An old Jewish recipe (It can or also be compared to Chinese Won Ton Soup or Italian Ravioli)

Materials:

3 or 4 cans of clear chicken broth

1 sprig of parsley	paper, plastic bowls
saucepan	marinara sauce
plastic spoons	grated parmesan cheese
electric fry pan or hot plate	

1 pkg.. of frozen ravioli or canned, not in sauce, or frozen Kreplach

Directions: - for school use:

(Homemade Kreplach, wontons, or ravioli consist of noodle dough, and filled with cheese, meat, or chicken)

1. Boil/heat frozen ravioli or frozen Kreplach (found in freezer section).
2. Add to heated, canned, clear chicken soup. Cook for 15 mins.
3. Sprinkle with parsley.
4. Serve in bowls with soup or serve in heated marinara sauce with grated parmesan cheese on top.

(In Jewish homes, this is served before the main meal. In many homes, with the marinara sauce, this can be a main course.)

KUGEL #1

Kugel means noodle/rice casserole this is served as a side dish or main dish in many Jewish homes. The modern translation becomes casserole combined with cheese, vegetables, and sour cream, or potatoes.

Materials:

2 noodle pkg. of wide noodles

1 grater	large bowl/spoon
4 cups water	1/2 cup of melted butter
salt	16 oz. sour cream
3 eggs	1/4 lb. of shredded cheddar cheese
sauce pan	salt, pepper
hot plate/stove	seasoned salt, garlic
oven	

Directions:

1. Clean hands, area, and equipment.
2. Boil noodles until tender, drain.
3. In large bowl, mix and add 1 lg. carton of sour cream, 2 eggs, shredded cheddar cheese, seasonings, and melted butter.
4. Grease baking dish.
5. Preheat oven to 325 – 350 degrees.
6. Combine drained noodles with ingredients in large bowl.
7. Spread into baking dish and bake for 50-60 minutes or until golden brown.
8. Serve warm and may be served cool.

Krazy Kugel (#2)

Materials:

2 or 3 cups of rice

1 teaspoon salt

4 cups boiling water

1/2 cup of sugar

1/4 teaspoon nutmeg

cup of seedless raisins, cherries, and/or cranberries

whipped cream

3 eggs

1/2 teaspoon cinnamon

1/4 cup of melted butter

1/4 cup chopped walnuts

Directions:

1. Clean hands, area, and equipment.
2. Cook rice as directed on box.
3. Combine nutmeg, walnuts, cinnamon, eggs, and either raisins, cherries, or cranberries in large bowl.
4. Grease baking dish.
5. Preheat oven to 325 - 350 degrees.
6. Combine cooked rice with items in large bowl and stir.
7. Spread into baking dish and bake for 45-50 minutes or until golden brown.
8. Serve with whipped cream.

Keebobs (#1)

Another version is "Skewer King." This can allow students an opportunity to try/taste combination or foods not in their own homes.

Materials:

meat, hot dogs

aluminum foil

1/4 cup onions

6 strips bacon

1 unpeeled apple

1/2 bell peppers

(or slices of onions,

bell peppers, zucchini)

rotisserie

8-10 olives

8-10 cherry tomatoes

metal or wooden skewers

6-8 mushrooms

table top or broiler, grill

Directions:

1. Clean hands, area, and equipment.
2. Allow each student to choose what they want on his/her keebobs.
3. Allow each student to put onto his/her own skewer what they have chosen.
4. If using table top broiler/rotisserie - put onto his/her own skewer what they have chosen.
5. Cook/broil until done.
6. If using table top broiler/put on metal skewer. (Be sure to mark name or initials with tape.) Use wooden skewer with aluminum foil.

KEEN FRUIT KEEBOBS (#2)

Materials:

wooden skewers	plain or fruit yogurt flavored
canned peaches	sections of oranges or grapefruits
canned pears	fresh pineapple
sliced bananas	apples
canned apricots	peeled kiwis
1/2 cup honey	1 tablespoon vanilla
1 cup orange juice	

Directions:

1. Clean hands, area, and equipment.
2. Combine orange juice, honey, vanilla, into sauce in small bowl.
3. Marinate (soak) fruit to be used into sauce.
4. Allow students to select his/her own fruit to be used.
5. Allow student to put on fruit onto their skewers with their initials on it.
6. Broil on table rotisserie or under broiler for about 5 mins with aluminum foil under the skewers. An alternative non-cooking recipe is to put fresh fruit on keebobs and dip into fruit yogurt.

KINGLY VEGETABLE KEEBOBS (#3)

Materials:

bell pepper (red, green, yellow) cut into pieces

8 mushrooms	slices of carrots
slices of jicama	8-10 cherry tomatoes
1 cucumber	1/2 cup lemon juice
1 teaspoon olive oil	1 celery stalk, cut into pieces
wooden skewers	herbs/garlic powder.

Directions:

1. Clean hands, area, and equipment.
2. Put vegetables on skewers (put initials on wood).
3. Marinate in lemon juice, olive oil, herbs, and garlic powder.
4. Place on grill with aluminum foil under it (until vegetables are tender: 10-15 minutes).

Kuick Kugelhopf (Swedish)

(A Kugelhopf is usually baked on the birthday of the saint that you were named after, rather than on your birthday!)

Materials:

7 inch tube pan
3-1/2 cups flour
1/2 teaspoon salt
1 cup butter
1 cup sugar
1/2 teaspoon sugar
spoon, mixer
3 teaspoon baking powder
pinch/sprinkle of confectioners' sugar or powdered sugar

5 eggs
1 cup milk
1 cup seedless raisins (or glazed fruit)
1 teaspoon grated lemon rind (fresh)
1 teaspoon vanilla
1/2 teaspoon nutmeg
grater

Directions:

1. Clean hands, area, and equipment.
2. Put flour, baking powder, salt, vanilla, cinnamon, nutmeg, and lemon ring into large bowl.
3. Cream butter and sugar in small bowl.
4. Add eggs, one at a time, mix in small bowl.
5. Add and mix small bowl to large bowl until smooth
6. Add raisins and glazed fruit.
7. Pour into greased tube pan for about 45 to 60 minutes or until golden brown.
8. When cool, take out of pan and sprinkle with conf./powdered sugar.

K-k Games/Activities

KICK THE CAN

This game is as old as cans. Open one end of four cans 16-19 ozs. Divide students into four equal lines. Have line 1 and 2 face each other with playground between them. Line 3 and 4 facing each other. This is a relay. Line 1 and 3 each have the cans. The first person in line must kick the can to lines 2 and/or 4. The first person in that line then kicks the can back to the 1st line (the person that has kicked the can goes to the end of the line and sits down). The line 1/3 or 2/4 which has all of it's contestants sitting down wins.

K-k RESEARCH REPORTS

In this activity, students locate and find all the areas listed on the word list and write about one of them. The students could divide into cooperative groups and decide which area they want to research and write about. All students in the group turn in one report. It contains a map, products, money, people, area, schools, and language.

K-k TASTES

Teacher/students could taste some/all of the items listed on the word list. They could compose/contrast the tastes. They could chart/graph which one they liked best. They could group into vegetables/fruits, bread/ grains, meats/cheese, etc.

K-k ANIMALS

Have students research about animals listed on the word list. Each student could write a one paragraph report about where they live, what they eat, how they live, and draw a picture of them.

KUDOS

Kudos — a large Hershey Kiss™ shape could be put on the black board. Attached to it could be little envelopes with the students' pictures on it. Each time a student displays being a) a kind kid, b) a keen kid, c) a kool kid he/she would get a small "Kiss"-shaped paper signed by the teacher. The child/student would have to write what others saw him doing to receive a kudo and the date. The winner for the month would have the most kisses/kudos. (If this happened at home, the parent could write a note about activity).

KONCENTRATION

Koncentration could be played with "memory-type cards" or teacher made cards that have pairs. The cards are played face down. The 2-4 players each get one turn to match two cards. If the cards match, they are called a "pair" and the players keep them. If the cards do not match, they are turned upside down again for the next player to try to match. The child with the most pairs wins.

K-k FLASH CARDS

Teacher reads all of the words on the K word list which have been written as flash cards. There must be other words on flash cards mixed in also. The instructor/aide/volunteer reads

K's in the Keg

Teacher puts items like a key, a Hershey Kiss™, a kit, a kite, a knife, a kernel, knitting needles, a kitchen item, and a knight in a keg. Students have to put hand into keg and describe what they feel and determine what the object is and if it starts with K-k sound. Other students may help guess what it is by its descriptions.

Kites

Students can make a kite with Popsicle™ sticks. The sticks could be joined by yarn on string. Cover the sticks with tissue paper and glue. Add crepe paper to make tail. These may not fly except in your room from attached yarn. If you want a less sturdy, but more flyable, kite, use balsa wood for the wood construction.

Kollectable Keys

Have each child bring in several keys that are no longer in use. Collect in a box. When there are several keys, sort by color, shape, size, and even function - if known. These can be used for math manipulatives to "unlock the answers." They can be used for story starters like "Once I found a key ..."

Kaboom

Children sit in square or circle. One child has an eraser (chalkboard) and is "it." The child says "Ka-Ka-Ka-Ka-Ka-Boom" and drops the eraser behind a student sitting down. That child must pick up the eraser and run after "it." "It" must sit down in other child's seat before other child touches (tags) "it" before he/she can sit down. If he/she is tagged, "it" must sit in the "Kaboom."

Knots

Students/children need to learn the skill of following directions either from a model or picture. Students could learn how to make knots using colored roving. Some knots that could be made are a figure-of-8 knot, a square knot, a granny knot, an overhand knot, a thief knot, a half hitch, a loop knot, a cats-paw, and a surgeon's knot.

King Kick Ball

King Kick Ball could be played. One student is the "King." He holds the ball, or places it on the ground, and kicks it to the other students situated in the field. If the student catches a fly ball it is worth three points. If a ground ball is gathered (caught) it receives one point. When a field member receives five points, he/she becomes "King." (Five points so everyone can have a chance to be "King" and the game is faster).

Kumquats

Kumquats are from China. The word means golden orange. It could be compared/contrasted to Kiwi from New Zealand.

K-k Word Lists

Area:

Kabul	Kabyle	Kadesh
Kagoshima	Kahoolawe	Kairouan
Kalahari	Kalamazoo	Kalimantan
Kalmar	Kalingrad	Kama
Kamchatka	Kampuchea	Kanzawa
Kanpur	Kansas	Kaohsiung
Kenya	Kashmir	Kauai
Knoxville	Kidron	Kiel Canal
Kokomo	Kumamoto	Kura
Kwangtung	Kyoto	

Food:

Kumquest	Kaki	kale
Kasha	kernel	ketchup
kidney beans	Kielbasa	Kiwi fruit
Kohlrabi	knockwurst	Kreplach Soup
Kugel	Kumquat	Kumiss

Animals:

Kalong	kangaroo	kangaroo rat
katydid	Kipper	Kingfish
kinkajou	koala	Kodiak bear
Kiwi	Komodo dragon	kookaburra
komondor	kudu	Kakapo

Verb/Action Word:

keep	kick	kill
kiss	knit	knock
know	kneel	

Noun or Object:

Karyo	Kendo	Kernel

123

Ketch	Kettle	Kabuki
Knot	Knuckle	kaleidoscope
kapok	kayak	keg
kelp	kerosene	kettle
keel	key	knot
kickball	kid	kidney
kilt	kimono	kind
king	kisses	kit
kitchen	kite	kitten
knee	knife	knight
knur	Kamikaze	Kakemono
Kamala	Kalazar	Kopek
kite	kitchen	Kumiss
Kwashiorkor	Kyphosis	

Descriptive Word:

keen	klutz	Khaki
Knowledgeable		

K-k Reading Resources

Kidnapped on a Star — J.L. Nixon

King of the Wind — Marguerite Henry — Rand McNally, 1949

Koko's Kitchen — Francie Patterson: Scholastic, 1985

Old King Cole — nursery rhyme

Katie Morag and the Two Grandmothers — Mairi Hedderwick: Little Brown, 1986

The King Has Horse's Ears — Peggy Thompson: Simon and Schuster, 1988

King Island Christmas — Jean Rogers: Greenwillow, 1985

Knee High Man: And Other Tales — Julius Lester: Dial/Pied Piper, 1972

Keep THE Lights Burning Abbie — Peter and Connie Roop: Carolrhoda, 1985

The Kid Next Door and Other Headaches: Stories About Adam Joshua — Janice Lee Smith: Harper and Row, 1984

Katie John — Mary Calhoun: Harper and Row, 1960

The Grey King — Cooper: Athenium, 1976

My Kitchen — Harlow Rockwell: Greenwillow, 1980

I'm King of the Castle — Shigeo Wantanabe: Philomel, 1982

Three Kittens — Mirra Ginsburg: Crown, 1973

A Kiss for Little Bear — Else Holmelund Minarik: Harper and Row —, 1968

Knots on a Counting Rope — Bill Martin, Jr. and John Archambaultt: Holt, 1987

The Great Kapok Tree — Lynne Cherry Harcourt & Brace Jovanovich, 1990

Kimako's Story — June Jordan: Houghton Mifflin Co., 1981

L-l Recipes

LEGIBLE, LIKABLE L's

Materials:

1/2 teaspoon yeast

1/2 teaspoon sugar

bowl rolling pin

salt shaker: could use Kosher or Sea Salt (larger pieces)

3 tablespoons warm water

8 tablespoons flour

Directions:

1. Clean hands, area, and equipment.
2. Add water, yeast, sugar, and flour into bowl.
3. Blend with hands.
4. Knead with hands.
5. Roll out into logs.
6. Link logs to form capital and lower case "L/l".
7. Sprinkle with salt.
8. Bake at 425 degrees for 15 minutes until golden brown.

LIKABLE LUCKY LATKES

Materials:

electric skillet

1 carrot

1 cold egg

parsley

knife

1/2 teaspoon salt

potato grater

cutting board

1 spatula

4 potatoes

1 onion

small bowl

1/2 teaspoon baking powder

2 tablespoons flour

dash pepper

cooking oil

applesauce or sour cream

Directions:

1. Clean hands, area, and equipment.
2. Grate potatoes and carrot.
3. Chop onion and parsley.
4. Add one egg.
5. In a small bowl, combine baking powder, flour, salt, and pepper.
6. Add contents of small bowl to potatoes, carrot, egg, onion, and parsley.
7. Drain some extra liquid and blend all ingredients.
8. Heat oil in skillet.
9. Drop batter into oil and brown. Then use spatula and flip until both sides are golden brown.
10. Drain on paper towel.

LOVELY LEMONY PANCAKES

Materials:

1 egg1/4 cup milk
2 tablespoons oil
1 cup flour
1 tablespoon sugar
mixing bowl
electric skillet
frying oil

1/4 cup plain yogurt
2 tablespoons baking powder
1 tablespoon grated lemon peel
1 tablespoon powdered sugar
spatula

Directions:

1. Clean hands, area, and equipment.
2. Add egg, milk, yogurt, and oil in bowl.
3. Beat lightly.
4. Add flour, baking powder, sugar, lemon peel and stir.
5. Heat frying oil in electric skillet.
6. Spoon batter into hot oil.
7. When pancakes are full of bubbles, flip over with spatula.
8. Cook until lightly browned on both sides.
9. Serve with sprinkled powdered sugar.

LOVELY LEMON LOLLYPOPS

Materials:

1/2 teaspoon of lemon zest (skin of lemon scraped with grater or zester)
stove or hot plate
3/4 cups light corn sugar
few drops of yellow food coloring
1/2 teaspoon lemon extract (in a bottle)
molds or aluminum foil
saucepan
red hots

2 cups sugar
1 tablespoon butter
1 cup water

candy
spoon sticks
life savers   hard candy

Directions:

1. Clean hands, area, and equipment.
2. Place sugar, corn syrup, and water in saucepan.
3. Cook over high flame.
4. Stir until sugar dissolves.
5. Continue cooking (without stirring until it reaches the hard crack stage (310 degrees) with candy thermometer) — drop a small quantity of syrup into ice water. Syrup will separate into threads that are hard & brittle.
6. Grease lollypop molds or foil.
7. Remove from heat and add oil of lemon and coloring.
8. Pour.
9. Press stick into lollypops.
10. Decorate with Red Hots™, Life Savers™, and hard candy.

LIVELY LEGUME SOUPS

There are more than 10,000 species of legumes: pods which open along two sides when the edible seeds are ripe. Some legumes are dried peas and beans. Packaged legumes must be washed and some packages recommend/require soaking. Bring beans to slow boil after soaked. Reduce heat and simmer. One cup of beans/peas will expand to 2 to 2-1/2 cups after cooking.

RECIPE #1

Materials:

6 cups water with beef stock or beef bouillon

medium-sized onion, chopped	1 large rib of celery, chopped
crock pot	salt and pepper to taste
cutting board	1/2 cup canned baked beans
1 carrot, sliced	1 potato cut up
barley (if needed)	1-1/2 cups stewed or canned tomatoes

Directions:

1. Clean hands, area, and equipment.
2. Using a crock-pot or hot plate with stock pot, add all ingredients except canned beans.
3. Cook for 2-3 hours or until the potatoes, carrots, and celery are tender.
4. Add canned beans and cook for 15-20 minutes longer.
5. This is lively.

LENTIL SOUP (RECIPE #2)

Materials:

1 smoked ham bone/or beef bones

8 cups of water	2 carrots, scraped, sliced
1 bay leaf	2 ribs celery, chopped
2 cups lentils, rinsed	salt/pepper to taste

herbs, such as: oregano, rosemary, basil, sage, thyme, & tarragon

Directions:

1. Clean hands, area, and equipment.
2. In soup kettle add lentils. Simmer for at least 1 hour.
3. Put kettle on stove or hot plate/or in a crock-pot. Add all the rest of the contents. Cook for 2 hours or until legumes are tender.
4. Take out bay leaf and ham or beef bone.
5. Serve in plastic bowls or ceramic bowls.

Light Lemony Gelatin Initials

Materials:

3 teaspoons grated lemon rind or lemon extract

baking dish	1 pkg. tablespoon gelatin (Knox™)
3/4 cup cold water	4-1/2 cup boiling water
2-1/4 cup sugar	alphabet cookie cutters
3/4 teaspoon salt	lemon drops/yellow life savers
shredded coconut	1-1/2 cup lemon juice
baking dish	whipped cream/cream cheese
plastic knives	plates

Directions:

1. Clean hands, area, and equipment.
2. Soak gelatin into cold water.
3. Dissolve it in boiling water in large bowl.
4. Add sugar, salt, and lemon juice to gelatin. Add grated lemon rind.
5. Pour into greased baking dish or dish sprayed with non-stick oil.
6. When gelatin has gelled, use cookie cutters or knife to cut initials.
7. Decorate with whipped cream or whipped cream cheese and use lemon drops or lemon Life Savers™ or other lemon candies, which can also be used.

Loretta Lion

Materials:

1 slice of bread per student

16 oz. cream cheese (softened) or peanut butter

Cheerios	nuts	Red Hots™
raisins	olives	black licorice
cutting board	knives	

Directions:

1. Clean hands, area, and equipment.
2. Cut off edges of bread.
3. Spread peanut butter or brown cream cheese (food colored with red, yellow, and blue).
4. Add Cheerios™, Cheetos™ or any round-like munchies for mane.
5. Use raisins or 1/2 olives for eyes.
6. A red hot for the nose.
7. Black licorice whips for whiskers.
8. Nuts for the mouth.
9. Children will sing, "La, La, La ..."

L-l Games/Activities

LOOK IT UP

This letter has a lot of words that are the names of areas. Students should look up some of the names in a dictionary or atlas and/or locate them on a World Map. It is a lively activity. This can be done in Cooperative Learning Groups, so that all the students can learn the location of several areas that begin with L-l.

L-L FLASHCARDS

Many of the L-l words could be written on flashcards. The teacher then has the children read/recognize/listen to the word and orally state or dictate a sentence to be written down and read to the class. The sentence is copied and may be illustrated. L-l books could be made and published. A library could be stocked with books.

L-L WORDS

Many words can be written onto flash cards. They can be sorted/classified/grouped into nouns, verbs, areas, foods, animals, etc. Students could then find pictures or draw pictures to illustrate the words. These words could be added to their word lists/dictionaries/charts. Then students can manipulate words and choose two to three words to write/dictate a sentence (adding as many other words as they need to make the sentence make sense). A game can be learned/played to see who/which learning group can make the longest sentence that makes sense.

LOG CABIN

Lincoln Logs™ are still available in toy stores. Students could make a log cabin. If it is not available, then allow students to find twigs and glue them to make a log cabin. A milk carton can be used for the frame. Many log cabins and stores can make a town. Several cabins glued together can make a community building and/or store. A church can also be made the same way.

L-L SONGS

"London Bridges Falling Down" can be played. Another L-l song that can be sung is "Let Everyone Clap Hands Like Me." This is great for rainy days or physical movements.

LEGENDARY LETTUCE SALAD

Students could make a "Legendary Lettuce Salad." Teacher could bring clean, cut up lettuce and each child could bring one thing to add to the "Legendary Lettuce Salad." The recipe could be written down. Children can decide which ingredients they like in their salad and which they didn't like. A chart/graph could be made with ingredients that they liked. They could then write their own "How To Make A Legendary Lettuce Recipe." (This is similar to a required test, so this is good practice).

LUNCHEON MEAT

Students can taste different kinds of luncheon meat. This is good for the child who is home

132

and gets hungry before mom/parent comes home. He or she can make a sandwich of bread, spread, lettuce, and luncheon meat. There are so many in the market that many mothers don't try a variety due to the cost. One package of several kinds could be purchased and samples tried ... another alternative is to send home notes for 1 package of bologna, salami, head cheese, etc. Samples (small bite size pieces) can be tasted and charted/graphed/described, and sorted (spicy, flavorful, boring, tasty, etc.) Students can also write about what they thought of the variety of luncheon meat in their journals. Students could write "How to Make A Luncheon Meat Sandwich."

LEAVES

Leaves can be gathered from around the school or from home. They can then be sorted by shape or color, one vein or several. The leaves can be mounted/preserved by ironing between two pieces of waxed paper (use old iron). A book could then be made with a paragraph written on a 3x5 card about the leaf: 1) what kind it is, 2) where it was found, and 3) who found it. Any sentence written by the child would be written, saying, "I like this leaf because ..." The book can stay in either the classroom library or in school library.

LIBRARY TRIPS

Many schools have libraries with schedules so that each class has its time in this valuable place. A trip to a local library could be taken. There would be more books and children could learn about library cards. They could check out books that have an "L-l" in the title.

LION HEAD

A game using any game board or a "Lion-head" with a start and finish indicators and path could be used. The flash cards made from the L-l lists could be placed face down. A child rolls the dice. If he can read/re-cognize the word/or tell if it begins with "L-l", he moves his marker to the number corresponding to the dice. The child who moves from start to finish first wins.

LOTS OF THINGS

Many times we say "Lots of things", lots of times ... many or a great number of times. Jars could be filled with marbles, tokens of some sort (rocks) students could guess which jar contains the most to understand the idea of lots. The jars could differ in shape. Boxes of items could also be filled and used to help comprehend what the word "lots" means. The number could be charted/grafted to see which had the most. Whose guess came closest? This helps students realize the association between the number (guess) and amount (items in the jar or box).

LOTTO #1

Lotto means an object used in deciding a matter by chance. Draw grids on tag board, 5 squares down by 5 squares across (similar to Bingo). Write a vocabulary word in each grid. (The word L-O-T-T-O could be written across the top.) A number of flashcards with the vocabulary words are placed in a container and then drawn out at random, one by one. Any child who has that word on their card then places a marker on the word. The first child that has five connecting markers either down, across, or diagonally, wins the game. They must read them back to the leader.

LOTTO #2

Using the words on flash cards, look for pictures to match from used textbooks, catalogues, newspapers, magazines, or hand drawn pictures. Place pictures and words together to help children relate to words. Then place 30 cards down — (15 pictures/15 words) to make a large square. Each player chooses two cards, shows it to all, and if they match, they are called a "Lotto" (or pair) and that player keeps it. The player keeps turning over cards until two do not match and the next player is up. The game proceeds until all the "Lotto" cards are matched. The player with the most pairs wins.

L-l Word Lists

Animal:

Labrador Retriever	lambs	ladybugs
Lemur	leech	ling (fish)
lizards	llama	lobo
lobster	locust	loon
long-horned beetle	long-horned grasshopper	
louse	lynx	Lyrebird
lark	lanternfly	lap wing
larder beetle	lubber grasshopper	luce
Lake-land terrier	Lake Trout	langur

Action words/Verbs:

lag	large	last
late	laugh	lay
lead	learn	lend
left	less	let
lick	light	like
limit	list	little
live	lock	long
look	loop	loot
lose	loss	lost
loud	love	low
luck	lug	luxury
lag screw	lash	lay
lallygag	lurch	lurk
leap	lack	lounge
lull	lumber	launder

Everyday/objects:

lab	label	lace
lad	ladder	lady
lagoon	lake	lard
last	lowboy	lurch
lure	luxury	land
lap	law	leaf
leg	legend	Leprechaun

letter	level	lever
lilac	lilly	line
link	lip	labor
loan	lock	lump
lung	lute	lather
lane	lark	lawn
Latch Key	latch	lattice
lead	language	lacquer
ladle	latchet	lane
lounge	lower	launch
lattice	lapel	launder
lamp	lance	lantern
lack	lash	luncheon
lumber		

Foods:

ladle	lasagna	latkes
leek	legumes	lemonade
lemon drops	lemons	lentils
lettuce	licorice	lima beans
lime	limeade	linguine
liver	liverwurst	lobster tail
Loganberry	lollipops	Lorain
lunch	luncheon meat	Lyonaise
lox		

Areas:

Labuan	Laccadive	Laconia
La Coruna	La Crosse	Ladoga
Lambeth	Libya	London
Lubeck	Lusaka	Luxembourg
Lydian	Lynn	lagoon
Lafayette	La-hore	Lahti
Lanchow	Lanchester	Land's End
Lapaz	Lake Charles	Lamancha
Little Rock	Lake of the Woods	Lachine
Labrador	Las-caux	Lake District
Lambeth	Lake Woods	Latvia

L-I Reading Resources

Lincoln (A photo-biography) — Russel Freedom: Clarion, 1887

The Little Prince — Antoinede de Saint — Exupery: HBJ/ Harvest, 1943

A Little Princess — Frances Hodgson Burnett: Lippincott/ Harper Collins, 1963

The Lucky Stone — Lucille Clifton: Del a Corte Press, 1976

Little Bear — Else Holmelund Minarik: Harper Collins, 1957

LuLu Goes to Witch School — Jane O' Connor: Harper Collins, 1987

Little Witch's Big Night — Deborah Hautzig: Random House, 1985

Lassie Come Home — Eric Knight: Dell Yearling, 1940

Learning to Say Good-Bye: When a Parent Dies — Eda Le Shan: MacMillian, 1976

My Little Island — Frane Lessac: Harper and Row, 1985

Land I Lost: Adventures of a Boy in Vietnam — Huynh Quang Nhuong: Harper & Row, 1982

Lentil — Robert McCloskey

Little House in the Big Woods — Laura Wilder: Harper & Row/Harper Collins, 1932

Little Red Riding Hood — Brothers Grimm: Holiday, 1983

Little Women — Louisa May Alcott: Little Brown/Penguin, 1868

The Lady and the Spider — Faith McNulty: Harper & Row, 1986

Latkes and Applesauce: A Hanukah Story — Fran Manushkin: Scholastic, 1990

Let's Go Swimming with Mr. Silly Pants — M.K. Brown: Crown, 1986

A Lion for Lewis — Rosemary Wells: Dial/Pied Piper, 1982

The Little Duck — Judy Dunn: Random House, 1976

The Little Fir Tree — Margaret Wise Brown: T.Y. Crowell/ Harper Collins, 1979

The Little Fur Family — Margaret Wise Brown: Harper & Row, 1951

Little Gorilla — Ruth Bornstein: Clarion, 1976

The Little House — Virginia Lee Burton: Houghton Mifflin, 1942

The Little Red Lighthouse and the Great Gray Bridge — Hildegarde Hoyt Swift: HBJ/voyager, 1942

Little Rabbit's Loose Tooth — Lucy Bate: Crown, 1975

The Little Island — Golden McDonald: Doubleday/zephyr, 1946

Louanne Pig in the Talent Show — Nancy Carlson: Penguin/Carolrhoda, 1986

The Little Red Hen — Paul Galdone: Clarion, 1974

Lon Po Po: A Red Riding Hood Story from China — Ed Young, Philomel, 1989

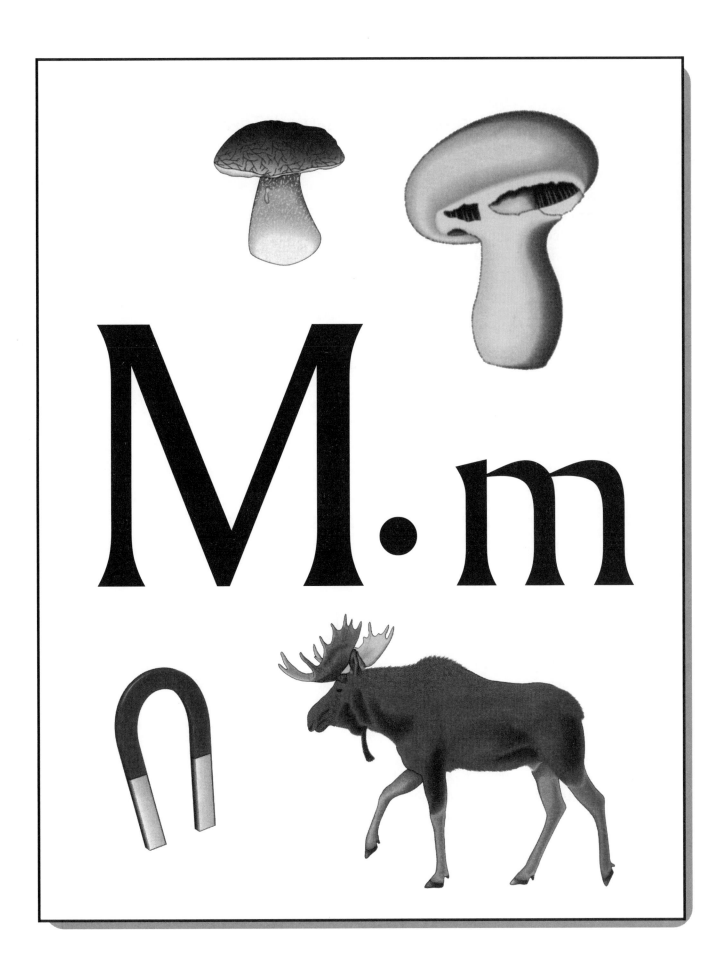

M∙m

M-m — Recipes

MAR-VEL-OUS MARSHMALLOW TREATS

Materials:

1/8 teaspoon of cinnamon
1/4 cup margarine or butter
10-1/2 oz bag (6 cups) miniature marshmallows
5 cups crispy rice cereal   bowls
1 cup of nuts (peanuts/walnuts)   knife
microwave oven   wooden spoons

Directions:

1. Clean hands, area, and equipment.
2. Melt margarine or butter in microwave bowl (high 45 seconds).
3. Add marshmallows, stirring until melted and very well blended. (High for 1-1/2 minutes-stir after 45 seconds)
4. Remove from heat.
5. Stir in cereal and nuts until well coated.
6. Press into greased baking pan.
7. Cool and cut.
8. M-m-m-m-m-m-m.

MILLIONAIRE'S MELBA SAUCE

Served over melons or marble cake.

Materials:

glass bowl   wooden spoon
1/8 teaspoon salt   1/2 cup sugar
double boiler or microwave   1 cup currant fruit jelly
1 cup raspberries, juice & pulp   1 tablespoon cornstarch
1 tablespoon cold water

Directions:

1. Clean hands, area, and equipment.
2. In clear bowl for microwave or top pan in double boiler add jelly, sugar, and raspberries. Cook until it reaches the boiling point (2-3 minutes in microwave).
3. Add cornstarch to water and mix. Add to syrup.
4. Continue to cook until it becomes thick and clear-stir often.
5. Cool.
6. Serve over melons or marble cake.
7. Marvelous.

MARVELOUS MAGIC MUFFINS

Muffins are easy and fun. Add beaten liquid ingredients to dry with very few strokes.

Materials:

small bowl
1/2 cup milk
1/2 teaspoon salt
1/2 cup sugar or honey
big bowl
2 large eggs
M & M's
1/3 cup raisins

1-3/4 cup flour
2-1/2 teaspoons baking powder
1 teaspoon pumpkin pie spice
1/8 teaspoon ground ginger
1/3 cup margarine or oil
1/2 cup chopped walnuts
muffin or aluminum cupcake holders
canned frosting/jar of peanut butter

Directions:

1. Clean hands, area, and equipment.
2. In a small bowl, combine flour, baking powder, and salt.
3. Add pumpkin pie spice, ground ginger, and sugar.
4. In a big bowl, combine margarine, milk, and eggs.
5. Add contents of small bowl to pumpkin mixture and add raisins and nuts.
6. Mix only until blended.
7. Pour into muffin holders or paper cupcake holders until 2/3 full.
8. Bake in preheated 400 degree oven for 20 minutes.
9. Use canned frosting or peanut butter and M&M's™ to decorate. (Optional)1/2 cup of apricots, nuts, bananas, apples, and 1/4 cup cheese as well as 1 cup blueberries & cranberries may also be added.

MYSTERIOUS MONSTER COOKIES

Materials:

cookie decorations-like dried fruit, raisins, coconut
canned frosting
toaster oven/oven
knife
flour

sugar cookie refrigerator dough
cutting board
foil

Directions:

1. Clean hands, area, and equipment.
2. Preheat toaster oven to 350 degrees.
3. Slice prepared cookie dough on cutting board.
4. Cut into slices 1/2-inch thick and then cut into quarters.
5. Flour the cutting board and shape cookies into "monster shapes."
6. Line the baking pan with foil.
7. Bake 7-10 minutes or until golden brown.
8. Allow cookies to cool.
9. Top with canned frosting and decorate.
10. Make M-m Monsters.

MAGNIFICENT MINESTRONE SOUP

An Italian soup made with many different kinds of vegetables and macaroni, or other pasta. It can be made in a crock pot or soup kettle.

Materials:

large soup pot or crock pot   2 qts. of water (or 2 cans or chicken/beef broth)
Lawry's seasoned salt, pepper, bay leaf, garlic powder
1 cup cooked macaroni/or other pasta
1 cup celery, chopped   1/2 cup peeled & diced potatoes
1 cup carrots, diced   1/4 cup onion
1 cup tomatoes, diced   1 leek diced
1/2 cup zucchini   any canned beans

Directions:

1. Clean hands, area, and equipment.
2. Add 2 cups of water/broth and fill measuring cup with water to make 1-1/2 to 2 qts. liquid.
3. Add cut up vegetables. Cook for 1 hour.
4. Add cooked macaroni or pasta.
5. Add seasonings to taste.
6. Cook until all is tender.
7. Season to your taste.

Marvelous Milk Nog

Everyone's favorite breakfast or special treat.

Materials:

blender
3-1/2 cups chilled milk
4 eggs (chilled until use)
1 tablespoon cocoa powder
1 teaspoon vanilla, almond, or mint extract

4 tablespoons honey
glasses/cups
3/4 cup cracked ice
1/8 teaspoon ground nutmeg

Directions:

1. Clean hands, area, and equipment.
2. Using a blender, add milk, eggs, and cocoa powder. Mix.
3. Add honey, vanilla (or other extract) with ice.
4. When mixed well and ready to serve, pour into cups/glasses and top with a sprinkle of nutmeg.
5. Mar-vel-ous.

M-M-M-M Marshmallow Pudding

Materials:

2 baking dishes, one which fits into the pan 1/4" filled with water
2 large eggs, beaten
1/2 teaspoon salt
1/4 teaspoon cinnamon
3 cups milk
1/4 cup soft butter
1 cup miniature marshmallows.

1/4 cup sugar
1 teaspoon vanilla extract
1/4 teaspoon nutmeg, ground
3-5 cups of cubed/diced bread
measuring spoons and cups

Directions:

1. Clean hands, area, and equipment.
2. Combine eggs, sugar, salt, and spices.
3. Add milk and mix well. Then add bread cubes.
4. Allow time for bread to soak up liquid-1 or 2 minutes.
5. Butter baking pan (butter first and then spray with Pam™ non-stick coating/spray).
6. Pour/spoon ingredients into baking pan.
7. Set baking pan into pan with water.
8. Bake in 350 degree oven for 40-50 minutes or until tester comes out clean.
9. Cover/spread with a layer of marshmallows and bake until marshmallows are melted and slightly browned (just a few seconds-watch carefully).
10. M-M-M-M-M.

M-m —Games/Activities

MARMALADE

There are many kinds of marmalade in the grocery stores today. Many children have not tasted it. It usually contains the fruit and sliced up peels in the jam. Spread on bread or crackers. Allow students to describe/tell which one they liked best and why. Chart/graph the results.

MEATS

Indians ate the meat from alligator, antelope, bear, beaver, buffalo, caribou, deer, elk, moose, rabbits, goats, squirrels, raccoon, opossum, and muskrats. Today, we have added cow, pig, lamb, and young cows or veal. Students can discuss their favorite meats and a chart/graph can be made. A questionnaire made of what's your favorite meat - students can collect data. The information can be included in your daily mail to the parents.

MAIL PERSON

Children can sit in a circle. One child is the "mailperson." The mailperson has an envelope which is held while the child chants, "I don't have a letter for you or you or you." But when the mailperson reaches the selected person, he or she says, "But I have a letter for you." The selected person grabs the letter/ envelope placed behind them and tries to catch the mailperson. The mailperson must run around the circle and sit down in the selected person's seat first. If tagged, the mailperson goes into the circle called the "dead letter office." The game continues until time is used up or all students/children have gotten to be the mailperson. A field trip to the Post Office to see how mail is delivered would be informational and very meaningful. A mailperson can be invited to your class to tell about their career.

M-M-M-M M & M's

Each student should trace large patterns of an upper case and lower case M-m. They can outline the letter in string or roving. Glue can be used to adhere M&M's™ to the patterns. When the group is finished, they can chart/graph how many yellows, oranges, greens, browns, or blue (dark or light) they have.

MYSTERY M-M HUNT

Each student/detective should each be given a magnifying glass. They must search the room for a designated time (2-3 mins.) and state/write down the objects or put them in a bag that they find which start with an /M-m/ sound. The student with most correct items wins. They are the M-m detective for the day.

MOUSE HUNT

Students can be "mouse detectives." They can search for items that begin/contain an /M-m/ sound. They can look on the way home from school, at home, in magazines, or on TV. They can orally dictate or list items that start with or have an /M-m/ in the name of the object (noun or descriptive word (adverb)). They can bring them in an /M-m/ bag. The student who wins can wear mouse ears (cut circles and leave a tab so it can be attached with hairpins) or a cap with mouse ears stapled on it would also work. The "mouse detective" could also be line leader

My Moving Musical Feet

The game "My Moving Musical Feet" may be played. Teacher/leader cuts out feet-shaped paper which need to be attached to the floor or carpet. Teacher cuts out enough feet (2 per child) for all the children playing except one child. When the music starts, the children must move his or her feet from one paper foot to the next foot until the music stops. The child who does not have their feet on two paper feet must sit down. The teacher then removes one or two feet and starts the music again. The child that is still moving when everyone else has sat down is the musical leader and he may work the record player or tape recorder.

My Many Moods Book

A My Many Moods Book can be written. Using the bottom from a coffee can lid, a circle can be traced and each child can draw in his/her face. The facial expression must match the child's mood. On the bottom, or the side, write the date and mood (happy, sad, depressed, unhappy, pleased, proud, good, bad, etc.) on that paper (plus, the reason for that mood). If the child is unable to write inventively then he or she can dictate and copy. The paper can then be corrected and given to the teacher. Each child must then help match the paper with their mood, read what has been written, and then add it to either a class or individual book. Do this for 1 month. It is marvelous to graph/chart the moods of each child. This is a good indicator/motivator for each child.

Multimals

Pictures from discarded textbooks, catalogs, magazines, and newspapers of animals can be used to cut up. The multimal may have a head of a zebra, body of a monkey, and feet of an ostrich. The multimal must have a name, whether it is a bird, insect, spider, mammal, or a one-valve shell or two. The child also must describe its habitat, where it lives, and what it eats.

Mammal Reports

There are several types of mammals listed under animals that start with the letter M-m or have the /M-m/ sound. Students can go to the library and research information about their Cooperative Learning group's choice. Included in the report may be: habitat, what they eat, their favorite food, and how they live. Their reports can be read to the class.

Animal Masks

There are several animals in the word list. Students can use socks, felt, and magic markers to make masks, like a mouse, mule, monkey, moth, moose, muskrat, mongoose, mammoth, mink, mosquito, and marmoset. Paper bags, construction paper, crayons, and magic markers can also be used. The students can then get into groups and write a skit/story using their masks as props. Also, paper plates are easily used to make masks.

Measuring . . . Mapping

Students can make maps of their own bedrooms using a 12 " ruler and then a yardstick. They can learn the reason for a universal/accurate type of measuring rather than by hands or feet. Students can then measure their classroom and draw a map of the way it is arranged.

At night, the teacher should rearrange the room to see if they can orally state what has changed, then more scientifically, compare with the use of their maps. They can measure the distance from their seat to: the office, drinking fountain, bathroom, and cafeteria. They can also practice measuring beans, rice, and colored water with a cup,   cup, ° cup and 1/8 cup. Remember, it must be level. Measuring spoons can also be used.

M-M MUSICAL CHAIRS

The teacher can label each chair with the letter of the alphabet. The teacher assigns each child to a letter except "M-m" which is musical. That chair is placed by the record player or tape recorder. The children move from one letter to another saying the sound/name out loud. When "M-m" stops the music, whoever does not have a lettered seat must sit down and they are out. Whoever doesn't identify/name the letter/sound of the chair/correctly is also out. The person who can get a chair and recognizes the letter/sound correctly the longest or is up last becomes Mr. or Ms. "M-m."

MILLIONS OF MAGNETS

Little magnets can be purchased inexpensively. Give each child a magnet and allow them to master the evidence as to what a magnet will and will not do. Graph/chart what they have learned.

MARVELOUS MACARONI MUSEUM-LIKE-PIECES

There are many, many shapes of macaroni in the market today. Students can dye it in food coloring and water (for just a few minutes), dry it thoroughly, and then string or thread it on elastic string or plastic thread to make a marvelous museum like jewelry. Necklaces, bracelets, and anklets might be suggested. A pattern can be established and repeated in all the pieces. (Also thin elastic can be used and knotted so a clasp would not be necessary.) Macaroni needs to dry thoroughly before used to make jewelry or used to make pictures or designs using glue and yarn. It can be glued to bottles or juice cans also.

MANDY MONKEY

Use 2 slices of bread. Cut off the edges of both slices of bread and make both of them round. Use one round slice for the face. Cut the second piece in half, and trim away a bit, so each piece becomes one of the monkey ears. Use peanut butter and spread it over the monkey face. Use a peanut for a nose, raisins for eyes, and a piece of licorice for a mouth.

M-m — Word Lists

Foods or food related:

meat	mug	meatballs
marshmallows	molasses	mustard
milk	macadamia nut	macaroni
macaroon	mutton	muffin
mint	marmalade	maraschino
mushroom	mango	mulligatawny
monkey bread	mix	manicotti
melon	mackerel	maple
marinara sauce	matzo	morel
mocha	margarine	Mincemeat
Mostacciol	Mussels	Maple Syrup

Geographical areas (rivers/places):

Macao	Macedonia	Mackenzie
Madhya Pradesh	Madison	Madrid
Mafeking	Macquarie	Magellan
Magdalena	Magyar	Missouri
Manhattan Island	Meerut	Melanesia
Mahican	Muscat	Muscovite
Moulmein	Moscow	Moselle
Morocco	Moravia	Monte Carlo
Moosehead Lake	Marshall Islands	Mobile Bay

Animals:

mouse	maggot	mite
mule	mag pie	manatee
mole	mutt	mammoth
mice	muskrat	mink
monkey	mussel	mantis
moose	mullet	marmoset
mosquito	moth	marten
macaque	mongoose	mayfly
macaw	mongrel	meloid

mackerel	minnow	musk ox
moloch	Monarch Butterfly	

Objects:

morning	month	motor scooter
mortar	moon	Mercury
mall	microphone	mackinaw
mark	measles	motor
moon	mess	magazine
me	manager	magma
mail	musician	mahjong
man	monster	mallet
map	magnet	mythology
mat	match	mystery
music	motorcycle	mute
museum	model	music
mop	mace	muscle
mother	machete	mural
mug	machine	mouth
mud	mortgage	mountain
monogram	mission	monopoly
mirror	monolith	minor
melody	minute	money
mandolin	mob	mantilla
mitten	mitt	maze
member	magnifying glass	

Descriptive words/action/verb:

mark	magnify	marry
mythical	maul	mystic
merry	mutilate	muster
made	mumble	make
multiplication	may	move
mad	mash	mourn
mean	monsoon	mow
monopoly	mother	modernize
marvelous	model	mastered
moan	much	mix
many	mistrust	mission
magic	miserable	magnificent
miss	mess	mischief
mighty	manipulate	marched

marine	mard	mean
measure	meager	meddle
meet	medium	mediocre
million		

M—m —Reading Resources

Mouse Soup — Arnold Lobel: Harper & Row, 1972

The Mitten — Alvin Tresselt: Lothrop, Lee, & Shepard, 1967

Marmalades' Nap — Cincy Wheeler: Knoph, 1982

Mama Went Walking — Christine Berry: Holt, 1991

Max's Chocolate Chicken — Rosemary Wells, Dial, 1990

The Mixed-up Mice Clean House — Robert Kraus, Warner, 1991

Monsters of the Sea — Rita Golden Gelman, Little Brown, 1991

Morris the Moose — B. Wiseman: Harper Collins, 1990

Mouse Paint — Ellen Stoll Walsh: Harcourt Brace Jovanovich, 1990

Mixed-up Sam — Elaine Moore: Milliken, 1990

Mathilda the Dream Bear — Nicholas Heller: Greenwillow, 1990

Movie Monsters — Tom Powers: Lerner, 1990

Merry Christmas Festus and Mercury — Sven Nordquist: Carolrhoda, 1990

Mummy Knows Best — Robert Kraus: Warner, 1989

Mail-Order Kid — Joyce McDonald: Putnam, 1989

My Mom Made Me Go to Camp — Judy Delton: Delacorte, 1991

Mike Mulligan and His Steam Shovel — Virginia Lee Burton: Houghton Mifflin, 1939

Molly's Pilgrim — Barbara Cohen: Bantam, 1983

The Mouse and the Motorcycle — Beverly Cleary: Avon, 1965

Many Moons — James Thurber: Voyager, 1943

Mazel and Shlimazel — Issacc Bashevis Singer: Sunburst, 1967

Minn of the Mississippi — Holling C. Holling: Houghton Mufflin, 1951

Mufaro's Beautiful Daughters: An African Queen — John Steptoe: Scholastic, 1987

Mrs. Moskowitz and the Sabbath Candles — Amy Schwartz: Jewish Publication Society, 1984

Miss Nelson Is Missing — Harry Allard: Houghton Mifflin, 1977

Madeline — Ludwig Bemelmans: Puffin, 1939

Moja Means One—Swahili Counting Book — Muriel Feelings: Pied Piper, 1974

Make Way for Ducklings — Robert McCloskey: Pufflin, 1941

Mama Don't Allow — Thacher Hurd: Harper Trophy, 1984

The Man Who Kept House — Katheleen and Michael Hague: Voyager, 1981

Millions of Cats — Wanda Gag: Sandcastle, 1928

May I Bring a Friend? — Beatrice Schenk de Regniers: Aladdin, 1964

Mitchell Is Moving — Marjorie Weinman Scharmat: Macmillian, 1978

Mouse Paint — Ellen Stollwalsh: HBJ, 1989

Moonlight — Jan Ormerod: Puffin, 1982

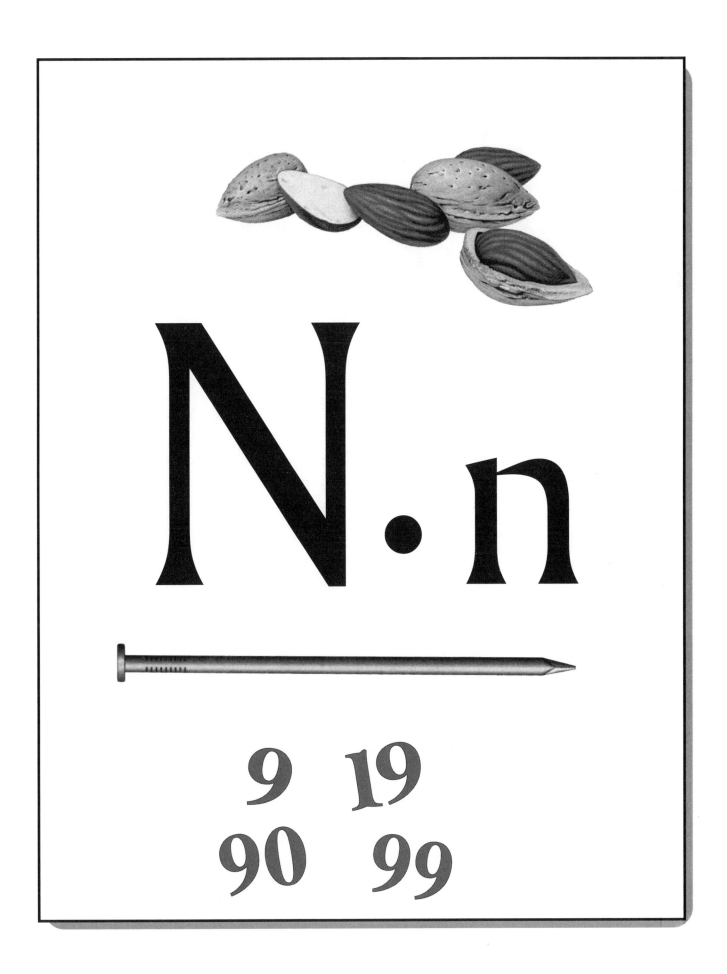

N.n

9 19
90 99

N-n — Recipes

NORMAN NEWTS

Norman Newts could be assembled to reinforce the sound of N-n.

Materials:

cutting board
toothpicks
raisins
gumdrops (or miniature marshmallows)
carton of solid cream cheese (or peanut butter)
cutting board

knife   paper plates
stalk of celery (per child)
1 large marshmallow (per child)

Directions:

1. Clean hands, area, and equipment.
2. Clean celery and cut into 3 inch long rectangles.
3. Spread cream cheese (or peanut butter) on each celery stalk.
4. Use toothpicks as legs and attach to a marshmallow or raisin for feet.
5. Attach a toothpick and large marshmallow for head. Eyes can be glued on with cream cheese or peanut butter. Raisins or cinnamon dots can also be used for eyes.
6. Use sprinkles to cover it and make him more "Newt-like."

NUTTY NOODLE NEST

Materials:

chocolate chips
peanuts
cookie trays
mixing bowl

1/2 cup chunky peanut butter
6 oz. package chow mien noodles
waxed paper

Directions:

1. Clean hands, area, and equipment.
2. Melt chocolate chips in bowl of hot water or in a microwave.
3. Stir chocolate chips well.
4. Add chow mien noodles.
5. Stir noodles well.
6. Add peanut butter.
7. Cover cookie sheets with waxed paper.
8. Drop spoonfuls of chocolate, peanut butter, and noodles onto cookie sheets.
9. Shape into nests and add five peanuts to each cluster.

NATIVE NACHOS

Materials:

electric fry pan
2 tomatoes
1 cup Jack cheese
1 lb. ground beef
diced chiles
microwave plate

1 package taco seasoning
1 can black olives
1 cup cheddar cheese
grater
tortilla chips

Directions

1. Clean hands, area, and equipment.
2. Brown and drain meat.
3. Place tortilla chips on microwaveable plate.
4. Follow taco seasoning package directions.
5. Sprinkle drained taco meat on top of tortilla chips.
6. Grate Jack and cheddar cheese.
7. Sprinkle cheese on meat.
8. Place in microwave on high for one to, 1 minute.
9. Add cut up tomatoes, sliced olives, and chilies.

NICE NIBBLY NOODLES

Materials:

1 tablespoon of chopped parsley, salt, pepper, garlic/onion powder
1 recipe of home made noodles, or 8 oz. package of noodles
3 qts. of boiling salt water
1 cup grated cheese
1 soup pot
spoon

3 tablespoons of butter
dish to serve/or dishes
1 colander

Directions:

1. Clean hands, area, and equipment.
2. Boil noodles in salty water until tender. Some people like it more tender and not al dente (firmer).
3. Use colander and drain. Some people like to rinse; it is up to you.
4. Add butter, seasonings, cheese, and stir.
5. Transfer to serving dish/dishes and sprinkle with parsley.

Nasty Nutty Treats

Materials:

12 oz. package of bakers semi-sweet real chocolate chips
10 oz. bag of large marshmallows   freezer
2 cups chopped walnuts/pecans/almonds
holders for nuts/coconut, other decorations
1 cup coconut(flaked)
wax paper/aluminum foil

Directions:

1. Clean hands, area, and equipment.
2. Place marshmallows on tray and freeze for, 15-30 minutes.
3. Microwave chocolate chips for, 1 minute—stir often.
4. Use skewer or pronged fork to dip marshmallow into chocolate until it is coated.
5. Roll into coconut, nuts or decorations.
6. Place on waxed paper or aluminum foil until eaten.
7. Nasty!

Neat Nut Bread

Materials:

2 cups flour   1/2 teaspoon salt
1 cup milk   3/4 cup sugar
1/4 cup oil   1 large egg, well beaten
1 cup chopped walnuts
1 tablespoon baking powder
bowls, spoon, loaf pan, oven measuring spoons, and cups.
oven or toaster oven

Directions:

1. Clean hands, area, and equipment.
2. Preheat oven to 350 degrees.
3. Stir flour, baking powder, salt, nuts, and sugar together in one bowl.
4. Stir milk, egg, and oil together in separate bowl.
5. Combine ingredients in both bowls. Mix until blended.
6. Pour into a greased and floured loaf pan.
7. Bake 45-50 minutes or until done.
8. Cool and enjoy.

N-n Games/Activities

Your Necessary Nose

All people have five senses and they are necessary for survival. Your nose smells and tells your brain whether what it has smelled should be eaten or not.

I.
1) Fill containers with water, white/clear vinegar, and white/clear ammonia.
2) Allow each child to tell you how they would be able to tell which one they can drink safely.
3) Let each child be blindfolded and see if he can guess which container has each liquid.
4) Chart/graph .

II. Place other object that smell, like oranges (peeled), bananas (peeled), lotion, coffee, milk, lemon, peaches (raw), and onions, in clear containers. Let each child guess (when blindfolded) what they are, using their nose to notice noxious/natural smells.

Our /N-n/ Word Book

1) Teacher writes some of the words from N-n word list on flashcards. She/he then asks the students if the words start with the /N-n/ sound. He/she work on comprehension/meaning of that word. Children/ students orally give that word in a sentence. Teacher writes it on the board.
2) Students choose words and write them into a sentence and illustrate it.
3) Pictures from magazines, catalogs, or newspapers could be used. Using dictation (or their own writing) about the object, its function could be written. This becomes a class book checked out and read many times and teachers may want to laminate it. This book helps with comprehension for all students.

Noodles

There are so many varieties of noodles in the grocery markets that a homework assignment may be to bring in a type of noodle. Atlas™ puts out a noodle maker for about $35-40. It is a hand-crank, which I've used for years. Students could also make their own with 3 cups flour and 4 large eggs unbeaten. Make a well of the flour, add eggs, and use your hands to combine. Then let it rest. Using your hands or a food processor, knead it. Then flatten into noodles with a rolling pin or pasta maker. Cut dry and cook in salted boiling water.

Nutty Noodles

Noodles can also be dyed with food coloring and glued, when thoroughly dried, to a tagboard capital "N" and lower case "n." Roving yarn may be glued around the edges to allow students to see/feel the shape better. Student can then, after thoroughly dried, feel the "N-n."

Newspeople

The students could pretend they are news reporters and gather facts. They could then type it into a computer or typewriter and publish as a class newspaper. Be careful—once this is done, you'll want to do another. Students' names could be placed on a square with a letter of

1) What his/her hobby is?
2) Favorite book?
3) Favorite food?
4) Favorite movie?
5) Favorite color?
6) Favorite car?
7) Favorite animal?

NEWSPAPER LOTTO

Students could find pictures from discarded books, old magazines, catalogs, or newspapers of objects that begin with or have an /N-n/ sound in the name. The picture could be glued to a 4"x6" card. The name of the object could also be written on a 4"x6" card. When enough cards with objects and names are made, a game of matching or concentration (lotto) could be played. (Lotto is played with the cards face down and each child takes a turn guessing, matching, then remembering where the pictures and words are.) If they choose two that match (are a pair), they get to hold them. The player with the most pairs wins.

NEWSPAPER FIND-SEARCH

Each child is given a sheet of newspaper and scissors or pencil. Students are given two, three or four minutes to circle or cut out words with an /N-n/ sound in it. The student with the most N-n's wins.

NUTCRACKER

Students could hear the story of E.T.A. Hoffman's tale of The Nutcracker and even watch the video. There are a variety of nutcrackers available, from collectibles made in Sweden and Germany to practical metal ones. Children could be given a chance to crack a walnut or almond shell. Also available is the old-fashioned rock and plastic bag. Students can then taste a variety of nuts and chart/graph their favorites.

A "NEAT NUT" TREE

This is a great activity to reinforce the sound of /N-n/. This is done after the different nuts are tasted and favorites are graphed/charted. Cut a 4"x5" cardboard (tag board) square roll to make a cone shape. Cut off the bottom rectangle so the cone sets flat on the desk. Cover paper tag with aluminum foil or wax paper. Generously glue nuts onto foil or wax pa-per cone (hint: start on the bottom). Allow each row to dry. When tree is completely dry and is well glued, take paper support out carefully. The nut trees can be decorated by sprinkles of glitter or tiny bows. These can be used for name place holders or mantle decorations.

NASTY NUTTY PAINT

This paint can be made and fingers, hands, arms, and feet can be the brushes. In a large saucepan, combine, 1 cup flour and one cup cold water. Then stir until smooth. Add three more cups of cold water. Cook and stir over *medium* heat until it thickens. Cook an additional minute over low heat. Use food coloring to color. Pour into bowl and cover bowl. Then let it cool.

N-n Word Lists

Foods/relation to food:

nut	nutcracker	nectar
Nubian	nutmeg	Nuba
nutrition	Nougat	nectarine
Navy bean	noodle	Newburg
Neufchatel cheese	non pareille	noodle

Descriptive/Action Words (verbs):

naked	napping	namby
next	name	nine
not	nervous	never
new	nibble	nippy
narrow	notice	nasty
notorious	national	noxious
near	nuisance	neat
nuzzle	necessary	numb
need	nudge	nice
notion	now	nag
new	natural	Neanderthal

objects (nouns):

nickname	nipple	noise
note	net	nerve
nail	nose	niece
napkin	night	nine
nation	needle	noon
native	nobody	noose
Navy	nightgown	north
neck	nutcracker	nose
net	nap	nostril
newspaper	neighbor	note
news	nephew	noun
nest	nickel	November
necktie	noble	number
nightmare	nurse	nova
nylon	nun	nugget
nursery	narrator	notion
necklace	nonesuch	nimbus
none		

Animals (or related to one):

nightingale	Newt	Narwhal
nightcrawler	nautilus	nighthawk
Nekton	night heron	nit
noctiluca	noctule	Nilgai
noctuid	Newfoundland Dog	numbfish
nurse bee	Norwegian elkhound	Nutria

Areas:

New Zealand	Nuer	New York
Nuevo Laredo	Nusa Tenggara	Nueces
Nuremberg	Nova Scotia	Notoguea
Narin	Nanning	Namaqua Land
Nam Tso	Namibia	Nan Tucket
Naples	Navaho	Nazarene
Nebraska	Nether	Netherlands
Neuchatel	Nevada	New Britain
New Hampshire	New Jersey	New Mexico
Niagara	New Orleans	Niger
Newport Beach	Nile	Nippon
Normandy	Nordkyn	North Pole
Northern Ireland	Norway	Newfoundland
Novaya Zemlpa	Nubia	Novi sad

N-n Reading Resources

Nail Soup — Harve Zemach: Sunburst, 1973

Nicolas, Where Have You Been? — Leo Lionni: Random House, 1967

Noah's Ark — Peter Spier or Nonny Hogrogian: Zephyr, 1977

Nothing Ever Happens on My Block — Ellen Raskin: Alad- din, 1966

Nothing to Do — Russell Hoban: Harper Throphy, 1960

Nate the Great — Marjorie Weinman Sharmat: Dell Young Yearling, 1972

No One Is Going to Nashville — Mavis Jukes: Knopf, 1983

Ned and the Joybaloo — Hiawyn Oram: Sunburst, 1989

The Nightingale — Hans Christian Anderson: Scholastic, 1986

No Star Nights — Anna Egan Smucker: Knoph, 1989

N Tombi's Song — Jenny Seed: Beacon Press, 1989

No More Monsters for Me — Peggy Parrish: Harper Collins (I can read), 1981

The Napping House — Audrey Wood: HBJ, 1983

Nana Upstairs and Nana Downstairs — Tomie De Poala: Puffin, 1973

No Nap — Eve Bunting: Clarion, 1990

Not So Fast, SongoLoLo — Nicki Daly: Puffin, 1986

Nutshell Library — Maurice Sendak: Harper & Row/Harper Collins, 1962

The Night Before Christmas — Clement C. Moore: Knopf, 1984

The New Teacher — Miram Cohen: Aladdin, 1967

Nutty for President — Dean Hughes: Bantam, 1981

Nothing's Fair in the Fifth Grade — Barthe De Clements: Puffin, 1981

Now We Are Six — A.A. Milne: Dell Yearling, 1924

National Velvet — Enid Bagnold: Avon, 1935

The Nutcracker — E.T.A. Hoffman: Crown, 1984

The Not-Just-Anybody-Family — Betsy Byars: Dell Year- ling, 1986

The Noonday Friends — Mary Stolz: Harper Trophy, 1965

The Night Journey — Kathryn Lasky: Puffin, 1981

Night Mare — Willo Davis Roberts: Atheneum, 1990

"Not Now!" said the Cow — Joanne Oppenheim: Bantam, 1990

O.o

O-o — Recipes

ONE OFFICIAL OH!

Materials:

sauce pan
large pan
strainer
1 box dried tortellini
1 can opener

bowl
hot plate
1/2 cup milk
1 can cheese sauce

Directions:

1. Clean hands, area, and equipment.
2. Cook tortellini as directed on package until tender.
3. Pour tender tortellinis into strainer and rinse with cold water.
4. Pour into bowl.
5. Heat cheese sauce as directed on can.
6. Mix milk into cheese sauce.
7. Stir heated cheese sauce over tortellinis.
8. Heat in cheese saucepan until O's are covered with sauce.
9. Oh!

ORANGE OZING

Materials:

blender
glasses/cups
1 raw cold egg
3 cans water to constitute
measuring cup/spoons

1 can of frozen orange juice
3, 4, or 5 ice cubes
1 cup orange sherbet
1 tablespoon of orange extract

opener for orange juice—if plastic strip is on can for easy opening.
If you do not want orange sherbet: 1 can orange juice, frozen water to constitute, 1 tablespoon sugar, 1/4 teaspoon vanilla extract, and pinch of nutmeg and cinnamon.

Directions:

1. Clean hands, area, and equipment.
2. Put ice cube into blender for a few seconds.
3. Open can of frozen orange juice, add to ice, and replace juice with water as the directions state.
4. Add sherbet, egg, and extract.
5. Blend
6. Serve and wait for Oh, Oh, Ohs!

Outrageous O'rtillas

Materials:

1 cutting board
1 can of olives
1 head of lettuce
2 tomatoes
1 grater
sauce pan
1 approved hot plate or microwave

1 can of cooked pinto beans
1 large block of cheddar cheese
1 tortilla (flour or corn) per student
2 large ripe avocado's
1 knife 1/2 onion
paper plates forks

Directions:

1. Clean hands, area, and equipment.
2. Heat canned pinto beans until warm.
3. Grate cheese.
4. Dice tomatoes.
5. Chop onions, very small.
6. Slice lettuce.
7. Dice up avocados.
8. Open olives, drain.
9. Have each item in #s (2, 3, 4, 5, 6) in bowls, arranged in a row.
10. Give each child a plate with a tortilla in it.
11. Allow him/her to put on his/her O'tortilla what he/she wants. Usually it is beans, lettuce, tomatoes, cheese, olives, and avocados.
12. Observe. Oh and Ohs.

Old Fashioned Orange Bread

This is a bread made for tea.

Materials:

1 cup boiling water to boil orange rinds either in strips or grated; if grated, you need a grater.
3/4 cup of sugar, less if oranges are sweet (to your taste).
2 well-greased loaf pans, margarine to grease.
1 egg 1/4 cup orange juice

1 cup milk
1/2 teaspoon salt
2 bowls
knife
oven

3 cups all-purpose flour
3-1/2 teaspoons baking powder
1 cup chopped walnuts
measuring spoons and cups
1 teaspoon orange extract

Directions:

1. Clean hands, area, and equipment.
2. Peel oranges.
3. Either grate rind (easier) or cut into very, very, narrow strips. Cover with hot water.
4. Combine flour, baking powder, and salt. Set aside in large bowl.
5. Combine milk, egg, extract, and drained orange rinds together in smaller bowl.
6. Grease loaf pans.
7. Combine large bowl with smaller bowl and stir until blended. Add nuts.
8. Pour into greased loaf pans.
9. Bake at 350 degrees for 50-55 minutes or until done.

Oh-Kee-Do-Kee Omelets

Today, an omelet is a word used to describe many kinds of egg dishes. Refrigerate the eggs until ready to use. Add seasonings last, as it toughens the egg dish. Also, they should be cooked at low to moderate temperature. This is a sweet baked omelet.

Materials:

8 egg yolks
1/2 cup sugar
baking dish
electric mixer
margarine

powdered sugar
canned/fresh fruit   8 egg whites
1/4 teaspoon cream of tartar
1/4 teaspoon cinnamon and basil

1 teaspoon vanilla extract or 1/2 teaspoon vanilla extract and 1/2 teaspoon almond extract
oven

Directions:

1. Clean hands, area, and equipment.
2. Using electric mixer, beat sugar and egg yolks until very light.
3. Clean mixer beaters well and whip egg whites until stiff. (When electric beaters are off, you lift beaters and the whites form a peak.) Then add baking powder/cream of tartar and mix.
4. Fold in vanilla, cinnamon and basil to yolks.
5. Fold whites into egg yolks.
6. Pour into greased baking pan (using margarine).
7. Slash top lightly or use a knife to make 1 cut in egg to allow to cook.
8. Bake until firm (middle doesn't move) 325 degrees for about 25 minutes.
9. Sprinkle powdered sugar on top.
10. Serve with canned or fresh fruit.

Observant Matzo Omelet

This one isn't sweet. It can be made all year long as Matzos are found in the market all year long.

Materials:

6 Matzos (whole or broken for easier manipulation)

1 lb. ricotta cheese

1/8 teaspoon pepper

measuring spoons

1 teaspoon sugar

baking dish

1/8 teaspoon of onion/garlic powder

5 eggs

1/2 teaspoon salt

2 tablespoons butter

1/2 teaspoon cinnamon

1/2 teaspoon seasoned salt

1 cup cheddar cheese, grated

oven

Directions:

1. Clean hands, area, and equipment.
2. Combine seasonings, sugar, and eggs. Mix well.
3. Combine cheeses.
4. Grease baking dish well.
5. Dip matzo into egg mixture.
6. Place matzo into buttered/greased dish.
7. Cover with layer of cheeses.
8. Add another layer of matzo, egg covered.
9. Add another layer of cheeses.
10. Continue until matzo and cheese are done.
11. Pour all extra egg mixture over last matzo.
12. Bake in 325 degrees for 30-45 minutes or until done.

OBESE OATMEAL COOKIES

These cookies may have been originally from Ireland.

Materials:

1 cup butter, at room temperature	aluminum foil
3/4 cup packed brown sugar	spatula
3/4 cup granulated sugar	1 large egg
1 teaspoon vanilla	bowl
1-1/2 cup all purpose flour	mixing spoons
1 tablespoon milk	1 teaspoon salt
2 cups chocolate chips	2-1/2 cups rolled oats
1 teaspoon ground cinnamon	oven
1 cup chopped walnuts or pecans	tray
1 teaspoon double-acting baking soda	cold milk to drink

Directions:

1. Clean hands, area, and equipment.
2. Preheat oven to 325 degree.
3. Add cream, butter, and sugar to a large bowl.
4. Add egg, vanilla, and milk. Then stir.
5. In a small bowl, combine flour, baking soda, salt, and cinnamon.
6. Combine the two bowls together and mix in oats, chocolate chips, and walnuts/pecans.
7. Line cookie sheet up with aluminum foil. (Use 1/4 to 1/3 cup to measure in order to save greasing.)
8. Scoop and drop dough onto lined baking pan. Flatten slightly to 5 inches in diameter. Leave space so that only 6 large cookies fit on sheet.
9. Bake until golden brown (10-12 minutes).
10. Allow to cool, slightly.
11. Try not to omit step 10, even if children can't wait! Cookies will burn their mouths, serve with milk. These are obese cookies— they can be made smaller by using a tablespoon to measure.

O-o — Games/Activities

/O-o/ Flashcards

O-o words can be written as flash cards. Students can write/dictate sentences using several to make a sentence. Student can then dictate/write it and illustrate it. It can be used to discriminate long/short O words or variable to make an O-o Book.

Orange Objects

Teacher could talk about objects. Students could mix orange paint using red and yellow (more yellow if lighter orange is what you want to obtain). Students could paint orange objects. When the paint is almost dry, a sentence could be dictated about their real/imaginary/obedient orange object and what functions it can perform.

Official O ... Ohs

Students could trace a pattern on to tag or railroad board of a capital and lower case O-o. Students could be given glue and must make an official O by gluing Cheerios™ or Fruit Loops™ onto the pattern and the objective is to cover the pattern with O's. The student may feel/observe the O's when dry.

Obedient "O" Orchard

Each child is given a whole orange. The objective is to peel the orange and section it. They must count the sections. Each child's number is put on the chart and graphed. Then each student must count the seeds in each orange. Those results are charted and graphed. Then the seeds are planted in potting soil & put into paper milk cartons with three to four holes in the bottom for drainage. The seeds should be placed about 1/2 to 1 inch into the soil. The obedient orange seed will become an orange seedling and grow into a tree. Place cartons in your room in a row facing the sun. Your room will become an orchard. Remember to water and measure before you chart and graph daily. See whose orange is the most obedient.

Offensive Ogre

An ogre is a giant or man-eating monster or very cruel man. Students love/hate ogres. To utilize this fact, puppets of socks or Popsicle™ sticks could be made. Plays or stories written in cooperative learning groups utilizing each ogre's name and what he does. These plays/ stories/skits could be read to each group/class and performed for other classes. Ogres are fun! Ogres can also be offensive.

Oscar Octopus

Using 1/2 of a navel orange per student, 8 toothpicks, 8 raisins/marsh- mallows/gumdrops for feet, and raisins for eyes, students could construct Oscars or Olivias to observe the 8 legs & reinforce the short /O-o/ sound.

Old Mac Donald or Old Gray Cat

These two songs, which are found in Silver Burdett, could be sung and acted out. Teacher

OBSTINATE OWLS – OWLETS

In this game, use an emptied half-walnut shell; felt eyes or moveable eyes could be glued on. Also, felt beaks, felt wings, and toothpicks or twigs can be glued on for feet (talons). These make darling owls or owlets. Paper bag pup-pets could be used to make owls. Students could research owls, osprey, oriole, ostrich, and the oven bird. Then they can obtain information about each bird and then use that and their puppets to write a play/skit/ book- let about their know- ledge of these birds.

OPPOSITE O's

Masking tape could be applied on the carpeting or floor in the shape of an O. The ogre is in the middle and all others are around the O on the tape. He gives a command like, "Touch your toes," and they have to touch/react/demonstrate the opposite like, "Touch your head," if the ogre says, "Don't touch your head," players must touch their head. If they cannot do it, they are o-u-t. The last one in is the ogre.

O-o OCTAGON BOOKS

Teacher could have discarded books, old picture books, old catalogs, or magazines and children/students must look up, find, cut out, and paste on paper, shaped like octagon objects that begins with or have an /O-o/ sound in it. The student must then name and state the function this object performs. (This can be written or dictated.) All the students' pages can be laminated and put into a book for the class library, or to go home.

O-o LOTTO

Students could play one-upmanship. Each child is given a magazine, discarded picture book, or catalog to find/cut out and paste on a 3 x 5 inch card, as many objects as he/she can find in 15 minutes. (A time must be set.) This can be a center activity without the timer as well. The one with the most correct is the winner. These cards may then be matched with the word and you have your own O-o Lotto game. Laminate cards and then place these pieces at a center or play as a game. It's better than a video to occupy their time.

OYSTER BEDS

Each student makes (after observing a real oyster shell) an oyster cover. Then students cut out three to four lined papers the same size. The pearls of wisdom or lined papers will be used to describe events, which are special/important that have happened to them. A needle strung with string can then be put through the middle of each pearl of wisdom and attached to the back of the oyster. A knot may be needed at the front/back of each pearl to keep it from being to close. These pearls could be arranged in order of importance in the oyster bed.

OUR OBNOXIOUS/OBSCENE OFFENSIVE OUTDOORS.

Each day, newspapers/magazines show pictures of how our outdoors is being ruined by man/nature. Pictures could be cut and mounted on heavy paper. Students could write/dictate either about the destruction and/or their opinion about it.

O-o — Word Lists

Long "O":

Oklahoma	overnight	oval
old	Ohio	O.K
owner	oyster	oath
oatmeal	oaf	owe
ownership	own	odor
coat	ocean	open
over	obey	omit
oboe	okra	oak
oats	oar	obey
object	oboe	ozone
over	boat	float
open		

Short "O":

of	out	olive
ostrich	ox	octagon
odd	October	octopus
otter	dot	opposite
oxen	opera	oxygen
occupy	off	oz
orange	oral	orchestra
order	orphan	orthodox
orphrey	ornament	organize
ordinal		

Variations:

off	office	often
on	odd	offer
onto	offset	onset
Ostrich	or	order
ore	orbit	orchard
Oregon	organ	ordinary
orchid	oar	other

169

official	observe	oppose
opossum	oven	oil
once	one	onions
other		

OU words:

out	our	ouch
outlaw	outrage	outer
ought	outline	outside
outfield	outfit	

OY words:

| oyster | oyster crab | oyster stew |

Animals:

okapi	oyster crab	oxpecker
ox	owlet	owl
oven bird	opossum	otter
osprey	oryx	orson
oriole	orangutan	octopus
opossum	ocelot	oxen
oarfish	oyster catcher	

Food:

omelet	oyster stew	okra
oxtail soup	oregano	orange
onions	osso buco	oatmeal
ozmazome	olive	oat
oatcake	octopus	opossum
orange	orange drink	olio
ogeat	ox heart	

Objects:

| odor | oar | office |
| oath | ogre | oboe |

oil	objection	oilcan
ocarina-instrument	ointment	occasion
oink	ocean	omen
octagon	onyx	opera
ozokerle	order	orchestra
opal		

Areas:

Oakland	Oaklawn	Oak Ridge
Oberland	Odense	Odessa
Oka	Oke	Okinawa
Omuta	Onondaga Lake	Oneida Lake
Oneida	Onega	Ontario
Oregon Trail	Ottoman Empire	Otztal Alps

Inventions:

oxacillin	oxytetracycline	opera
overtrain	overshoe	overlap
outrigger	open-heart surgery	Olympic games

Descriptive Words:

oasis	obedient	obese
obey	only	objective
obnoxious	one-up	obscene
obscure	one-upmanship	observant
obsolete	one	obstinate
obstruct	open	obtain
opaque	occupy	odd
opinion	offend	oval
open	official	open-end
oily	okie	operate
old	olive green	oppose
ominous	opposite	oxymoron
omit	once	outrageous
outlandish		

O-o — Reading Resources

On My Mother's Lap — Anne Herbert Scott: McGraw Hill, 1972
Oh a Hunting We Will Go — John Langstaff: McElderry, 1974
Old Henry — Jean Blo's: Mulberry, 1987
On Christmas Eve — Peter Collington: Knopf, 1990
On Market Street — Arnold Lobel: Mulberry, 1981
Once a Mouse — Marcia Brown
One Fish, Two Fish, Red Fish, Blue Fish — Dr. Seuss: Random House
One Frog Too Many — Mercer Mayer: Pied Piper, 1967
One-Eyed Cat — Paula Fox: Dell Yearling, 1984
Onion John — Joseph Krumgold: Harper Thropy. 1959
Old Arthur — Liesel Moak Shorpen: Harper & Row, 1972
Old Mother West Wind — Thornton Burgess: Little Brown, 1910
Owl Moon — Jane Yolen: Phiomel, 1987
Owl at Home — Arnold Lobel: Harper Collins, 1975
Over and Over — Charlotte Zolotow: Harper & Row, 1957
One Fine Day — Nonny Hogrogian: Aladdin, 1971
One Gorilla: A Counting Book — Atsuko Morozumi: Forrar, Straus, and Giroux, 1990
One Monday Morning — Uri Shulevitz: Aladdin, 1967
The Old Synagogue — Richard Rosenblum: Jewish Publican Society, 1989
One Day in Paradise — Helme Heine: McElderry, 1986
Oxford Book of Poetry for Children — Edward Blishen: Bedrick, 1986
Child of the Owl — Lawrence Yep: Harper Throphy, 1977
Oatmeal Is Not for Mustaches — Thomas Rockwell: Dell Yearling, 1973
Once There Were Bluebirds — Bill Martin, Jr.: Henry Holt, 1986
One Fine Day — Nonny Hogrogian: Aladdin, 1971
One Wide River to Cross — Emberley: Simon & Schuster Books for Young Readers, 1967
Oscar Otter — Nathaniel Benchley: Harper Collins, 1969
Outloud — Eve Merrian: Morrow Jr. Books, 1989
Ox-Car Man — Donald Hall: Puffin, 1979
Oats and Wild Apples — Frank Asch: Holiday House, 1989
Oh My Baby Bear — Audrey Wood: Harcourt Brace Jovanovich, 1991
Oh, the Places You'll Go! — Dr. Seuss, Random House, 1991
Oh, Sister!: Giggles, Gasps, Groans, and Growing Up Together — Debra Solomon: Warner, 1990
One Sister Too Many — C.S. Alder: MacMillian, 1990
Over the Steamy Swamp — Paul Geraghty: Gulliver, 1990

P-p — Recipes

POPULAR PEANUTY POPCORN

Recipe #1

Materials:

baking pan
electric fry pan
spoon
3/4 stick of butter
6 cups popped corn

bowl
measuring cup
1/4 cup of honey
3/4 cup shelled peanuts

Directions:

1. Clean hands, area, and equipment.
2. Preheat oven to 350°.
3. Put six cups of popped corn and 3/4 cup of shelled peanuts into large bowl.
4. Melt 3/4 stick of butter and, 1/4 cup of honey in electric fry pan.
5. Stir until blended.
6. Pour honey-butter over the popcorn/nuts and stir to coat.
7. Place mixture on baking pan.
8. Spread to about one inch thick.
9. Bake for ten minutes.
10. Cool before eating.
11. Perfect.

Popcorn Recipe #2

Materials:

Microwave
bowl
wooden spoons
greased cookie sheet

28-30 wrapped/unwrapped caramels
2-1/2 tablespoons water
2-1/2 qts. popped corn
1 cup roasted peanuts

Directions:

1. Clean hands, area, and equipment.
2. Microwave caramels and water in bowl for, 1 minute.
3. Stir until sauce is smooth; continue stirring every 30 seconds.
4. Pour over popped corn and toss well.
5. Spread onto greased or aluminum foiled lined cookie sheet. Allow to sit until set.
6. Break apart and you'll know why it is popular.

PERFECT PARTY PICKLES

Information: Pickles require salt & water or brine to preserve cucumbers. Pickles can also be made with vinegar either plain or spiced. Americans eat more than 28 billion pickles a year. Middle Europeans used salt. Russians use vinegar. Scandinavians use a bit of both. There are three ways to make pickles: fermentation, fresh packed, and refrigerated.

Materials:

one large jar
1 tablespoon salt
sharp knife
2 teaspoons celery seed
1/2 cup lemon juice

1 green pepper, finely chopped
3 large green cucumbers
1 onion, finely chopped
3/4 cup sugar
1 lemon sliced into circles

Directions:

1. Clean hands, area, and equipment.
2. Cut cucumbers (unpeeled) into slices about, 1/16" thick.
3. Mix with pepper, onion, salt, celery seed.
4. Let stand for one hour at room temperature.
5. Mix sugar with lemon juice until sugar dissolves.
6. Pour sweetened lemon juice over cucumbers.
7. Add lemon slices.
8. Stir to blend.
9. Cover and refrigerate 24 hours.

PHANTOM PEANUT PRETZELS

Materials:

rolling pin
pastry brush
measuring cups
spoons
knife2 teaspoons baking powder
1 teaspoon sugar
bowl 1 egg, beaten
1-1/2 cups all-purpose flour-unbleached

bread or cutting board
aluminum lined cookie sheet
2/3 cup milk
2 tablespoons crunchy peanut butter
spatula
1 teaspoon salt
coarse salt

Directions:

1. Clean hands, area, and equipment.
2. Mix flour, milk, peanut butter, baking powder, sugar, and salt into a soft dough in a large bowl with fork or hands.
3. Smooth dough into a ball in the bowl.
4. Divide the dough equally.
5. Knead, 10—12 times.
6. Allow each child to make a pencil/pen roll. Then shape into a pretzel shape. Place seam side down on cookie sheet.
7. Brush pretzel with beaten egg. Sprinkle with coarse salt.
8. Bake in oven at 400 degrees for 20 minutes or until golden brown.
9. Use spatula to take off the sheet.
10. If put out on a dish—only the phantom knows who ate it.

PHOTO-PERFECT PIZZA

(Students love pizzas. They take home The recipe and make It At home. Great For professional/student relations. This is a great snack for the whole family.)

Materials:

1 toaster oven and bowl   1 English muffin per pizza (per student)
1 jar of pizza sauce (I use Pizza Quick™ regular or traditional)
1 teaspoon of pizza seasoning (Lawry's™)
2 pounds of Mozzarella cheese — either as a ball and use a grater or purchased already grated.
1 package of sliced pepperoni (or 2 packages depending on the number of students and amount per student).
1 can of black olives — sliced (for eyes)   1 purple onion, diced

Directions:

1. Clean hands, area, and equipment.
2. If need be, grate Mozzarella cheese into a bowl or put grated cheese into bowl.
3. Slice olives and dice onions.
4. Separate muffins and spread sauce evenly on each muffin.
5. Lightly season with pizza seasoning.
6. Sprinkle Mozzarella cheese
7. Add pepperoni, olives, and onions to make a perfect pizza.
8. Bake until cheese melts and pepperoni curls.
9. Take a picture.

PUFFY PLUMB POTATO CHIP COOKIES

Materials:

1 pound butter   oven — potholders
1 cup granulated sugar   2 teaspoons vanilla extract
2-1/2 cups all-purpose flour, unbleached
2 cups potato chips, crushed   1 cup chopped pecans
cookie sheets/aluminum foil   spoons
spatula

Directions:

1. Clean hands, area, and equipment.
2. Cream butter, sugar, and vanilla extract.
3. Blend in flour.
4. Stir in potato chips and pecans, gently.
5. Preheat oven to 350 degrees.
6. Line or use ungreased cookie sheet.
7. Drop the dough from teaspoons and flatten the drop to make it even. Round edges, if you prefer.
8. Bake until edges and bottoms are golden brown. Allow to cool.
9. Remove with spatula onto cookie rack.
10. Dust with powdered sugar.

PEANUT BUTTER

Materials:

blender

crackers

stalks of clean celery

sprinkles (chocolate chips, cake decorations, raisins)

bread

1 tablespoon oil

1 package or roasted peanuts in the shells

apple slices

Directions:

1. Clean hands, area, and equipment.
2. Remove peanuts from shells.
3. Take off red skins.
4. Add oil into blender (before putting in the peanuts).
5. Put in three handfuls of peanuts.
6. Blend until smooth — salt may be added.
7. Spread on crackers, celery, apple slices, or bread.
8. Decorate.

POWERFUL PUMPKIN PECAN COOKIES

Pumpkin cookies/pies/cakes were served at the first Thanksgiving in America. That's pretty powerful.

Materials:

2 large bowls

measuring spoons

cups 5 teaspoons baking powder

spatulas

1/2 teaspoon salt

1 teaspoon vanilla extract

5 cups all-purpose flour, unbleached

3 cups granulated sugar or, 1, 1/2 cups each of brown and granulated sugar.

1/2 cup pecans, chopped

aluminum lined cookie sheets

3 teaspoons pumpkin pie spice

oven   2 teaspoons baking soda

2-1/2 cups canned pumpkin

1 cup butter   2 eggs, beaten

1 cup raisins

Directions:

1. Clean hands, area, and equipment.
2. Combine flour, baking soda and powder, salt, and spices in, 1 bowl and set aside.
3. Add cream, butter, sugar(s), and eggs; mix in vanilla and pumpkin.
4. Blend dry ingredients (#2) into creamed ingredients (#3). Add raisins and pecans.
5. Drop by teaspoons about 2" apart on lined cookie sheet.
6. Bake in 350 degree oven for about, 15 minutes or lightly browned.
7. Remove with spatula on racks.
8. These make you feel powerful.

P-p — Games & Activities

PANTRY:

The teacher selects all the words from the P-p word list that the students are to learn/need to know/should read. Then the teacher makes flash cards. The children can then illustrate the cards or use pictures from magazines, discarded books, pictures, dictionaries, or catalogs. The pictures can be attached to the back. The children can dictate or write sentences/stories using these words. They can be used to check spelling or sequencing sounds. All the words should be placed in a box named "Pantry".

PARSLEY PALS:

Students can sprinkle parsley seeds onto sponges/wet paper towels or towels on top of cotton. Then they can watch the growth. They can also record the growth on paper with a pen. The plants can be their pals. Photos can be taken and students can chart/graph the growth of their pals. They can then be placed in potting soil where they will continue to grow. Students can then eat the product.

PIG PUPPETS:

After reading *The Three Little Pigs, Perfect The Pig, Petunia Piggins, Mr. & Mrs. Pigs, Evening Out Pigs from A to Z,* and *The Pigs' Wedding,* students can make pig puppets out of paper bags. They can then write their own skits/plays and put them on for others to watch their performances. Take pictures! They could also do A Reader's Theater about any Of The pig books.

PICTURES & WORDS:

Distribute to students discarded picture books, magazines, or the newspaper. They are timed to find either words or pictures of objects that have the initial consonant or final consonant /P-p/ sound of in the word. The winner gets the prize of putting it on the construction paper marked with a Pp. The students can also make a P-p with the pictures and dictated/written lines describing each picture and its performance/ function. This book can be published as A class book and passed around.

PREDICTABLE PECULIAR POPCORN:

The teacher should place butcher paper on the floor. Circles need to be drawn around the electric popcorn popper (the one with the glass top). As soon as the colored circles are drawn, students predict which colored circle most of the popped corn will land in. Teacher then takes the top off and popcorn pops on the butcher paper. Kernels are counted and the circle with the most kernels wins. Good predictions.

PARTNER PEANUT BUTTER

Peanuts are grown underground. Each pod may contain one-to-three edible seeds. The plant is a vine. The vine has yellow flowers. Peanut oil is made from these seeds. You will need: a blender/food processor, 1 tablespoon oil, crackers, knife, salt, and one package of roasted peanuts in shells. Clean hands, area, and equipment. One partner removes peanuts from shells. The other partner takes the red skins off of the peanuts and puts the peanuts into a bowl. Another partner takes the peanuts collected in the bowl to the teacher. The teacher adds oil, then three handfuls of peanuts into the blender. Blend until smooth. The partner brings back the spread to all. Spread on crackers and say, "Partner, Partner, Partner Peanut Butter."

PUZZLE PASTA

There are so many shapes/kinds of pasta that students could bring one bag from home. They could be classified/sorted by names, like: spaghetti, cockaigne, fusilli, penne, rigatoni, farfalle, fettuccine, zita, macaroni, and Mostaccioli. One of each kind/shape could be glued on and each student at a center could try to find a similar one & match it. Also, the pasta could be glued to a tag/cardboard shaped P-p and then feel to reinforce the shape and recognition of P-p. While gluing, they could make the sound of P-p. The puzzle is why there are so many shapes/kinds of pasta?

PEACEFUL/PENNY PIPE CLEANERS

Pipe cleaners could be manipulated/shaped/moved to make P-p's. This equipment (pipe cleaners) is quiet/peaceful and can be used over and over. It costs less than a penny to use, as it can be used over and over. Have students make capital and lower case letters. Other P's could be made of pretzels and squares of cheese.

PICK P-P INVENTIONS

Popcorn poppers, potato chips, park, pattern, penny, pistol, playdough, pools, pens, pencils, paper, purses, pumps, pulleys, plastic, pillows, pup- pets, paint, and photos are inventions that start with P-p. Can you name others? These inventions could be written on the board and one student or teacher is "it." "It" gives three clues and students try to pick the "p" invention. They have 20 guesses. Whoever guesses correctly wins. They are then "it." This game helps with comprehension and critical thinking.

PALE PEBBLE PICTURE

Students could draw a picture of a home/house/palace and glue pebbles onto it. The picture could be of anything as long as pebbles (they have each collected) are glued/pasted on.

POWERFUL PUMPKIN SEEDS

(Pumpkin was served at the first Thanksgiving.) Children or teacher could bring in pumpkins and measure them. Draw faces on them. Have children draw or paint pictures of pumpkins. Children also need to know pumpkins grows on a vine from the seeds. The pumpkin(s) could be cut open and seeds counted, graphed, and charted. Predictions could be made as to which pumpkin has the most seeds. The seeds could be planted. The other seeds could be washed thoroughly and placed on lined cookie sheet and baked until golden brown at 350 degrees. They can be salted.

PLAYFUL PEANUT BUTTER DOUGH
(This can be eaten, but only if you want to.)

In a bowl, put 2 cups of peanut butter, 2 cups of powdered milk, and 2, 1/2 tablespoons of honey. (Raisins, nuts, and dried fruit can be used to decorate.) While mixing, if it is not the desired consistency, add a bit more powdered milk. Then, sculpt into Ps, or pigs, or pennies, or pickles, or, whatever.

179

P-p — Word Lists

Noun-Objects:

pack	pad	page
pagoda	pair	pal
palace	palm	pan
panic	pansy	pantry
pants	paper	parchment
parent	park	partner
party	paste	pastry
path	patrol	pattern
peace	peak	pearl
pedal	peg	pellet
pen	penny	people
perfume	person	pest
phantom	phone	photo
piano	picnic	picture
piece	pilgrim	pillow
pin	pine	pipe
pirate	pistol	pit
pity	place	plan
plane	planet	plant
plaster	plastic	Playdough
pond	pool	porridge
portrait	possess	prejudice
premium	president	press
price	priest	prince
print	prison	poker
police	poppy	portfolio
postage stamp	poultry	pouch
pound	powder	products
progress	proof	property
protein	protractor	pulley
pump	punch	pupil
puppet	purple	purse
pus	puzzle	pajamas
puttees	pyramid	

Animals:

pandas	parakeet	parrot
peacock	pelicans	penguin
pheasant	pig	pigeon
pike	platypus	pointer
Pomeranian	poodle	porcupine
prairie dog	prawn	porpoise
pronghorn	pupa	pussycat pupa
pussycat		

Foods or Food Related:

pancake	papaya	parsley
parsnip	passion fruit	pastrami
pate	peaches	peanut
peanut butter	perch	pears
peas	pepper	pepperoni
persimmon	picante sauce	pickle
pie	pig	pike
pimentos	pineapples	pine nuts
pizza	plantain	plum
poi	polish sausage	pollock
pomegranate	popcorn	pork
potatoes	potato chips	pot roast
pretzels	prune	pudding

Verbs:

pace	pack	paint
pale	pant	pass
paste	patch	pause
pay	perform	pet
pick	play	please
plead	plot	plunder
poach	postpone	power
pray	precook	preheat
prepare	press	prevent
prick	print	provide

provoke	pry	publish
pull	punch	punish
purge	push	put
pray		

Descriptive Words (Adjectives or Adverbs):

pair	paradise	passion
peculiar	perfect	pink
pioneer	pious	plenty
polite	poor	popular
pretty	pride	primary
primitive	private	proud
puffy	pure	purple

P-p — Reading Resources

The Three Little Pigs — Paul Galdone: Clarion, 1983

The Popcorn Book — Tomie de Paola: Prentice Hall, 1970

Peter's Chair — Ezra Jack Keats: Harper and Row, 1967

Perfect the Pig — Susan Jeschke: Scholastic, 1981

Paul Bunyan — Steven Kellogg: Mulberry, 1984

Each Peach, Pear, and Plum: An "I Spy" Story — Janet and Allan Ahlberg: Puffin, 1978

Pickled Peppers — Nancy McArthur

The Tale of Peter Rabbit — Beatrix Potter: Frederich Warne, 1902

Petunia — Roger Duvoisin: Knopf, 1958

Pinkerton, Behave — Steven Kellogg: Pied Piper, 1979

Smashed Potatoes — Jane G. Martel

Push, Pull, Empty, Full — Hoban: Puffin, 1980

Pretzel — H.A. Rey: Houghton Mifflin, 1946

Pancakes for Breakfast — Tomie de Paola: Harcourt Brace Jovanovich, 1978

Mr. & Mrs. Pig's Evening Out — Mary Rayner: Atheneum, 1967

A Pair of Red Clogs — Masako, Matsuno: World Publishing, 1960

The People Could Fly: American Black Folktales — Virginia Hamilton: Knoph, 1985

The Patchwork Quilt — Valerie Flournox: Dial, 1985

Patrick's Dinosaurs — Carol Carrick: Clarion, 1983

Puss in Boots — Charles Perrault: Farrar, Strauss and Giroux, 1990

Pamela Camel — Bill Peet: Houghton Mifflin, 1984

Peter and the Wolf — Sergei Prokofier: Knoph, 1986

Peter Pan — J.M. Barrie: Puffin, 1987

Pigs From A-to-Z — Arthur Geisert: Houghton Mifflin, 1986

The Polar Express — Chris Van Allsburg: Houghton Mifflin, 1985

Potatoes, Potatoes — Anita Lobel: Harper Collins, 1984

Panda, Panda — Tana Hoban: Mulberry, 1978

Pat the Bunny — Dorothy Kunhardt: Golden/Western, 1942

The Pilgrims of Plymouth — Marcia Sewall: Antheneum, 1983

Pippi Longstocking — Astrid Lingren: Puffin, 1950

Princess Furball — Charlotte Huck: Scholastic, 1989

Pyramid of the Sun — Leonard Everette: Four Winds, 1986

Pyramid of the Moon — Fisher: Four Winds, 1986

Panda — Susan Bonners: Young Yearling, 1978

The Purple Coat — Amy Hest: Four Winds, 1986

Piggy Book — Anthony Browne: Knopf, 1986

The Pearl — Helme Heine: McElderry, 1985

Paddy's Evening Out — John Goodall: McElderry, 1973

Pollyanna — Jean Stratton Porter: Dell Yearling, 1913

Q-q — Recipes

Quadruple "Q" Cookies

You will have enough dough to make eight (four capital and four lower-case) "Q" Cookies.

Materials:

2 cups sugar

4 eggs well beaten

1/2 teaspoon salt

4 teaspoons baking powder

1 cup or 2 sticks of butter

2-4 tablespoons milk, divided

5 cups all-purpose flour

2 tablespoons almond/vanilla extract

Directions

1. Clean hands, area, and equipment.
2. In one bowl, beat butter and sugar.
3. Beat in eggs, 1/2 of the milk, and vanilla/almond.
4. In another bowl, mix flour, baking powder, and salt.
5. Mix flour mixture (#4) into butter mixture (#2).
6. Gather dough and cover with plastic wrap and refrigerate overnight.
7. Flour hands and surface.
8. Give each student a handful of Q cookie dough.
9. Roll into snake, or pencil, and form Q-q's.
10. Decorate — put names on each cookie.
11. Bake 10-12 minutes until lightly browned in 350 degree oven.

Quest Quiche

Materials:

6 beaten eggs

toaster oven

garlic powder

1 prepared pie crust (frozen)

1 cup whipping cream

1 cup mozzarella cheese

seasonings-Lawry's™ seasoned salt and pepper

additives: bacon bits, chiles, onions, mushrooms, and even cut up broccoli

Directions:

1. Clean hands, area, and equipment.
2. Use frozen pie crust, prick several times and bake at 350 degrees for 8 minutes.
3. Combine eggs, cream, cheese, and additives.
4. Mix well.
5. Pour mixture into cooked pie shell.
6. Bake at 375 degrees for 30-45 minutes or golden brown.
7. Cool and eat quietly.

QUACKED QUEEN-LIKE SNACK
(No cooking required)

Materials:

knife1 tablespoon lemon juice
8 oz. carton of sour cream
8 oz. bottle of taco sauce
2 10-1/2 ounce cans of bean dip
1 bag of tortilla chips
1 cup of shredded jack cheese

cutting board
grater
3 small avocados
pie dish
measuring spoons
2 green onions, chopped

Directions:

1. Clean hands, area, and equipment.
2. In a pie dish or plate, spread a layer of bean dip.
3. Mash avocados, add lemon juice and spread over bean layer.
4. Layer sour cream over avocado.
5. Sprinkle jack cheese and onions.
6. Use tortilla chips to scoop.
7. Eat quickly.
8. Feel like a queen or king.

QUAINT-QUICK-BREAD

Quick breads are made with baking soda/baking powder instead of longer acting yeast. Quick breads rise quicker and you don't have to wait or knead). Try to keep ingredients at room temperature ... a hint.

Materials:

1 egg
1/2 cup ginger
1/4 tablespoon salt
loaf pan
measuring cups
1 cup milk
3/4 cup sugar
1 cup nuts
1 teaspoon vanilla extract
3/4 cup cranberries, fruits, chocolate chips, bananas

1/4 teaspoon cardamom
1/2 teaspoon cinnamon
toaster oven/regular oven
1-1/2 teaspoon baking powder
1/4 cup butter/margarine (shortening)
1 cup diced/dried apricots
flavorings/additives
1-1/3 cups unbleached all-purpose flour
1 cup blueberries/grated carrots

Directions:

1. Clean hands, area, and equipment.
2. Measure and combine dry ingredients.
3. Measure and combine shortening extract, milk, sugar, egg, and your choice of flavorings/additives.
4. Stir until just blended.
5. Pour into greased loaf pan or pan from toaster oven.
6. Bake at 350 degrees until golden brown and tester comes out clean (35-50 minutes).
7. Eat quickly with margarine or butter or by itself.

QUARTERED QUICK QUESADILLAS

Materials:

grater
toaster-oven
knife
2 olives, chopped
4 tablespoons cheddar cheese or Mexican white cheese

1/2 teaspoon onions
1/2 flour or corn tortilla
1/2 teaspoon bell peppers (optional)
mild salsa or hot sauce

Directions:

1. Clean hands, area, and equipment.
2. Combine tortilla with cheddar cheese, onions, olives, and bell peppers.
3. Place in foil-lined tray in toaster oven.
4. Heat for 1-3 minutes or until cheese melts.
5. Take out salsa or hot salsa and dip.
6. Quarter and serve.

QUIET QUENELLES

This is a Russian dish called Knel.

Materials:

skillet
cheesecloth/string
1 egg1/2 finely chopped onion
1-2 tablespoon flour
Seasonings: Salt, pepper, nutmeg, All-Spice™, onion and garlic powder

2 small French rolls - crusts removed
3/4 lb. ground chicken

2 tablespoons softened butter

Directions:

1. Clean hands, area, and equipment.
2. Soak bread in water for about 10 minutes, then squeeze out excess water.
3. Combine soaked bread and chicken.
4. Sauté onions in 1 tablespoon butter until soft.
5. Combine 1 tablespoon butter, meat, & bread and mix.
6. On a floured board, form two rolls wrapped in cheesecloth with string.
7. In low pan, bring three inches of salted water to a boil and then simmer. Cook rolls uncovered for 10-15 minutes.
8. Remove rolls, still wrapped, into boil with boiled, salted, cooled water and allow rolls to cool.
9. Unwrap and cut on an angle.

Q-q — Games/Activities

Q-Q FLASHCARDS

The teacher makes flash cards of the "Q" words. Students can discriminate if the word has a /Qu/ sound. Teacher can give students a noun, verb, and adjective/adverb and have each child arrange the words in correct order and orally give a sentence. If desired, the teacher can write the sentence on the board and students copy it. Each student can read their own sentence.

Q-Q COMPREHENSION

The teacher can give the meanings or have students use the dictionary to look up and understand/comprehend flash cards. Allow students to choose one to two or three to four words and orally dictate/or write a sentence. Then they can illustrate the sentence to gain Q-q comprehension.

QUILT LESSONS

Students can learn about quilt making and patterning. They might be shown books on quilting, so they understand why and how quilts are made. Each child could also be given a paper square (3 x 3 inches). Then glue all the squares together to make a quilt. Each student might write their name or draw an event or a design. A border could be glued on. (Material and material pens could also be used instead of paper. It would have to be sewed together.) The squares could also be sewn together using large needles and yarn.

QUITTING TIME

Students could play "Quitting Time." One person is "it" and closes their eyes. Another person uses the tape recorder/record player. When "it" says "Start," students move. When "it" says "Quit", all movement must stop. Those who will/can not stop are out. The last person still playing is "it" for the next game.

I'VE GOT A QUESTION

Students could play this game. Pictures/flash cards could be used. "It" states function, description and any other hint. "It" states, "I've got a question. It has, it does, it's _____ (color)." The students have 20 guesses to try to determine what the answer to the question is.

Q-Q PUPPETS

Students could make paper sack or felt puppets of a duck called Quacker, a dog called Queen, and a cricket called Quicket. They could write plays to go with their puppets.

QUICK-QUIET BIRD HOUSE

A Quick-Quiet Bird House could be made. Use a bleach or liquid laundry soap bottle— cut round holes across from each other. Tie/hang a cord onto a branch. Put birdseed on the bottom of the bottle.

Quizo

Using the words in the word list like: queen, quack, qualify, quart, quiz, quote, quilt, quit, quiet, quick, quarrel, quality, and quantity. Put words on 2 x 4 inch cards and write each word two times. Shuffle the cards and then place them face down. Each player can choose two cards to find a match. The person who finds a match can keep the pair and has another turn. The person with the most pairs wins.

Q-tip Paintings

Using Q-tips™ instead of brushes, allow students to paint with tempera paint mixed with liquid starch. Be sure to use a new Q-tip for each color.

Quill Painting

Many, many years ago when the U.S. Constitution was written, people used pen and ink. The pen was called a quill. It was usually a feather from a turkey which/had been cut on a diagonal and trimmed to a point. Today, you can make your own quill. Colored feathers can be purchased and ink can as well. (Remember: you can't erase it or control the ink as well as a marker or ballpoint.)

Quarters

Students can collect quarters or purchase them from the bank. Students could hold them, learn to recognize a quarter, learn how to make coins equal to a quarter, and how many quarters make a dollar ($1.00) and $1.50 and $2.00 and so on up to $5.00. They can also learn that quarter relates to time. They can learn about one quarter after and one quarter to the hour. Also in measuring is one-quarter cup and teaspoon.

Q-q — Word Lists

Nouns:

Quartermaster - corps		quotient
quest	queen	quarantine
quill	quilt	quarrel
quiz	quarry	question
quarterback	quarter	quarterhouse
quid	quartette	quorum
quartile	quote	quart
quintar	quatrain	quack
query	quad	quota
quadrangle	quip	quadruple
question	quagmire	quantity
quantum	quirt	quartz
quirk	quicksand	

Verbs:

quack	quit	quandry
quarrel	quibble	quaff
quake	quash	queasy
quell	quench	quiver
quicken	questioned	

Adverbs/descriptive words:

quiet	quick	quaint
quality	qualify	quantify
quarrelsome	quartered	quasi
quite		

Areas:

Quebec	Quechua	Queretaro
Quirites	Quintana Roo	Quilmes
Quezon City		

Foods/cooking related:

quart	quince	quesadilla

quiche	Quaker Oats	quandong
quenelle	Quinine	quickbread

Animals:

quail	quetzal	quillback
quahog	quarter horse	
Quinnat Salmon		

Q-q —Reading Resources

Quick Chick — Julia Hoban: Dutton Children's Books, 1989

Quiet Time — Gary Rosen: Random House, 1990

Quick! Turn the Page — James Stevenson: Greenwillow Books, 1990

Queen of the Sixth Grade — Illene Cooper: Puffin Books. 1992

The Queen's Goat — Margaret Mahy: Dial Books. 1991

Quacky Quack-Quack — Ian Whybrow: MacMillian, 1991

Quick Moves — Dean Hughes: Random House, 1993

The Cat's Quizzer — Dr. Seuss, 1976

Q is for Duck (Alphabet Guessing Game) — Elting & Michael Folsom

Quick as a Cricket — Don Wood — Child's Play International, 1990

The Quarreling Book — Charlotte Zolotow

The Quicksand Book — Tomie de Paola: Holiday House, 1977

Quentin Corn — Mary Stolz: David Godine, 1985

Queen's Necklace: A Swedish Folktale — Jane Langton: Hyperion Books for Children, 1994

The Queen's Nose — Dick King-Smith: Harper Collins, 1994

In a Quiet Night — Jill Murphy: Candlewick Press, 1994

The Queen with Bees in Her Hair — Cheryl Harness: Holt, Henry & Company, 1993

The Quiet Noisy Book — Margaret W. Brown: Harper Collins, 1993

R·r

R-r —Recipes

REAL RED RINGS

(In Russian — "Red" means beautiful.)

Materials:

peeler
appleknife
1 cup water
spatula
whipped cream

electric fry pan

8-oz package cinnamon red hots
few drops red food coloring

Directions:

1. Clean hands, area, and equipment.
2. Wash, peel, and core apple(s).
3. Slice apples crosswise.
4. Combine red hots, water, and food coloring to make syrup.
5. Cook apple rings in electric fry pan in syrup until tender.
6. Use spatula to remove apple rings.
7. Serve with whipped cream.
8. This is really rad!

REGAL RICE S'MORES

Materials:

microwave
peanut butter
banana slices
cinnamon

paper plates
rice cake
1/2 chocolate bar
miniature marshmallows

Directions:

1. Clean hands, area, and equipment.
2. Put rice cake on microwave/safe plate.
3. Spread peanut butter evenly on rice cake.
4. Sprinkle cinnamon to taste.
5. Place chocolate bar on top.
6. Place marshmallows on top of chocolate.
7. Place in microwave at high for 20 seconds.
8. Let set for 25 seconds.
9. Place banana slices on marshmallows.
10. Relish like a ruler.

RELUCTANT RUDOLPH REINDEER
(No Cooking Recipe)

Materials:

2 raisins

paper plate

peanut butter

1 piece of white bread

1 red hot candy

6 stick pretzels   knife

Directions:

1. Clean hands, area, and equipment.
2. Cut each slice of bread into a large triangle.
3. Spread triangle with peanut butter.
4. Place two raisins for eyes.
5. Place red hot for nose.
6. Place three pretzels per antler.
7. Remember with a photograph.

RICE PUDDING

Materials:

saucepan

2 cups milk

1/3 cup sugar

1 teaspoon vanilla

refrigerator

3 eggs, beaten

colored sprinkles

1-1/2 cups cooked rice

1 tablespoon butter or margarine

stove top

ground cinnamon

bowl

Directions:

1. Clean hands, area, and equipment.
2. Combine rice, milk, and sugar in saucepan.
3. Bring to a boil, stirring constantly.
4. Remove from heat.
5. Stir in margarine and vanilla.
6. Slowly stir 1/2 cup hot rice into eggs.
7. Blend with rest of rice in saucepan.
8. Cook over medium low heat, stirring constantly, until it thickens.
9. Do not boil!
10. Remove from heat and stir.
11. Pour into serving dish.
12. Chill, then sprinkle with cinnamon and/or colored sprinkles.
13. Make 5 to 6 servings.

RECKLESS ROCKY ROAD
(It is reckless because it is easy to make & easily eaten)

Materials:

8" square pan
1 tablespoon milk
microwave
measuring cups
measuring spoons

16 oz milk chocolate
1 Snickers™ bar (Kingsize).
1-1/2 cups walnuts, chopped
1/2 cup miniature marshmallows
aluminum foil to cover pan

Directions

1. Clean hands, area, and equipment.
2. Break chocolate bar into pieces as well as a Snickers™ bar.
3. Melt milk chocolate and Snickers™ in microwave until chocolate mixes/melts.
4. Pour half of chocolate into foil lined pan.
5. Sprinkle/place nuts and marshmallows on chocolate.
6. Pour 1/2 of chocolate mixture over nuts and marshmallows.
7. Chill or leave out until set (in a cool area).
8. Cut and eat recklessly.

RAVENOUS RELISH #1

During Pioneer Days, crops were harvested and if not preserved, the food was lost. The following are great activities for Pioneer Days. This can be made ahead of time and served with chicken, beef, or fish. This is a non-cooking recipe.

Materials:

1 lemon
1 navel orange
1 zester
knife
1 can of whole cranberry sauce

bowl   spoon
1/2 cup raisins
1/2 teaspoon cinnamon, nutmeg
1/2 cup chopped almonds/walnuts

Directions:

1. Clean hands, area, and equipment.
2. Open can and put into large bowl.
3. Using a zester or peeler, skin, and cut lemon peel into very fine sections.
4. Peel and section orange.
5. Cut orange sections into small pieces.
6. Rinse raisins and add to the bowl.
7. Chop/cut walnuts or almonds and add to bowl.
8. Mix in cinnamon and nutmeg.
9. Refrigerate and relish—spread on bread/cracker or rice cake.

Relishes were made during the summer to preserve the crops so it could be eaten all year long.

#2. ROBUST CABBAGE RELISH

Materials:

1 shredded carrot
1 tablespoon sugar
bowls
grater
spoons

1 apple optional (shredded)
2 tablespoons mayonnaise
1 tablespoons fresh lime juice
1/8 teaspoon salt/pepper adjust to taste
4 cups shredded cabbage (red & white)

Directions:

1. Clean hands, area, and equipment.
2. Combine in small bowl, sugar, lime juice, mayonnaise, and salt and pepper.
3. Shred apple, carrot, and cabbage in large bowl with grater.
4. In large bowl, add dressing.
5. Great relish.

#3. ROBUST DILL PICKLED BEAN RELISH

Materials:

2/3 cup lemon juice
1/8 cup raw dill
1 clove garlic
1 cup pearl onions

1/2 cup vegetable oil
2 teaspoons salt and pepper
1 teaspoon chopped mustard seeds
1 to 1-1/2 pound of fresh green beans

Directions:

1. Clean hands, area, and equipment.
2. Clean, sort beans.
3. Boil juice with seasoning for at least five minutes.
4. Cook (add green beans) slightly in juice (hot) with seasonings (about 10 min.) until slightly limp.
5. Place in clean container with tight seal.
6. Allow to stand for 4 days.
7. Refrigerate after that.

#4. ROBUST PICKLED PEACHES RELISH

Materials:

1/4 cup vinegar
1 teaspoon all spice
2 3" cinnamon sticks

3/4 cup brown sugar
1 teaspoon whole cloves
1 pint canned peach halves.

Directions:

1. Clean hands, area, and equipment.
2. Boil seasonings for five minutes.
3. Add peach halves and cook for 1 minute.
4. Pour into clean container.
5. Chill overnight.
6. Great with meats or over cake/ice cream.

R-r — Games/Activities

RINGO

The teacher uses words on word list (35-40) and writes them on little 2 x 4 inch cards. A "Ringo" card is made for each player, which has five words down, five across, and words to fill in. Across the top write the letters R-I-N-G-O. Each card needs the words placed differently with a few different words so that there is only one or two winners when all the cards are shown. This teaches sight words and visual perception.

"R" IS FOR RAISINS

An uppercase "R" and lower case r could be cut for a pattern. Each child is given either a cup filled with raisins (dried grapes) or a snack pack of raisins. The student must glue all the raisins to the letter. Of course some will be eaten, so have plenty. There are several varieties of grapes and they could be shown/identified and tested. Chart/graph the results (golden, white, seedless, red, flame, currents). The student must then try to remember and retrieve them by naming all of them.

R-r ANIMAL REPORTS

In the word list, there are several animals whose name starts with the /R-r/ sound. Students could check out books/encyclopedias and write page (one to two paragraphs) on their favorite animal. It could be completed in a cooperative learning group. Each animal report requires: picture, habitat, foods, identification, and any relevant facts.

RULE OF THUMB

Long ago, measurements were explained by hands (five hands tall: horses, cows) feet, or thumbs. This proved to be inconsistent/inaccurate and unreliable. Rulers were made so that when someone orders a bed, bookcase that is 3 feet 4 inches, it's exact. Have the students measure or use rulers to measure desks, books, bookcases, pencils, hands, and feet. They could also measure their friends and other staff to see who has the largest hands and feet as measured by rulers.

RHYTHMIC ROLLING

The teacher could use chalk or duct tape to write/draw an upper case and lower case R-r on the ground. Each student must rapidly roll on the shape to get the configuration of the letter. They could also roll around the room to music.

RICE - O

There are many kinds of rice. There is the kind preprocessed from long grain. There is wild rice, which is a seed from a wild grass; flavored rices for chicken or beef; there is brown rice, which keeps its bran coat and germ which makes it more nutritious; there is short grain, which cooks up more tender and faster; there is long grains, which is good for soup, molding, and stuffing as they hold their shape; finally, there is Chinese rice, which uses a lot of water and may stick together. Children/teacher could purchase these boxes and compare taste/texture and write/dictate why they liked each kind and what they would cook at home. The Chinese say "May your rice never burn."

R-r INVENTIONS

Inventions help make our life better, easier, and more technological. What inventions can you think of that start with the "R-r" sound: rolling pin, rubber bands, rake, recess, racket, radar, radio, raft, rails, rice cooker, ratchet, rattle, razor, ruler, rug, robe, rudder, rope, room, roof, rocket, robot, ring, report, refrigerator, ramp, ranch, register, rifle, roads, rubber tires, and restaurant. The words could be written on the board and explained. "It" can be thinking of an invention beginning with the "R-r" sound. "It" must give two to three hints about it. The class tries to guess it in 20 or less tries. The one who guesses it becomes "it."

R-r PICTURES/BOOKS

Students look through old catalogs, discarded books, magazines, and newspapers to find objects that start with the "R-r" sound. They must either write/dictate two to three sentences about the object (name) its function and why they chose this. These could be displayed or made into a book. Place it in the class library so each student could read it by him/ herself.

REALISTIC RECIPE BOOKS

Each child should bring to school a recipe from home. This can be planned as a multicultural activity. The recipes are copied along with favorite recipes from the teacher(s) and principal's office, along with custodial staff. They can then be sold to buy books for the class library or used as gifts for Christmas/Mother's Day. (This is a class favorite.) Children can read them and even make up one of their own. A recipe is a formula and must be followed to get the results consistently. A recipe can be changed, but the consistency/results may change.

RELAY RUNNING

Relay running is a great activity if done respectfully. It keeps your heart muscles and lungs strong while keeping you physically fit. Always run with good strong, safe shoes. Do warm-up exercises first. Run for 15 minutes (around the course) three times a week. Jog (slow run) first. Pace yourself. Run on a track, grass, or beach. Run during the day. Use a stopwatch and race yourself only. When in condition, races against others in class can be held. Relays are a classic example of a running game. Divide into four teams. Each team must have equal numbers. Arrange the teams so that Team One has two parts (A and B) and Team Two has two parts (A and B). When the bell/whistle gun fires, a shout is heard - Team One A runs to B, which is across the playground and equal to/next to Team Two's B and vice versa. Team One's and Team Two's runner runs to B and then sits down. The first runners from B run back to A and then sit down while the first runner from A goes to B. This continues until all the relay players are sitting down. The first team (one or two) whose players are all sitting down, wins.

R-r — Word Lists

Nouns:

rayon	razor	Ranger
receipt	recess	recorder
rectangle	red	reed
railroad	refrigerator	rings
Rhinestones	rage	ragtime
raid	rail	rainbow
rainfall	ramp	ranch
rattle	ray	ream
rack	rid	race
rudder	racket	ruby
radar	rose	radio
rosary	raft	rope
rag	roof	raid
room	rail	roof
rain	romance	rake
rocket	ramp	rock
rampart	robot	range
river	ransom	ring
ratchet	riddle	rattle
rigmarole	reward	ruler
retort	rear	retaliation
rebate	result	rebel
rest	rural	respect
rule	residence	rugby
Republic	rug	report
rota	rent	robe
religion	remark	rein
Rabbi	reef	race
reason	recruit	

Verbs:

realized	recite	recognize
record	ramble	rally
revolt	rage	reveal

202

rain	revenge	raise
return	rank	real
ransack	rap	rapid
retreat	rate	rest
ration	reach	respond
read	reason	rut
resent	rust	resemble
rush	resent	rescue
run	range	rummage
ruin	reply	rub
repel	row	rent
rot	remove	roll
remorse	rob	remind
risk	relish	riding
rejoice	ride	refer
rid	redeem	remember
responsible	receive	recruit

Adj/adv-descriptive Words:

rackle	rustic	royal
responsible	rapture	round
rare	rotten	rascal
racial	ready	racy
real	radiant	rude
radical	royal	rancid
rapid	rough	rap
rogue	rave	robust
rash	right	rational
ridge	raunchy	rich
ravenous	rhythm	raw
rhetoric	readable	rhapsody
readily	revise	realistic
reverberate	receptive	reluctant
reckless	rely	recluse
reddest	redundant	regal
relevant	revolting	rickety
romantic		

Animals or descriptive words about Animals:

rabbit	ram	rat
raven	rodent	robin
roach	rhinoceros	raccoon
rattlesnake	raccoon dog	road runner
rat fish	rat kangaroo	red admiral
red bird	red breast robin	red deer
red ear	red eye	red fish
red fox	red snapper	red spider
reindeer	remora	reptile
rhebok	Rhesus Monkey	rice bird
rock fish	ring-necked duck	roe
ring-necked snake	Rocky Mountain Goat	
red-winged blackbird		

Foods or food-like words:

radish	raisin	raspberry
ravioli	raw	russet potato
rosemary	roast	ripe
rice	ribs	restaurant
relish	reduce	recipe
refrigerator	Rye	rhubarb
roasted	rarebit	ricotta cheese
rind	rutabaga	rabbit
ratatouille	reindeer	red snapper
Rennet	Roe	Roll
radicchio		

R-r —Reading Resources

Red Riding Hood — James Marshall: Dial 1987

Rip Van Winkle — Washington Irving, 1819

Runaway Bunny — Margaret Wise Brown: Harper Trophy, 1972

Rosies Walk — Pat Hutchinson: Aladdin/MacMillian Co., 1968

Rain and Rainfall — Peter Spier: Doubleday, 1982

Mr. Rabbit and the Lovely Present — Charlotte Zolotow

Rosie and Michael — Judith Vorst

The Relatives Came — Cynthia Rylant: Bradbury, 1985

Raggedy Ann and Andy — Cathy Dubowski

Rain Makes Applesauce — Julian Scheer: Holiday, 1964

Rabbit Hill — Robert Lawson: Puffin, 1941

Rapunzel — Brothers Grimm

Rumpelstiltskin — Brothers Grimm, 1986

The Red Shoes — Hans Christian Anderson

Rainbow of My Own — Don Freeman

Rainy Day Kate — Lenore Blegvad McElderly, 1989

Rap — Keith Elliot Greenberg: Lerner, 1989

Rats — Pat Hutchins: Greenwilloe, 1990

Rotten Ralph's Show and Tell — Jack Gantos: Houghton Mifflin, 1990

Rufus M — Eleanor Estes: Yearling, 1941

Rumble Fish — S.E. Hinton: Dell, 1967

A Rose for Pinkerton — Steven Kellogg: Pied Piper, 1979

Rookie of the Year — John R. Tunis: Odyssey, 1940

Roar and More — Karla Kuskin: Harper Trophy, 1990

Rasco and the Rats of Nimh — Robert C. O'Brien: Aladdin, 1971

Rachel Fister's Blister — Amy McDonald: Houghton Mifflin, 1990

Read-Aloud Rhymes for the Very Young — Jack Prelutsky: Knopf, 1986

Rotten Ralph — Jack Gantos: Houghton Mifflin, 1976

Raffi Singable Song Book — Raffi Crown, 1987

Rain Forest — Helen Cowcher: Sunburst, 1990

Rainy Day Max — Hanne Turk Studio, 1984

Ralph S. Mouse — Beverly Cleary: Avon, 1965

Ramona Quimby, Age 8 — Beverly Cleary: Avon, 1952-1984

The Real Mother Goose — Blanche Fisher Wright: Checkerboard, 1916

The Red Balloon — Albert Lamorisse Zephr, 1957

The Red Pony — John Steinbeck: Penguin, 1937

Rosalie — Joan Hewett: Lothrop, Lee, and Shepard, 1987

Rose in Bloom — Louisa May Alcott: Penguin, Bantam, Signet, 1868

Robin Hood — Donald Cooke: Holt, 1961

Rotten Island — William Steig: David Godine, 1984

Rabbit's Morning — Nancy Tafuri: Greenwillow, 1985

Round Robin — Jack Kent: Prentice Hall, Inc., 1982

Rabble Starkey — Lois Lowry: Dell Yearling, 1987

The Rainbow People — Lawrence Yep: Harper Trophy, 1989

The Reluctant Dragon — Kenneth Grahame: Holiday, 1938

Roll of Thunder, Hear My Cry — Mildred Taylor: Puffin, 1976

The Ruby in the Smoke — Phillip Pullman: Knopf, 1985

Raven — Gerald McDermott: Harcourt, 1993

Raindrop Stories — Preston Basset: Four Winds, 1981

S•s

S-s —Recipes

SPECTACULAR STONE SOUP

Materials:

1 very clean stone
knife
ladle
3 carrots
1 cup barley or rice
2 tomatoes
1 can tomatoes
crock pot/soup pot
1 can broth

garlic powder
seasoned salt
pot
3 potatoes
1 celery stalk
4 cups water
1 can peas
1 can corn
stove

Directions:

1. Clean hands, area, and equipment.
2. Wash and cut into pieces (carrots, potatoes, celery stalk, and tomatoes).
3. Add water.
4. Combine all into large soup pot and add 1 clean stone.
5. Simmer until tender.
6. Ground or squared beef, pork, turkey, or chicken can be added.
7. Add 1 can of tomatoes, 1 can of peas, 1 can of corn, and 1 can of broth.
8. Add salt and pepper to taste.
9. Herbs, garlic powder and seasoned salt can be added, if desired.
10. Serve and sip.

SERIOUSLY SPECIAL SALSA (No Cooking)
Served with tortilla chips.

Materials:

cutting board
1/4 cup lime juice
knife1 stalk of celery (diced)
1 large carrot-shredded

tabasco sauce
1 bunch cilantro-chopped
bowl
1 teaspoon of vegetable oil

6 ripe tomatoes or 2 cans cooked/diced tomatoes

1/2 yellow onion diced small/fine or 1 bunch of green onions-diced

1 jalapeno chili-cut lengthwise, all seeds removed and diced very small (remember, use sparingly!)

Directions:

1. Clean hands, area, and equipment.
2. Using the cutting board and knife, chop all the ingredients.
3. Put into bowl.
4. Add lime juice.
5. Mix
6. Serve with tortilla chips or flour tortillas, which have been baked.

Sammy Snake Salad (No Cooking)

Materials:

2 or 3 apples

1 stalk celery

1/4 cup mayonnaise

1/4 teaspoon vinegar

2 large carrots

1/2 cup raisins

1/4 cup sour cream

Directions:

1. Clean hands, area, and equipment.
2. Peel 2 or 3 apples.
3. Peel 2 large carrots and grate them.
4. Cut 1 stalk celery into small pieces.
5. Add 1/2 cup raisins.
6. Combine apples, carrots, celery, and raisins into a small bowl.
7. In large bowl mix mayonnaise, sour cream, and vinegar.
8. Combine contents of small bowl with contents of large bowl.
9. Refrigerate before eating.
10. Serve and smile.

Spicy Saucy Spaghetti

Materials:

electric fry pan

sauce pan

wooden spoons

plates

diced tomatoes with basil

1/4 onion, diced very fine

1 can of Italian-style tomatoes

-3/4 cup of Parmesan cheese

14-16 oz. of spaghetti noodles cooked (hot)

1 lb lean ground beef/turkey or 2-3 Mild Italian Sausages

4 jars or 2 packets of Italian spaghetti sauce (two 8-oz. cans of tomato sauce with packages of mix)

seasonings: Italian herb, pepper flakes, oregano, basil, and salt and pepper to taste.

Directions:

1. Clean hands, area, and equipment.
2. Add brown Italian sausages (remove casing and crumble) or ground beef/turkey/chicken.
3. Add diced onion and cook/sautÈ for 5-7 minutes or until meat is thoroughly cooked in electric fry pan.
4. Add sauce mix with tomato sauce or jars of prepared sauce.
5. Add diced tomatoes with basil.
6. Add seasonings to taste.
7. Cook for several hours.
8. Serve over cooked spaghetti noodles.
9. Sprinkle with Parmesan cheese.
10. It's a favorite.

SUCCESSFUL SALAD
Served in bowls with choice of salad dressings.
(No Cooking)

Materials:

2 large tomatoes
1 large carrot, diced
cutting board
knife
grater
1 cup cheddar cheese
Several bottles of salad dressing

1 head of Romaine lettuce
1 head of butter lettuce
1 head of red leafed lettuce
1 bunch of green onions
1 stalk of celery, diced
1 cup of sliced olives, black and pitted

Directions:

1. Clean hands, area, and equipment.
2. Clean and cut up lettuce by hands.
3. Cut tomatoes, score first.
4. Slice green onions.
5. Dice celery.
6. Grate cheese and slice olives.
7. Using a large bowl, add all ingredients.
8. Toss with large utensils.
9. Give each person a bowl to fill, and allow their choice of dressings.
10. Very successful.

SAVORY SUMMER SALAD

Materials

2 avocados
3 or 4 leaves of lettuce
knife
bowl
plate
1-1/2 cups of zucchini slices or cucumber
2 tablespoons green onion slices

1/4 cup Parmesan cheese
1 bottle of Italian salad dressing
3 cups of cooked shell macaroni
2 cups of tomato wedges
1 can pitted olives-sliced
1/4 tablespoon cilantro and/or parsley

Directions:

1. Clean hands, area, and equipment.
2. Put cooked shell, macaroni, tomato wedges, zucchini/cucumber slices, parsley and/or cilantro, green onion slices, and olives in bowl.
3. Refrigerate for two hours.
4. Arrange avocados, tomatoes, and lettuce.
5. Top with pasta mixture.

SUREFIRE SUGAR COOKIES

Materials:

canned frosting
1 cup sugar
2 eggs
1/2 teaspoon milk
3 cups flour
little candies
sprinkles to help decorate

1 cinnamon and cardamom to taste
2 teaspoons baking powder
2/3 cup butter, softened
1 tablespoon milk
1 teaspoon vanilla
ungreased baking sheets

Directions:

1. Clean hands, area, and equipment.
2. Combine flour, baking powder, and salt.
3. Cream butter and sugar until light and eggs one at a time and beat after each addition.
4. Add vanilla.
5. Add flour and milk alternately until blended.
6. Wrap and chill for several hours or overnight.
7. Roll or give each child a ball on lightly floured foil or board. Have dough about 1/8" thick.
8. Cut with floured cookie cutters.
9. Bake on ungreased sheets or aluminum lined sheets.
10. Bake at 400 degrees for about 8 to 10 minutes or lightly browned.
11. When cooled, frost, and decorate.
12. Stand back and smile.

SMART AND SWIFT STRAWBERRY SHORTCAKE

Materials:

1 pkg. frozen strawberries or 2 pints fresh strawberries

1 cup sugar
1/2 teaspoon salt
cookie sheets
cutting board
aluminum foil
3/4 cup milk
oven fork

2 cups all purpose flour
2-1/2 tablespoons of sugar
3-1/2 teaspoons of baking powder
1/3 cup of melted butter
2 tablespoons of powdered sugar
1 cup whipping cream

Directions:

1. Clean hands, area, and equipment.
2. Rinse fresh berries, sprinkle with sugar (allow to stand for 1/2 hour to 1 hour).
3. Mix flour, baking powder, salt, and 2-1/2 tablespoons of sugar.
4. Stir in milk and butter until just blended.
5. On floured board, knead dough ball for only 20-25 times (do not work dough!).
6. Cut into 3 to 3 1/2" circles, 1/2 to 3/4" thick.
7. Place on lightly greased cookie sheet or aluminum foiled sheet.
8. Place into 400 degree oven and bake 10-15 minutes, until golden brown.
9. Split warm biscuits in half with fork. Place strawberries and whipped cream (2 teaspoons powdered sugar and 1 cup cream).

S-s —Games/Activities

STREGA NONA SURPRISE

The teacher reads *Strega Nona*. In this story Anthony does not listen and is suggestible, so he tries out the spell. He does not hear the end, and there is spaghetti everywhere. For the activity, the teacher boils spaghetti (which is a pasta served in many countries) and students then add any of the following: flavored butter (garlic and salt), spaghetti sauce (in jars, warmed), cream sauce (pkg. or jars) and any other toppings. Children can predict, taste, and vote (decide). A chart/graph can be created to illustrate results. Have others join in. Also, take one piece of spaghetti and manipulate it until it forms an S and glue it down.

SAD SACKETS

Two paper sacks (small) are provided for each child. One side is a "sad" or a "silly" face. On the other side is a "Sunny" or a happy face. Children could get into groups and discuss what makes them sad, angry, silly, sunny (happy) and scared. The groups then present their ideas, which are then charted. Each child writes a paper or "I Feel" book about what makes them feel sad, silly, sunny, scared, stubborn, strange, strong, or smart.

SHOW-OFF SNACKS SACKS

Children get time for nutrition or recess before lunch, when they can each have a nutrition snack. Students could talk about what a nutritional snack consists of: vegetables, fruits (fresh/dried), nuts, raisins, cheeses, peanut butter, and etc. Each child could bring a snack in an unlabeled sack. They could each get one and rate it (5 being best and 1 being lowest). Illustrations or realia is shown/discussed as to what a 5-point snack sack consists of. They could then be displayed so others can "see" what a 5 point snack sack is.

SUCCESSFUL SQUARES

Each child/student is given several squares of different sizes and colors. Students spread, swap, spin, scatter, show, and glue them into a collage/ picture. Students write a story about his/her own squares.

S-s SCRAMBLE

One child is "it". All the students form a small square. When the music starts, the students scramble. The child who is "it" has a blindfold on his/her eyes as he/she counts to 10. When the music stops, the students stop. The child who is "it" is in the middle of the square. When the music stops, "it" tries to touch as many students as he/she can. Students who are caught become the substitute squares and direct "it" by saying "cold, hot, right, left" until "it" has touched snarled each player. The last student snarled (caught) is "it."

SCOOP/SUPPORT THE SUNFLOWER SEEDS

Sunflowers are very available today. Not all sunflowers produce seeds. Show students sunflowers and explain to them that the seeds are collected and then baked with salt. Each bag of seeds is sold by weight, not number. Students predict how many seeds are in each package. (Chart) Each student then counts the seeds in their package. Students can see/show the difference. Chart/graph actual count. Students can eat the seeds, not the shells.

SHOW-OFF SHAMROCKS

You will need a toaster-oven, shamrock-shaped cookie cutters, cutting board, flour, refrigerator, cookies or recipe for sugar cookies (in this chapter, made and cooled), icing, and sprinkles. Have students: clean hands, area, and equipment. Then have them preheat oven to 350 degrees, flour (lightly) on cutting board with hands and cutters, flatten dough to 1/2" thick, cut with cutters, bake until golden brown (7-9 minutes), and decorate them with either cream cheese, powdered sugar, butter, and milk. Beat until smooth or buy canned frosting. Sprinkles are fun.

SUPERFINE SPONGES

Sponges can be purchased in different shapes and even in shapes of the alphabet letters. Pour tempera paint into flat containers (lids) using either shaped sponges or sponges that are cut into different shapes. Students can spin, swap, set, scatter, shape, smear, share, and supply sponges to make a patterned paper, design, or a picture. Be sure to have students write or dictate about their creation.

"S-S" SHARE STORIES

Teacher writes words from "thing" (nouns) list, "does" (verb) list, "descriptive" (adverbs, adjectives) list. Each student chooses five to seven, one of each, and writes a story about (including) the words. The stories could be published as S-s Stories from Room _____ and students could share them with their families or other students.

SWEET OR SOUR

Students could be blindfolded. They are asked to smell several samples and state if the sample is sweet or sour. Teacher could chart answers. The next group would have a different sampling of items.

S-s —Word Lists

Nouns:

sachet	sweetheart	solarium
sack	swing	story
storm	stomach	sabot
sand	string	set
spot	sweat	sound
skirt	stripe	shirt
screen	spring	survey
school	seat	scarf
shin	space	surgery
scar	spirit	scholar
sea	sports	supper
scout	scab	stem
snack	superstition	ship
step	surf	sombrero
sun	shot	steel
snow	sonar	secret
shell	sap	snowball
sheet	socket	shop
snowman	sunflower	sunglasses
screw	static	sled
smoker	sundae	slave
smokestack	Sunday	slate
shoe	saber	slipper
sweater	Summer	skull
shot	system	suitcase
skeleton	silk	swamp
smile	symptom	suit
store	surprise	stretch
sunbeam	stick	sense
sympathy	stone	substitute
story	signal	symbol
sunshine	stroller	street
skin	stroke	star
stem	schedule	scope
scout		

Verbs:

switch	strip	strike
stab	save	strum
scram	set	sweat
sob	stole	snuggle
suspend	sip	study
see	slap	snore
said	stood	set
swab	sneeze	sound
settle	state	say
sweep	swim	scratch
stay	scatter	sat
swell	scramble	step
scrape	swept	screw
scared	support	spend
scoop	sweep	scrub
spoke	shall	show
strike	spin	shape
strangle	swung	shop
spell	shut	swam
stink	spread	slip
swap	slice	speak
slam	show	slit
skid	snap	smile
spin	smell	snarl
smother	sift	smash
snip	smear	smack
shout	squeal	scoot
scream	skip	stole
saw		

Descriptive Words:

strange	stingy	saturated
strong	stubborn	still
same	secret	sensuous
side	sure	same
surly	sea	surprising

215

scarce	surefire	short
supreme	slant	supposedly
slope	supply	slim
supple	sly	supernatural
sleek	superior	slimy
superfluous	skinny	superfine
strategy	smooth	superficial
small	superb	strong
super	spark	sunless
speed	sultry	special
suggestible	shallow	sudden
swelter	such	swift
succinct	soon	successful
some	subtle	slim
substitutive	sap	submissive
serious	subjective	stiff
sturdy	smart	stupid
specific	stunning	stuffy
stylish	skate	

Animals:

snails	seahorse	schnauzer
scallop	scorpion	seal
sea otter	salamander	sheep
sardines	squirrel	skunk
secretary bird	sand dab	salmon
snake	Siamese cat	shrimp
sloth	sea urchin	swan
sable	shark	sheath bill
Shetland pony	swordfish	barn swallow
surgeon fish	Sturgeon	Struma
stork	stomatopod	stockfish
stickleback	sand piper	sand hopper

Areas:

Sun Valley	San Francisco	San Jose
San Jacinto	San Juan	San Marino
San Remo	San Salvador	Sarajevo

Sacramento	Switzerland	Swaziland
Swamp	Swahili	Suwannee
Svalbard	Sussex	Lake Superior
Sumatra	Suez Canal	Styr River
Stonehenge	Stockholm	Stockport
St. John	St. Joseph	St. Laurent
St. Martin	St. Mary	St. Helens
San Antonio	San Bernardino	Samoan
Salvador	San Diego	Scandinavia
Seoul	St. Lawrence Seaway	
San Iago De Cuba	Sugar Loaf Mountain	
San Fernando Valley		

Foods — Cooking Terms:

spinach	squash	syrup
succotash	salad dressings	salami
Salisbury steak	salmon	salsa
sand dab	sardines	sapodilla
savertraut	scallop	seafood
shallot	sherbet	shortening
shrimp	snails	stuffing
stroganoff	strawberry	sweet potato
sweet oil	sweetener	sweet bread
sugar beet	sugarcane	succulent
strudel	strain	stout
stir	sole	stir-fry
stiff	sticky	stew
steam	sassafras	sauce
sausage	scallion	scald
scone	sea lettuce	soybean
sunflower oil	sage	snow peas
sturgeon	sugar maple	sugar apple
sour cream	soup	spaghetti
sauce		

S-s —Reading Resources

Dragon Stew — Tom McGowen

Strega Nona — Tomie DePaola

Chicken Soup with Rice — Maurice Sendak

The Snowman — Raymond Briggs — Random House, 1978

The Seven Chinese Brothers — Margaret Mahy: Scholastic, 1990

Sheep in a Jeep — Nancy Shaw: Houghton Mifflin, 1968

Snuggle Piggy and the Magic Blanket — Michelle Stepto: Unicorn, 1967

Swimmy — Leo Lionni: Knopf, 1963

Swan Sky — Tejima: Philomel, 1988

Sam the Minuteman — Nathaniel Benchley: Harper Collins, 1969

Surprises — Lee Bennett Hopkins: Harper Trophy, 1984

Something Sleeping in the Hall — Karla Kushin: Harper Collins, 1985

Where's Spot? — Eric Hill: G.P. Putnam's Sons, 1980

Chicken Soup with Rice — Maurice Sendak: Scholastic Press, 1962

Shoes — Elizabeth Winthrop: Harper & Row, 1986

It Looked Like Spilt Milk — Charles Shaw: Harper & Row, 1947

Spring Fellow — Robert Kraus: Windmill Books, 1978

Strega Nona — Tomie De Paola: Free House, 1975

Stone Soup — Marcia Brown: Aladdin, 1947

The Selfish Giant — Oscar Wilde: Picture Book, 1984

Sounder — William H. Armstrong: Harper, 1970

Summer of the Swans — Betsy Byars: Viking, 1971

The Surprise Picnic — John Goodall: Atheneum, 1977

Skates — Ezra Jack Keats: Scholastic, Inc. 1981

The Silver Pony — Lynd Ward: Houghton Mifflin, 1973

Spider Jane on the Move — Jane Yolen: Coward, McCann, and Geoghegan, 1980

The Trumpet of the Swan — E.B. White: Harper, 1970

Seven Little Rabbits — John Becker: Scholastic, 1973

Simon's Song — Barbara Emberley: Prentice Hall, 1969

Shadow — Blaise Cendraras: Aladdin, 1982

Shaka—King of the Zulus — Diane Stanley and Peter Vennema: Morrow Junior Books, 1984

The Stupids Have a Ball — Harry Allard — Houghton Mifflin

Swan Lake — Margot Fonteyn: HBJ, 1989

Susanna of the Alamo: A True Story — John Jakes: Voyager, 1986

Stevie — John Steptoe: Harper Trophy, 1967

The Something — Natalie Babbitt: Sunburst, 1970

Sayonara, Mrs. Kackleman — Maira Kalman: Viking, 1989

The Snowy Day — Ezra Jack Keats: Puffin, 1963

Song of the Swallows — Leo Politi: Scribners, 1950

The Big Snow — Berta and Elmer Hader: MacMillian, 1949

White Snow, Bright Snow — Alvin Tresselt: Lothrop, 1948

Sylvester and the Magic Pebble — William Steig: Windmill, 1970

Saint George and the Dragon — Margaret Hodges: Little Brown, 1985

Strawberry Girl — Lois Lenski: J.B. Lippincott, 1946

Smoky, The Cowhorse — Will James: Scribners, 1927

The White Stag — Kate Seredy: Viking, 1938

Shadow of a Bull — Maia Wojeiechowska — Atheneum 1965

Slugs — David Greenberg

Sammy the Seal — Syd Hoff: Harper Collins, 1958

The Snow Queen — Eva LeGallinenne: Harper & Row, 1985

Soup — Robert Newton Peck: Dell Yearling, 1974

The Secret Garden — Frances Hodgson Burnett: Harper Trophy, 1912

Scary Stories to Tell in the Dark: Collected from American Folklore — Alvin Schwartz: Harper Collins, 1981

Slime Time — Jim & Jane O'Connor: Random House, 1981

Stars and Planets — Christopher Lampton: Doubleday, 1989

Sports — Tim Hammon: Knoph, 1989

The Soup Bone — Tony Johnston: H.B.J., 1990

T-t —Recipes

TASTY TOP-O-THE LINE TACO
(This could be used as a multi-cultural experience recipe)

Materials:

2-2 1/2 pounds of ground beef

2 packages taco seasoning mix

electric fry pan

1 can olives

1 small container of sour cream

chopping board

1/2 head lettuce

3 tomatoes

2 lbs. of cheese (cheddar)

2 packages-taco shells

1 avocado (opt.)

knife   grater

Directions:

1. Clean hands, area, and equipment.
2. Read and follow directions on taco seasoning mix (hint: drain fat with turkey baster and put fat in plastic container).
3. Grate cheese with grater.
4. Chop tomatoes, olives, and avocado.
5. Shred lettuce with knife on chopping board.
6. Allow each taster to toss into his/her taco shell what he/she wants.
7. All together say, "This is tasty."

TANGLE-TWISTY-TACO CASSEROLE

Materials:

1 jar of Kraft Cheese Whiz⌀ or 1 can of Campbell's Cheese Sauce

1 pkg.. of twisty-type macaroni (cooked/drained)

1 package of taco seasoning mix or taco sauce

seasonings-pepper, flakes, salt, pepper and garlic

2 pounds of ground beef   frying pan

plates   forks

Directions:

1. Clean hands, area, and equipment.
2. Brown and season taco meat according to taco seasoning mix or brown meat (drain). Season with taco sauce (hint: be sure to drain fat).
3. Add cooked macaroni.
4. Blend meat and macaroni.
5. Add cheese.
6. Season to taste.
7. Terrific!

TROUBLELESS TOSTADAS

Materials:

1 carrot
1 stalk of celery
1 food processor
1 chopping board
1 can of olives
2 tomatoes
1 knife
1 grater
cilantro

2 cups dry pinto beans
1 can diced/cooked chilies
4 raw sausages (suggested: hot)
1 small onion, diced
2 pounds of cheddar or jack cheese
1/2 to 1 head of lettuce
carton of sour cream
1 package of corn/flour tortillas

Directions:

1. Clean hands, area, and equipment.
2. Rinse, sort, and soak beans.
3. Put into a 4 qt. pot.
4. Add six cups of water and let soak. (4 to 8 hours)
5. Simmer and add cooked sausage and onions (I crumbled and browned with onions).
6. Add carrot and celery and cook until tender (Make sure beans are covered with water).
7. Cool, then add beans to food processor or mash with potato masher.
8. Grate Jack/Cheddar cheese.
9. Shred lettuce.
10. Chop tomatoes/olives.
11. If using corn tortillas, take out of box and assemble tostada-beans, lettuce, cheese, tomatoes, and one scoop of sour cream.
12. If using flour tortillas, heat (bake) until firm or golden brown and then assemble.
13. True love.

TRUE-HEARTED TUNA-SANDWICH

Tuna is caught on large fishing boats. It is cleaned and processed into cans for retail selling.

Materials:

3 large tuna cans
1 head of lettuce
2 stalks of celery
1 loaf of bread
fork bowl

1 bunch green/purple onions
1 jar of mayonnaise 1 lemon
2 tomatoes 1 can of olives
can opener spoon
plates

Directions:

1. Clean hands, area, and equipment.
2. Use fork to drain and takeout tuna. Put into bowl.
3. Crumble with fork.
4. Add mayonnaise and lemon juice to taste.
5. Chop onion, olives, and celery.
6. Add to tuna mixture.
7. Slice tomatoes and clean leaf lettuce.
8. Put 2 slices of bread on each plate. Put lettuce, tomato, and tuna on both slices.
9. It is true love.
10. Remember the process.

NOT TYPICAL TURKEY

Materials:

3 cups thinly sliced vegetables: carrots, celery, peppers, zucchini, mushrooms, jicama, & green beans

1-1/2 pounds turkey breast (raw)	knife
2 tsp. soy sauce	1/2 cup water
cutting board	2 tsp. corn starch
1 green onion	wooden spoon
steamed rice	electric fry pan
plates	forks
oil	

Directions:

1. Clean hands, area, and equipment.
2. Cut turkey into bite-sized pieces. Marinate in soy sauce (1 tsp.).
3. Combine 1 tsp. soy sauce, water, corn, starch plus ground ginger, mustard, onion, and garlic to taste. Allow to sit.
4. In large fry pan add 1/2 tsp. of oil and stir fry vegetables until tender.
5. Add green onions and stir-fry for one minute.
6. Stir in turkey until no pink remains.
7. Stir in cornstarch mixture #3 and cook/stir until thickened.
8. Serve over steamed rice.
9. Terribly terrific.

TRIUMPHANT-THREE JUICE TWIRLS

Materials:

1 carton of strawberries (washed and cut into halves) or pears (peeled and quartered).

1 apple: quartered, peeled	3 oz paper cups
1 banana, peeled & cut up	aluminum foil
food processor or blender	wooden sticks
1/2 cup orange juice	freezer

Directions:

1. Clean hands, area, and equipment.
2. In blender or food processor, add orange juice and fruit pieces.
3. Process until smooth.
4. Pour into cups.
5. Cover each cup with foil.
6. Insert wooden stick into cup.
7. Freeze for 4-6 hours until firm.
8. Remove foil and tear from pops.
9. Enjoy.

T-t — Games/Activities

TROMBONE/TRUMPET/TUBA

In this activity children listen to instrumental music. Real instruments or just pictures of them could be displayed. Students can then identify/compare/ contrast the sounds of these musical instruments all having the names that begin with T-t.

TRUCKS/TRANSPORTATION

Have students bring in models, pictures, or cut pictures from discarded books, magazines, or catalogs. Sort and classify them as trucks, cars, boats, and airplanes. Transportation means ways to move (carry) people or things from one place to another. Today most items are transported by large ships. Read about it. It is fun to learn about transportation. Make a city and transport goods.

TALKY TELEPHONE

Have the children sit in a circle. One child is the telephone. The telephone whispers a message to the person (transmitter) next to him/her and that person tells the message to the next. The last person repeats the message out loud. All hear the original message and the transmitted message. It's tricky.

TRICKY-TIC-TAC-TOE OR 3 IN A ROW

Children love to play games. This is a game for children and adults. It is easy to play, but becomes a critical thinking game. Four T's are constructed to make an open block of 9 squares. One person moves/draws X's and the other moves/draws O's. The trick is to connect three (X's or O's) in a row (this can be straight or diagonally).

THANK YOU NOTES

There are many people on the school staff that never get thanked for the extra effort/time they put into their job. Your class could write the bus driver, cafeteria staff, custodial staff, clerical staff, and anyone else (principal, assistant principal) a little note to thank him/her for all their time/effort.

T-ANIMAL-O-RAMA

Refer to the "Animals" section in the Word List; it lists several animals starting with the letter T-t. Make flashcards with copies/pictures of those animals. Allow each child/student to choose three to five animals like: turtle, tiger, tree squirrel, toucan, Tasmanian devil and toad. Children can color/cut copies of that animal or draw their own pictures. They can be pasted into a shoebox. They can then write/dictate a story about these T-animals.

THREES

3 Little Pigs, 3 Little Kittens, Billy Goats Gruff, The 3 Robbers, and The Three Bears are some of the stories about threes. Have students make puppets out of paper bags, or paper with

Popsicle™ sticks and write their own or even have a class puppet show using three characters.

TUG-O-WAR

You will need tape and a tug rope. Children/students form two teams. The teams should have the same number of students. The team leaders stand on the tape and team members hold each other by the waist. When the number "3" or "10" or "12" is said, the teams try to pull the other team over the taped line.

TRICK-O

The teacher makes flashcards that are skill and/or age appropriate, and then makes a game board. Each student rolls the dice and must decode/ read the word to move their marker the number of squares/moves that correspond to the number on the dice. The player that goes from start to finish wins.

TACKY TRIANGULAR DESIGN

Each student can cut and paste as many triangles as they need to make a shape/design/item. The child/student may then write one line sentence about their creation.

TOOL TIME

Each student is to bring one tool in a bag to school. Teacher charts or graphs how many different tools are brought and how many are the same. Tools could also be found around classroom and school. Other classes/people could join to see/find out the most popular tool.

THOUGHTFUL TRUFFLES

These truffles could be made and given to people who are thoughtful. They are easy, fun to make, and it may even make our world more thoughtful. The ingredients are one 8-oz. package of cream cheese, 1 tsp. of honey, 1/3 cup of chopped raisins, 2 tablespoons chopped nuts, 2 table- spoons graham cracker crumbs, and colored candies. The directions are:
   1) Clean hands area and equipment,
   2) chop nuts and raisins,
   3) combine cream cheese, honey, raisins and nuts,
   4) roll into a ball,
   5) roll on crumbs,
   6) roll in candies,
   7) chill,
   8) taste, and
   9) tell others (be thoughtful).

TREE LEAVES

The teacher could make a Tree Trunk on the board. The books A Tree Is Nice and The Giving Tree could be read. Each time a student is observed doing a nice thing, a helpful thing, a cooperative thing, or type of behavior that is positive, then his name is put on a leaf (and date and task) and the leaf goes on the tree. The student with the most leaves wins.

T-t —Word Lists

Nouns:

telephone	toaster	teaspoon
traffic signal	T-shirt	truck
truth	tax	trust
tent	trustee	table
trumpet	tab	tabernacle
Trump	tablet	tennis
truce	tabloid	taboo
tabor	tabulator	trowel
tacamahac	tachistoscope	trousers
tachometer	tack	tropic
tackle	trophy	tack room
trombone	tact	tactics
trooper	tael	taffeta
trouble maker	tag	tag board
troop	tyrant	Tyrannosaurus
typist	tugboat	tuck
typhoon	typhoid	trouble
typewriter	tympanum	tympani
twister	twill	twilight
twig	twerp	twenty-one
tweak	tutu	tuxedo
tutor	tusk	turret
turquoise	turbulence	turban
tunnel	tunic	tune
tumor	tumbler	tuba
Tuberculosis	tub	tripper
tobacco	traditions	temple
trace	track	trade
thunder	throne	throat
thermos	thread	thought
thorn	thirst	thing
troll	television	trivia
tank	trigger	trifle
trick	tricycle	tribute

tribe	triangle	trial
trestle	trench	treat
tray	treasure	trash
trauma	trap	transportation
transmission	translation	transformation
trampoline	tallit	tail
tailor	tale	talent
tambourine	traffic	trail
traitor	train	tramp
trampoline	tape	tooth
tar	toe	target
tarnish	task	tonsil
tow	tissue	town
test	technology	tire
timber	television	tepee
telegram	telescope	totem pole
touchdown	term	tour
team	title	tot
ten	top	temper
team	teacher	time
tear	taxicab	towel
tee	tramp	

Verbs:

tap	trap	tag
tell	tax	tired
table-hop	tabulate	typify
type	twist	twitch
twirl	twinkle	twinge
twiddle	tweeze	turn
tuck	try	trudge
trouble	trot	triturate
trisect	trip	trim
trifle	trick	trench
tremble	treat	trash
transport	transpire	transmit
take	tailing	talk
transact	transfer	trail
trade	track	trace
tour	toss	tote
torment	top	tatting
tax	tear	tease

228

team	thank	thaw
tell	thrust	throw
throb	threw	think

Animal:

tadpole	terrier	toad
tarantula	tripletail	termite
triggerfish	tiger	turtle
triceratops	trout	tree shrew
tortoise	tree squirrel	tree frog
Tachina fly	treehopper	tsetse fly
tyrant fly catcher	turtle dove	tailor bird
turkey buzzard	tern	turkey cock
toucan	turbot	tamarin
tapir	tuna	tapeworm
tumble bug	tui	tarpon
tubifex	tarsier	trout-perch
trout	tortoise beetle	trotter
tropic bird	tropical fish	tortoise
Tasmanian devil	trypanosome	trunk-fish

Foods or food related:

tortellini	tortilla	tomato
tea	tofu	tea biscuit
turnip	tangerines	tapioca
tuna	teaspoon	toast
tenderize	tacos	tarts
trepid	tabasco	thyme
tablespoon	turbot	tableware
taffy	T.V. Dinner	tutti frutti
turmeric	turkey	tarragon
turbinado sugar	truffle	truck farm
tripe	tangerine	tart
tartar sauce	taco	tangelo
tartar steak	taste	taste bud
tasteful	T-bone steak	tea
tempur	torte	tortellini
tortilla	tortoni	torula

turmeric	turn	tea biscuit
turbot	truss	Tabasco
table ware	taco	taffy
toffee	tea cup	tea spoon
tenderloin	thirsty	tester
thorn apple	Tex-Mex	thrust
thermos	timer	thick
thicken	tin-foil	tin-ware
thimble berry	T.L.C.	thin
thinner	toast	toaster
tomato	tongue	toothpick
top	top-heavy	

Adjectives/adverbs:

tired	tacit	taciturn
tacky	tactful	tactic
tactile	tactless	tactual
typical	two-sided	two-tone
two-legged	two-handed	thirsty
twit	thirteenth	two
twice-told	thousand	twice-laid
twenty-fold	thousandth	twenty
thoughtful	twentieth	twelve
thoughtless	tweedy	thirty
turbulent	third	turbid
thin	trustful	thick
truthful	these	trying
touchy	tenth	terribly
telling	terrify	terrific
thready	three	tight
total	trumped-up	truly
true-love	true-hearted	true
truculent	troublesome	trivial
tense	triumphant	trite
tristful	teenage	triple
toxic	trickish	tricentennial
triangular	trendy	transparent
translucent	tall	tragic

touching	tedious	telling

Areas:

Table Mountain	Tacna	Tacoma
Tadzhik	Tennessee	Taegu
Tijuana	Taejon	Taganrog
Thuringia	Tagalog	Tzupo
Tyumen	Tyrian	Tuskegee
Tuscany	Turkmen-USSR	Turkey
Turin	Tupi	Tungus
Troy	Transvaal	Taiwan
Tamatave	Tamayo	Tampa
Tampico	Tanganyika	Tanzania
Taos	Tasmania	Trafalgar
Tortuga	Taunton	Tibet
Thailand	Thornburi	

Animals:

tiger salamander	tilefish	tiger cat
toad fish	thread worm	tardigade
terrapin	toad	tamarin
tarsier	terrier	tachinafly
tanager	tarantula	tadpole
Tasmanian devil	thread fin	tapir
Tasmanian wolf	thrush	tailor bird
tapeworm	turtle	termite
tick	teredo	tuna
thornback	tiger	tigerbeetle
tomato worm moth	tom cod	tortoise
tortoise beetle	tortricid	toucan
tree frog	touraco	Tuatara
tragopan	trapdoor spider	treehopper
tree shrew	turn spit	tree squirrel
turbot	tree frog	tarpan
triceratops	tent caterpillar	Tyrannosaurus
trigger fish	theropod	Tussock moth
turtle dove	trumpeter swan	

T-t — Reading Resources

Two Bad Ants — Chris Van Allsburg: Houghton Mifflin, 1989

Thanks a Lot, Triceratot: A Tiny Dino's Story about Helping Others — Guy Gilchrist: Warner 1961

Transportation, Transportation — Keith Brandt

The Tuesday Elephant — Nancy Garfield

Three African Tales — Adjal Robinson

Tangle and the Firesticks — Benedict Blathwayt

They Were Strong and Good — Robert Lawson

Tikki, Tikki, Tembo — Arlene Mosel: Holt, 1968

A Tree Is Nice — Janice Udry: Harper, 1956

Telephone Time — Ellen Weiss

Toba — Michael Mark, Bradbury, 1984

Trig — Robert Peck, Little, 1984

Tikhon — Margaret-Ilse Vogel, Harper, 1984

Twenty Thousand Leagues Under the Sea — Jules Verne

This Old Man: Pam Adams — Grosset & Dunlap, 1974

Teammates — Peter Golenbock, HBJ, 1990

Tacky the Penguin — Hester Lester, Houghton Mifflin, 1988

Ten Little Bears — Scott Foresman & Company, Scott Foresman, 1976

The Trumpet of the Swan — B.B. White: Harper And Row, 1989

Ten Black Dots — D Crews: Greenwillow, 1986

Time to Go — B&D Fiday: HBJ, 1990

Ten Potatoes in a Pot and Other Counting Rhymes — M.J. Katz, Harper & Row, 1990

Tyrannosaurus Was a Beast — J. Prelutsky: Greenwillow, 1988

Tuesday — D. Weisner: Clarion, 1990

The True Story of the Three Little Pigs —J. Scieszka, Viking, 1989

Ten Little Rabbits — V. Grossman, Trumpet, 1991

A Treeful of Pigs — A. Lobel, Greenwillow, 1979

Teeny-Tiny Woman — Paul Galdone, Clarion,, 1984

There's a Boy in the Girl's Bathroom — L. Sachar: Knoph, 1987

Thank You, Santa — M. Wild, Scholastic, 1992

The Turkey's Side of It — J.L. Smith, Harper, 1990

Through Our Eye — L.B. Hopkins: Little, Brown, 1992

This Old House — K. Ackerman

Twas the Night Before Thanksgiving — D. Pilkey, Orchard, 1990

Exploring the Titanic — R. Ballard, Scholastic, 1988

The Three Bears and, 15 Other Stories — Anne Pockwell, Harper Throphy, 1975

The Three Billy Goats Gruff — Paul Galdone, Clarion, 1973

The Three Little Pigs — Margot Semach: Sunburst, 1988

Thunder Cake — Patricia Polacco, Philomel, 1990

Today Was a Terrible Day — Patricia Reilly Giff, Puffin, 1984

Twenty-Six Letters and Ninety-Nine Cents — Tana Hoban, Mulberry, 1978

Turkeys, Pilgrims, and Indian Corn — The Story Of Thanksgiving Symbols — Edna Barth: Clarion, 1975

The Talking Eggs — A Folk Tale from American South — Robert D. San Souci: Pied Piper, 1987

The Three Robbers — Tomi Ungerer, Aladdin, 1962

Tortillitas Para Mamma: And Other Spanish Nursery Rhymes — Margot Griego: Holt, 1981

The Twelve Days of Christmas — Jan Brett: Dodd, Mead/ Putman, 1986

The Twenty-One Balloons — William Pene du Bois: Viking, 1948

One, Two, Three: Ahchoo — Marjorie Allen: Coward, McCann, and Geoghegan, 1980

Treasure Island — Robert Louis Stevenson, Scribners, 1939

The Little Red Hen — Paul Galdone: Scholastic, 1973

Titch — Pat Hutchins: Collier Books, 1971

Ten Bears in My Bed — Stan Mack, Pantheon, 1974

Timothy Goes to School — Rosemary Wells: The Dial Press, 1981

The Great Big Enormous Turnip — Alexi Tolstoy: Franklin Watts, Inc., 1968

The Giving Tree — Shel Silverstein: Harper & Row, 1964

Timothy Turtle — Al Graham, Welch, 1947

T-Bone, The Baby Sitter — Clare Newberry, Harper & Row, 1951

The Thanksgiving Story — Alice Dagliesh, Scribner, 1955

A Time of Wonder — Robert McCloskey, Viking, 1958

Tom Tit Tot — Evaline Ness, Scribner, 1966

Treasure — Uri Shulevitz, Farrar, 1980

Truck — Donald Crews, Greenwillow, 1981

The Trouble with Tyrannosaurus Rex — Lorinda Bryan Cauley: HBJ, 1985

A Toad for Tuesday — Russel Erickson: Lothrop, Lee & Shepard, 1974

Tool Book — Gail Gibbons: Holiday House, 1982

Three-to-Get-Ready — Betty Boegehold: Harper And Row, 1965

U.u

U-u —Recipes

ULTIMATELY UNEQUALLED SQUARES

Materials:

2 cups of dried apricots, raisins, dates, currants

9 in. square pan   margarine
2/3 cup honey   1 tablespoon lemon juice
1/2 cup oil   1 cup whole wheat flour
3/4 cup oat bran   1-1/2 cup oatmeal
spoon   3/4 cup sunflower seeds
2 tablespoons sesame seeds

Directions:

1. Clean hands, area, and equipment.
2. Mix honey, oil, and lemon juice in a small bowl.
3. Combine oats, oat bran, and flour in big bowl.
4. Mix big bowl with small bowl.
5. Stir until moistened.
6. Add sunflower seeds and dried fruit.
7. Press into greased 9" square pan.
8. Bake 350 degrees for 20 to 25 minutes.
9. Cut and eat this unequalled treat.

UNBELIEVABLE UNTOSSED SALAD (NO COOKING)

Materials:

luncheon meat   8 strips of cooked bacon, cut up
plastic wrap   chunks of tuna (drained)
1 tomato, quartered   left over pieces of meat
4 hardboiled eggs   3/4 cup chopped celery
2 teaspoons sugar   grated Romano or Parmesan cheese
1/4 cup chopped green, red, yellow peppers (optional)
1 head of lettuce shredded (or torn into bite size pieces)
1 package of frozen peas, thawed
1/4 cup chopped purple onion
rectangular baking dish

Directions:

1. Clean hands, area, and equipment.
2. Add first 6 layers in the dish (lettuce, celery, onions, peppers, and top with frozen peas).
3. Mix sugar and mayonnaise.
4. Cover salad evenly with mayonnaise mixture.
5. Layer Romano/Parmesan cheese over mayonnaise.
6. Cover with plastic wrap and refrigerate for at least 8 hours.
7. Do not mix.
8. When serving, have eggs, tomatoes, and meat available to add to salad.

UPGRADED, UPPER CASE "U"- LETTERS #1

Materials:

1 cookie sheet or sheet from toaster oven

aluminum foil

frosting decorations

1 large egg

alphabet cookie cutters

1/4 teaspoon almond extract

2 cups all-purpose unbleached flour

1/4 teaspoon vanilla extract

ground cloves

ground ginger, to taste

1/2 cup softened butter, not margarine

3/4 cup sugar

oven or toaster oven

1 tablespoon milk

extra flour

1/4 teaspoon salt

ground cinnamon

spices

Directions:

1. Clean hands, area, and equipment.
2. Cream sugar, butter, and spices.
3. Add egg and extracts, as well as milk.
4. Mix salt and flour together.
5. Add flour mixture to butter mixture.
6. Make dough into balls.
7. Chill.
8. Give each student a square of foil and a little pinch of flour and dough.
9. Allow students to knead ball of dough.
10. Flatten dough and cut out letters, but make sure each child cuts an upper case U.
11. Bake at 350 degrees, 8 to 10.
12. Allow to cool.
13. Use frosting and decorate.
14. Each student must have a U to be upgraded.

UPGRADED, UPPER CASE "U"-LETTERS #2

Materials:

1 cup sugar

1 egg1 teaspoon baking powder

1 cup butter, softened

extra flour

oven or toaster oven

2-1/2 cups all-purpose unbleached flour

1 tablespoon vanilla extract

2 tablespoons orange juice

1 teaspoon orange zest

1 square of aluminum foil

Directions:

1. Clean hands, area, and equipment.
2. Cream butter and sugar together.
3. Add egg, juice, and extract.
4. Add flour and baking powder.
5. Beat until well mixed.
6. Cover, refrigerate.
7. Give each student a square of foil and a pinch of extra flour.
8. Knead and roll until 1/4 inch thick; then cut upper case U's or roll and form an upper case "U" and a lower case "u."
9. Put each square on a cookie sheet and place them an inch apart from each other as these will rise.
10. Bake at 350 degrees for 8-10 minutes or until edges are lightly browned.

UTTERLY UPSIDE-DOWN SUNDAES

Materials:

electric mixer

raisins

peanuts

ice cream

cherries

1/2 cup peanut butter

mixing bowl

2 cups milk

trail mix

coconut

dessert dishes

4 oz package chocolate instant pudding mix

Directions:

1. Clean hands, area, and equipment.
2. In a small bowl, combine milk and peanut butter.
3. Beat with electric mixer on low until blended.
4. Add chocolate instant pudding mix.
5. Beat according to package, scraping sides frequently.
6. Pour 1/4 cup of pudding mixture into 10 dessert dishes.
7. Top each with one scoop of ice cream.
8. Sprinkle with peanuts, raisins, trail mix, coconut and a cherry.
9. Unique.

UKHA

This can be a one-course dinner. Russian peasants used many vegetables, grains, occasionally a chuck of meat or fish, and a lot of ingenuity to produce superb soups. Ukha is a clear fish soup and should be translucent containing a piece of fish, a sprinkling of parsley, and dill.

Materials:

1 onion
1 carrot
1 parsnip
1 parsley rook
2-3 bay leaves
1 leek (white only)
soup bowls & spoons

1 pound of fresh or frozen smelts
1 teaspoon of garlic powder
1 bunch of parsley and/or dill
10 pepper corns
1 teaspoon salt
1 soup pot (4 qt)

Directions:

1. Clean hands, area, and equipment.
2. Combine vegetables, salt, and water into pot.
3. Bring to a boil — then simmer for 30 minutes.
4. Add fish, pepper corns, bay leaves, garlic powder, and simmer for 20 minutes.
5. Strain the stock and add parsley or dill.

U-u — Games/Activities

Uni Means One

Have students make a paper upper and lower case "U" or if too expensive, make one or "uni" U-u for the class. Glue univalve shells on them. They may be collected at the ocean or purchased.

U-u Upper/Lower Case "U" Game

Teacher/parent could make flash cards of long and short vowels. This is an oral auditory discrimination game. Students face the teacher. They must hear the word and determine if the vowel is long or short. Teacher could make two cards with a 1 or 2 on it and have students either point to the card, or put up 1 or 2 fingers (one is for short and two is for long). This also helps with spelling.

Ultimate Unequalled Letter U-u

Students could write a poem about this letter, using as many words beginning or containing a U-u. Poems do not have to rhyme. The poems could be written around the shape/words forming the shape of a U-u.

Untold, Unused, Understanding of movement with U-u's

There are many verbs/action words, which begin with the letter U-u. Students could dramatize or manipulate objects to show the meaning of up, under, uncover, undo, use, upper, uprise, uplift, unveil, untwist, until, unthread, unsnap, underfoot, underground, undo, unfold, until, and undress. Words could be written on flash cards. There could be several groups who demonstrate word. Other teams guess and team with most points...wins.

Umpire/Guardian Angel Books

Many times, mothers, fathers, and teachers feel that they must act like umpires. Each student could draw a picture of what makes them see purple or makes the student feel unhappy, like an unexpected event, makes them feel uncertain or an unforgettable moment when their parent(s) or teacher was needed to help settle/learn what to do. The students can describe the situation and tell what the umpire/guardian angel did to solve the problem. These pages could be published into a class book and checked out to share with each family.

Fortunately/Unfortunately Books

Each child is given a 4 x 5 inch paper or 8-1/2 x 11 inch with the headings: fair/unfair, urban/country, do/undo, bend/unbend, easy/uneasy, pack/ unpack, usual/unusual, common/unique, dress/undress, ugly/pretty, use/don't use, believable/unbelievable, equal/unequal, upper/lower, cover/ uncover, up/down/above/under. The student then illustrates these concepts to learn U-u vocabulary and connect their meaning with a visual image.

Use All of Your Senses Game

An item is placed in the paper bag. The student may/must use most of their senses. He/she may use their sense of touch, smell, hearing, and taste if it is safe. The student may only use fifteen guesses or the item is unveiled. The person who is "it" selects the student guesser and can utter words like: close, cold, hot. It also writes the tallies on the board. When 15 tallies are up, the guesser loses. If the guesser guesses right, he/she becomes "it."

A UNIT OF MEASURE

The teacher explains what a unit is: amount of quantity or measurement that has been adopted as standard. Long ago, a foot, hand, pinch, tad, bit, was used. Since these change from person to person, there needed to be a standard set. Now we have measuring cups (1/4 c, 1/2 c, 1-cup), 1 teaspoon, 1 tablespoon, 1/2 teaspoon, a quart, a gallon, a pint, and a pound. Don't forget an inch, a foot, and a yard. Students then can use rice, beans, sand, and water to measure capacity and how it does not change. They could also measure items in the room.

UNANIMOUS LOVED GLAB

4 oz. white glue, 1 cup of water, food coloring, 1 teaspoon Borax. Add glue to 1/2 C of water in a bowl. Add Borax, 1/2 cup of water. Add food coloring to the desired color. Stir until it forms one large glob. There will be extra water — pour it off. The glob gets thicker as you work/play with it.

U-u — Word Lists

unit	united	Utah
uniform	universe	usual
University	unify	unique
utilize	use	

Short Vowel:

udder	us	up
under	until	ugly
uncle	unhappy	upon
usher	unusual	uproar
upset	unless	umpire
umpteen	undercoat	underarm
unfed	upper	uproot
underhand	unfair	unbelief
underwear	understand	unarm
unfriendly	unhappy	unique
universal	unexpected	unforgettable
unfortunate	undone	uneasy
unemployed	uneven	underhanded
underneath	underprivileged	uncial
uncertain	undecided	uncommitted
unconditional	unconscious	unkempt
untrue	untouchable	unbeaten
unused	unusual	untold
untimely	unthankful	unbelievable
unsuspected	unsuitable	unsocial
unstable	unsophisticated	unknown
unkempt	unkindly	unknowable
uncouth	ulterior	ultimate
ultra marine	ultra microscopic	ultrasonic
ultraviolet	umbrageous	unanimous
unaware	unavoidable	

Short Vowel Above or Next to Medial Position:

but	run	much
just	cut	funny
number	must	study
hundred	sudden	sun
such	hunt	summer
jump	gun	lump
bump	dust	rust
jumbo	crush	hush
sung	fund	bug
hug	dug	rug
hut	stub	suds
trust	runt	

Long Vowel Next to Medial Position:

future	human	valuable
humor	January	pupil
community	humid	museum
fuel	bugle	cubic
menu	puny	musician
unusual		

Ur Sound:

Urn	urge	urgent
turn	burn	curl

Nouns:

unison	unit	urchin
utensils	uniform	union
U-boat	U-bolt	Uvula
U-turn	usher	urgency
upswing	up-state	upmanship
upbringing	upgrade	upgrowth
upheaval	upholstery	upbeat
universe	ulcer	ulna
ulster	ultimatum	ultraism

ultramicroscope	umpire	uncle
undertaker	underwear	unicycle

Descriptive Words:

ugh	ugly	utopia
usual	upwind	upward
uptown	up-to-date	uptight
upstairs	upside down	uproarious
upright	uppercase	upper
upgrade	upcoming	uphill
up-and-down	up-and-coming	up
unwritten	unworthy	unwilling
unwholesome		

Verbs:

utter	utilize	usurp
use	urge	upset
uproot	uprise	uplift
upheave	unyoke	unwish
unwind	unvoice	unveil
untwist	untread	untie
unthread	unswathe	unteach
unstrung	unsnap	unsettle
unlearn	ululate	undercut
underdevelop	underbid	underemployed
underfoot	underground	understand
undo	unfold	uniform
unify	untie	

Areas:

Ucayali	Uele	Ufa
Uganda	Utah	U.S.S.R.
Uttar Pradesh	Utica	U.S.A.
Urundi	Uruguay	Urdu
Ural Mountains	Upper Volta	Unter Walden
United Arab Rep.	United Kingdom	Umbria

Inventions/Musical Instruments/Animals:

Ukelele	Umbrella Bird	Upbow
Universal joint	Umiak	Umpire
unicycle	urn	undershirt
umbrella	utensils	unit
ulu		

Foods:

Udo	uglifruit	utensils
uppercrust	ukha	

U-u — Reading Resources

Underwear — Mary Elise Monsell: Whitman, 1988

Umbrella — Taro Yashima: Viking Press, 1959

Uneasy Money — Robin F. Brancato

Under the Moon — Joanne Ryder

Under the Sea — Brian Williams

Tales of Uncle Remus — Joanna Reiss/Julius Lester: Dial, 1987

Understanding Yourself — Leicht

Up a Road Slowly — Irene Hunt: Follett, 1969

The Yellow Umbrella — Henrik Drescher: Bradbury, 1987

Upon the Head of a Goat: A Childhood in Hungary (1939-1944) — Aranka Siegal: NAL, 1981

Up the Road Slowly — Irene Hunt: Follett, 1968

Over, Under, Through, and Other Spatial Concepts — Tana Hoban: MacMillian,, 1973

The Umbrella Day — Nancy Evans Cooney: Philomel, 1990

The Ugly Princess — Nancy Luen: Little, 1981

Up and Up — Shirley Hughes: Prentice, Hall, 1979

The Ugly Duckling — Hans Christian Anderson: Knopf, 1986

Uncle Elephant — Arnold Lobel: Harper Collins, 1981

Under the Sunday Tree — Eliose Greenfield: Harper And Row/Harper Collins, 1988

Up Goes the Skyscraper — Gail Gibbons: Four Winds, 1986

Up North in the Winter — Deborah Hartley: Dutton, 1986

Underground — David McCaulay: Houghton Miffin, 1976

Up from Jericho Tree — E.L. Konigsburg: Atheneum, 1986

The Upstairs Room — Johanna Reiss: Harper Collins, 1982

V · v

V-v Recipes

VALID VEGETABLE SOUP

(Stone Soup without the stone or one could be added)

Materials:

1 knife	2 cups of tomato juice
seasoned salt	4 cups beef or chicken stock
1 cutting board	Parmesan cheese, grated
2 carrots	1/2 cup bell pepper (opt.)
1/2 lb. green beans	1 celery stalk
garlic	1 potato
1 tomato	bowls
spoons	salt
pepper	1 crockpot, or pot, or electrical unit, or stove
1 zucchini	

Directions:

1. Clean hands, area, and equipment.
2. Place stock into pot (can use canned soup).
3. Peel and chop onions, carrots, green beans, and potatoes.
4. Add to stock and cook for 1-1/2 hours.
5. Add zucchini and tomato.
6. Season to taste.
7. Add water if necessary.
8. Simmer 30 minutes more.
9. Serve in bowls with bread/crackers.

VOLCANIC VEGETABLE SALAD

(The taste and tossing makes this explode) — No Cooking

Materials:

2 heads of clean lettuce torn into bite size pieces	
1/4 red onion, cleaned, peeled, sliced, and chopped	
Parmesan cheese	1/4 cup jicama, peeled and chopped
large bowl	1/2 cup sliced black olives
spoons (lg. or reg.)	2 carrots cut into bite size pieces
fork 2 tomatoes, cleaned and sliced	cutting board
1/2 cucumber, peeled and sliced	knife
1 stalk of celery, clean and sliced	salad dressing
1 pkg. shelled sunflower seeds/pignolias	

Directions:

1. Clean hands, area, and equipment.
2. Put clean torn lettuce into bowl.
3. Carefully place cut up vegetables into bowl (scattering).
4. Toss up vegetables like a volcano exploding.
5. Pour on the dressing (slowly) and allow volcano to explode again (toss).
6. Serve with bread, crackers.

Very Velvety Valentines

Materials:

refrigerator

oven heart-shaped cookie cutters

2 envelopes of unflavored gelatin

1 cup frozen strawberries, mashed

potato masher

1-1/2 tablespoons margarine/cooking spray

6 oz. package of cherry, strawberry, or red colored flavored gelatin

shallow 8" or 9" glass square pan

1 bowl

1 spoon

stove/heating unit

refrigerator

Directions:

1. Clean hands, area, and equipment.
2. Fill bowl with cool water.
3. Pour unflavored gelatin into the water.
4. Stir until dissolved (almost).
5. Heat one cup of water to a boil.
6. Add flavored gelatin.
7. Add dissolved cold water gelatin to hot flavored gelatin.
8. Mash strawberries with potato masher.
9. Add 1/2 cup cold water to now warmed gelatin mixture.
10. Add strawberries.
11. Spray or grease glass square pan.
12. Pour in mixture.
13. Cool (refrigerate) for four hours.
14. Cut with heart-shaped cookie cutters.
15. Very velvety.

"Vis - a - Vis" Orange Potatoes

Materials:

knifebaking dish

salt potato masher

pepper

cinnamon

nutmeg

4 sweet potatoes — boiled and mashed, or buy canned

bowl

1 sprig mint

1-1/2 tablespoons butter

1/2 orange per serving

1 cup margarine

Directions:

1. Clean hands, area, and equipment.
2. Boil and mash sweet potatoes in a bowl.
3. Cut oranges into half. Scoop out oranges cut into small pieces and add to sweet potato mixture.
4. Add butter, salt, pepper, cinnamon, nutmeg, marshmallows, and cut up oranges.
5. Brush the insides of orange halves with butter.
6. Fill with potato mixture.
7. Bake for 20 minutes in 350 degrees oven.
8. Add sprig of mint.
9. This is great with chicken or anything. A great way to get Vitamin C from vegetables.

VILE VEGETABLE LOAF
Easy meal to fix while others and you are busy.

Materials:

1 onion, chopped

1 carrot, chopped

1 teaspoon salt

1 large egg

garlic powder

1/4 cup milk

Pam Spray

oven loaf or heat proof pan

1 teaspoon of crushed/ground chili powder

1 Russet potato, peeled and cubed

1 1/2 lbs. ground chicken, turkey, beef

1 can or marinara/tomato sauce

1 celery rib chopped

1 cup cracker crumbs

1 tablespoon season salt

1/4 teaspoon black pepper

Directions:

1. Clean hands, area, and equipment.
2. Lightly grease pan with Pam, or butter/margarine.
3. Combine meat, crumbs, milk, egg, and seasonings. Blend in vegetables.
4. Pour 1 cup of marinara sauce on the bottom of the pan. Add the loaf of meat plus vegetables.
5. Cover with the remaining sauce.
6. Heat oven to 350 degrees and cook until done (160 degrees on meat thermometer or about 1 1/4 hours).

VIVACIOUS CARRIBEAN VEGETABLE- PLANTANOS

Green Plantanos are eaten like potatoes in Puerto Rico. This recipe calls for the yellow/ripe plantains. The yellow/ripe plantains are easy to peel. Cut away any spots that don't peel easily with a sharp knife. Most grocery stores carry this vegetable/fruit. This is a multicultural experience.

Materials:

4 yellow-ripe plantains - peeled and cut lengthwise

1 slotted spatula

1 tablespoon salt

salt 4 cups lukewarm water

1/4 cup vegetable oil

powdered chili pepper

1 large electric fry pan

1 roll of paper towels

dried coconut

raisins

Directions:

1. Clean hands, area, and equipment.
2. Allow plantains to soften in salted water.
3. Heat oil in electric fry pan. Cook on medium (medium high heat), turning once, until golden brown on both sides. This takes about 4-5 minutes.
4. Transfer with slotted spatula to paper towel.

V-v Games/Activities

VICTORY SYMBOLS/SIGNS

Children/students could collect craft sticks/Popsicle™ sticks and glue them together to form V's. A variety of buttons, rocks, or macaroni could be added. They could then be painted and shown off, so others could view the various V's. Also, play dough recipe is given in "D" chapter. Students could make, form, and decorate V's to display or have others view them.

VIVID VALENTINE JEWELRY

Each student should:
1. Select 30 pieces of various colors of construction paper cut into the shape of a heart or valentine.
2. Glue each shape on top of each other and make sure the glue secures the papers to each other.
3. Dry thoroughly.
4. Sand the edges so that the different colors show.
5. Coat with glue, which is dry/clear.
6. Make a hole and thread with yarn or ribbon through the hole to make a necklace.
7. Present to your valentine.

A VIVID, VISIONARY VISIT

Each cooperative group has a pad and paper. They are to go and view anything at school that they want (nurse's office, office, cafeteria, library, resource room). They take notes on what they have visited. They visit the same place for three to four days. Each visit is somewhat pre-arranged. The students then come back and write one vivid, visionary paragraph or story about what they viewed. Each story is then published and even presented to the school library. Be sure to allow for their own point of view and students may write book to the stories explaining his/her own point of view, which may be different. This needs to be published also.

VITAL VIBRANT VESTS

Each cooperative group or group of students chooses a core literary work or book with a "V" in the title. They should read the book, discuss it, and cooperatively write a Reader's Theater or play about that book. Each student selects a character and/or narrator and draws/colors/paints a vest to signify, validate that character. The vest is made of a large paper bag. The front is slit and the reinforced rectangle becomes a circle to fit the character's neck. It's great because when he/she puts on the vest, he/she becomes that character.

VERY VALUABLE BOARD GAME

Flash cards from the word list can be matched and illustrated by each child or group. Pictures can come from discarded books, catalogs, magazines, and newspapers. These could also be laminated and used to play video, which is a memory game. Each picture is then

V-V's Only

There are many alphabet cookies and macaroni (dry letters in a bag). The timer is set and many letters are spilled into a tray. Each child has one to two minutes to find V's and the student with the most V's wins.

Villanelle vs. Virelay

A villanelle is a short poem consisting of five 3-line stanzas and a final 4-line stanza having only two rhymes.

A virelay is a short poem consisting of short lines with two rhymes and having two opening lines repeated as intervals or any verse with stanzas made up of alternating long lines and short lines. The rhyme of the shorter lines echo the lines of the longer lines.

Try both types of French poems and compare/contrast which works out best.

Volumes of Rhymes Games

Class could be divided into four teams. Teacher or "it" gives a "V" word from the list and the team with a correct word that rhymes with the "V" word first gets the point. These words can be made from the word list or flash cards already made. The card is viewed and then they must be decoded. Each team voluntarily discloses a rhyming word.

Vibrant Valuable Vase

Each student brings in bottles or jars and colored tissue paper. The tissue paper can be cut up into small squares. The squares can be attached to the bottles and jars with white glue. These become vases for dry or fresh flowers. (hint: an additional coat of white glue is to be added and when dried, it is a valuable vase.) The vases are as vibrant as the color of tissue paper you use.

Visible Veins

Many times, students do not understand how the heart and veins function. Students can see their veins, which are vessels that carry blood from the body to the heart vs. arteries that carry blood from the heart to the body. A white carnation could be a visual way to show this. Cut the stem diagonally. Put into water with food coloring. As the water is carried into the flowers, the petals turn green/red/purple. Color really is visual.

Vegesaurus

Cut up pieces of carrots, celery, cucumbers, olives, cherry tomatoes, and potatoes. Each group gets a zucchini, plastic knife, and toothpicks and as many pieces as they need to develop/construct/make a vegesaurus (hint: since saurus aren't alive, they can be any shape). The group must work together. The creatures are then viewed by each of the groups and voted upon. The group with the most paints wins. (Sometimes other classes can vote, also.)

V-v Word Lists

Nouns:

valentine	verb	vase
valley	varsity	varnish
variety	verdict	verbose
vent	venom	velvet
velour	vest	vessel
vertigo	vein	vacancy
vacation	vaccine	vacuum
vacuum cleaner	veil	vacuum pump
vacuum tube	vagary	vagrancy
vagrant	vagus	vair
valance	valediction	valence
valedictorian	valet	valetudinarian
valgus	valor	validity
valise	vallation	valley
valorization	value	valve
vampire	van	vandalism
vane	vulgarity	vulcanite
voyage	vowel	vow
voucher	voter	vortex
vomit	veto	veterinarian
vehicle	Victoria	victim
vicinity	volunteer	volume
volt	volleyball	volley
volcano	volcanic rock	voice
vocal cords	vocal	vocabulary
vixen	vitamin	vitality
vista	visor	visitor
visa	virus	virtuoso
virtue	vine	violet
violence	vinyl	vinegar
villanelle	villain	village
villa	vigor	view
vigil	video	victory
vial	version	verse

vermin	vault	vaudeville
variation	vapor	

Verbs:

vacate	vacillate	validate
valuate	vamoose	vamp
vouch	vote	vomit
vociferate	vivify	visit
violate	view	vie
vibrate	verify	vent
veneer	vend	veer
varnish	vanish	vaporize
visit	view	

Descriptive:

vacant	vacuous	vagabond
vagrant	vague	vain
valedictory	valerian	valiant
valid	valorous	valuable
valued	value free	valvate
valvular	vulnerable	vulnerary
vulgar	vulcanian	voluptuous
volcanic	voluntary	volumed
voluble	volatile	void
voiceless	vogue	vociferous
vocal	vivid	vivacious
vital	violent	visual
visionary	visible	vindictive
vis-a-vis	virtual	vile
villainous	vigorous	vigilant
video	Victorian	vicious
vicarious	vibrant	vertebrate
veteran	very	vertical
versatile	vernacular	verbal
venerable	velvety	vegetable
vascular	vary	various

Areas:

Valley Of Ten Thousand Smokes		Virgin Islands
Vaishnava	Valdai Hills	Valdemar I
Valdez	Valence	Valencia
Valenciennes	Valens	Valladolid
Vallejo	Valletta	Valley Forge
Valparaiso	Vancouver	Vandal
Vulgate	Volta	Vologda
Volgograd	Voleano Islands	Vitievu
Vitoria	Vitebsk Visayas	Virginia City
Vindhya Range	Vienna	Viet Cong
Vietnam	Vera Cruz	Ventura
Venice	Vatican City	

Animals:

vampire bat	vicu a	vulture
volvox	vole	viper
Virginia deer	vinegar worm	

Musical Instruments & Inventions

violin	violin cello	viola
vacuum	vina	vase
vat	van	vest
velvet material cleaner		vehicle

Foods or food related:

vinegar	vinaigrette sauce	veal
vegetables	vat	variety meat
vegetarian	voracious	variation
vacuum-packed	vegetable oil	value
vaporize	vegetable butter	vein
vegetable marrow	vanilla	
Vitamins A, B, C, D, E, H, K, and P		

V-v Reading Resources

A Very Special House — Ruth Krauss: Harper, 1953

Visit to William Blake's Inn & Poems — Nancy Willard: Voyager, 1982

The Village of Round and Square Houses — Ann Grifalconi: Little, 1987

The Very Hungry Caterpillar — Eric Carle: Philomel, 1983

Vicki — Renate Meyer: Atheneum, 1969

Voices of the Wild — Wayne McLoughlin, 1994

The Velveteen Rabbit — Margery Williams: Zephyr, 1926

The Very Busy Spider — Eric Carle: Philomel, 1985

A Visit to the Sesame Street Hospital — Deborah Hautzig: Random House, 1985

Very Last First Time — Jan Andrews: Atheneum, 1986

Volcano: The Eruption and HealIng of Mount St. Helens — Patricia Lauber: Bradbury, 1986

The Valentine Star — Patricia Reilly Giff: Dell Yearling

The Very Worst Monster — Pat Hutchins: Greenwillow, 1985

The Very Young Dancer — Jill Krementz: Dell Yearling, 1976

The Visitor — Helme Heine: Aladdin, 1982

The Visit — Diane Wolkstein, Alfred A. Knopf, 1977

Valentine Blues — Jeanne Betancourt: Bantam, 1991

Vampires Don't Wear Polka Dots, or Do They — Debbie Dadey and Marcia Thornton Jones: Scholastic, 1991

A Visit from Dr. Katz — Ursula K. LeGuin: Atheneum, 1989

Village by the Sea — Paula Fox: Orchard Books, 1988

Visions — Donald R. Gallo: Dell, 1987

Venus — G.L. Vogt: Millbrook, 1994

Arthur's Valentine — Marc Brown: Joystreet/Little Brown, 1976

I Like Vegetables — Sharon Lerner: Lerner Publication Co.

Growing Vegetable Soup — Lois Ehlert

W . w

W-w —Recipes

Wonderful, Wacky "W" Cake

Materials:

small bowl
3 tablespoons flour
1/3 cup butter
1 egg1/2 teaspoon vanilla
1/3 cup mixed fruit, cut up

14 graham cracker squares
1 teaspoon baking powder
1/3 cup sugar

Directions:

1. Clean hands, area, and equipment.
2. Crush 14 graham cracker squares.
3. Pour into small bowl.
4. Combine with flour and baking powder to make graham cracker mix.
5. In a big bowl, beat butter 30 seconds with an electric mixer on medium.
6. Add sugar and beat with butter until fluffy.
7. Add 1 egg and 1/2 teaspoon of vanilla.
8. Beat well.
9. Add graham crackers, mix, then add to big bowl.
10. Then add mixed fruit.
11. Spoon into greased and floured loaf pan.
12. Bake in toaster oven at 350 degrees for 30 minutes or until center is done.
13. Cool before heating. (Boy is this wacky!)

Well Thought-of Waldorf Salad

Can be served with anything or well-thought-of by itself. Served first at famous Waldorf Astoria Restaurant (N.Y.C.) This is my version.

Materials:

1 cup grapes
cutting board
knife
bowl
3/4 cup mayonnaise—with ground cinnamon, nutmeg, and a whisk of chutney
(hint—this could also contain chunks of chicken or feta cheese)
1 large spoon

1 cup diced red apples—do not peel
1 cup of diced celery
1/2 cup chopped walnuts
1 cup drained pineapple tidbits

Directions:

1. Clean hands, area, and equipment.
2. Dice celery and apples.
3. Combine with chopped walnuts.
4. Combine mayonnaise with cinnamon, nutmeg, and chutney.
5. Combine and toss.
6. Can be served with clean dry lettuce.
7. Well?

WILD THINGS' WINNER

(After visiting *Where the Wild Things Are* book, Max could have eaten this.)

Materials:

toaster oven
bowls
1 cup milk
spoons
bowls
grater
salt 1/2 cup chopped carrots
10-3/4 can of cream of chicken soup
onion powder to taste
margarine to grease pan

4 cups diced cooked chicken
measuring cups and spoons
4 oz. of sliced water chestnuts (canned)
1 cup shredded/grated cheddar cheese
3 cups cracker crumbs
1/2 cup chopped celery
pepper
garlic powder
1/2 chopped onion

Directions:

1. Clean hands, area, and equipment.
2. Use chopping board and knives to prepare everything. Grate cheese.
3. Combine all ingredients into bowl except for 1/2 of cracker crumbs.
4. Pour into greased pan that fits into toaster oven, or any oven.
5. Spread evenly.
6. Top with other half of cracker crumbs.
7. Bake 350 degrees for 45 minutes or golden brown.
8. Would you leave the Wild Things for this dinner?
   (Hint—to make the casserole go further, serve over rice)

WONDERFUL WATERMELON SALAD

(This makes a great patriotic salad.)

Materials:

1 small cantaloupe, cubed
1 large bowl
knife
cutting board
plates
measuring cups
1 melon baller
1/8 tsp pepper
1 tablespoon lemon juice

3 cups watermelon, cubed
3 cups honeydew melon, cubed
1 package/tray of fresh strawberries
1 package/tray of fresh blueberries
1 sprig of mint per serving
mint fruit dressing (if desired)
1/4 cup orange juice

Directions:

1. Clean hands, area, and equipment.
2. Cube or use melon baller and ball/cut all three types of melon and put in bowl.
3. Wash and check strawberries and blueberries; then add to big bowl.
4. Make mint fruit dressing.
5. Add and lightly toss.
6. Serve and glamorize with a sprig of mint.
7. Wonderful.

WARM-HEARTED WALNUT BREAD WITH WHIPPED CREAM

Materials:

1/8 teaspoons cinnamon, nutmeg, and cardamom

1 cup butter	4 cups all-purpose flour, unbleached
2 cups sugar	1-1/2 cups chopped walnuts
4 eggs	2 teaspoons vanilla
1/2 teaspoon salt	2 cups sour cream
9"x5" loaf pan	1 teaspoon powdered sugar
whipping cream	1 large carton of heavy cream
2 teaspoons soda	bowls spoons

1 plastic jar, plus 2 clean marbles or whisk

Directions:

1. Clean hands, area, and equipment.
2. Cream butter and sugar.
3. Slowly add and beat with eggs in big bowl.
4. Mix flour, baking soda, salt, and spices in small bowl.
5. Mix dry (small bowl) into large bowl.
6. Add nuts, vanilla, and sour cream.
7. Pour butter into 2 greased and floured 9"x5" loaf pans.
8. Bake at 350 degrees for about 50-60 minutes—use cake tester to be sure.
9. Cool.
10. Put heavy cream into bowl with whisk or jar with marbles and shake. When cream becomes slightly thick, add powdered sugar and continue a whisper more until it becomes thick or stiff.
11. Spread whipped cream over sliced walnut bread, individually.
12. It does warm hearts.

WACKED WIENERS

Kids like to say this name. It's a favorite.

Materials:

plates	1 package potato chips
aluminum foil	4 teaspoons of melted butter
baking brush	4 teaspoons mustard
toaster oven	ketchup (or taco sauce)
knife	8 wieners (hot dogs)

1 package of refrigerated crescent rolls
(1 slice of cheese can also be added.)

Directions:

1. Clean hands, area, and equipment.
2. Open package of rolls and separate carefully. You may need a knife.
3. Brush/spread melted butter.
4. Spread/brush with mustard and ketchup or taco sauce.
5. Place on ungreased baking sheet covered with aluminum foil.
6. Crush potato chips and sprinkle over each wacked wiener.
7. Roll each wiener into a roll.
8. Bake at 375 degrees for 10-13 minutes or until rolls are golden brown.

W-w — Games/Activities

WHO AM I?

The teacher writes several names on the board or suggests names from the books the class has read. "Who" comes forward and gives two to three clues. Students guess. Whoever guesses correctly becomes "Who" and the game continues. Teacher may want to keep score of guesses. Usually 10 to 20 guesses are Wright.

"WILD THINGS" BOOK

After reading *Where the Wild Things Are*, by Maurice Sendak, have each student take "20 Winks" or close their eyes for two to three minutes. They need to visualize their own version of a "Wild Thing" book. Have each child draw with pencil, then color in wild colors. They can write or dictate the name of their wild thing, what it does, and what it likes to eat. Publish as a class book.

WHACKED, WEIRD, AND WIGGLY

Give each child a half of an orange or apple. Provide toothpicks, marshmallows, gumdrops, candy corns, popcorn, licorice, M&Ms™, and other assorted items. Allow them to weld/whip/wring/wrist/wrap these items into a whacked, weird, and wiggly thing. Student then draws it and writes its name and what it can do (waddle, wag) using as many "W" words as they can.

W-w ANIMAL BOOKS

In the word list, under animals, there are many, many of them. Have each cooperative group or divide class into 3s and allow them to choose 2 animals to research. Have each group name animals, location/habitat, food/choice of food, mammal/bird/insect/spider or other type of animal. Have them illustrate it. Publish as W-w animals.

WHATEVER "WORDO"

Teacher lets students find pictures/illustrations of items that begin with or has the "W" sound in it. Some of these words are: washing machine, wastepaper, waterfall, wax, wedge, wreath, waiter/waitress, whale, wood, etc. These pictures could be glued to tag board and then matching words could be written on tag board and both laminated. The game is played with all the cards are turned face down. Each player takes a turn and turns over two cards/pieces. The players keep turning over cards until the word matches the picture. Then it becomes a set. The player with the most sets wins.

WELL-KNOWN WOMEN IN HISTORY

There are many women who have changed history and/or are well-known like Agatha Christie, Jackie Cochran, Judy Bloom, Louisa May Alcott, Oprah Winfrey, Barbara Walters, Barbara Streisand, Mary Harris Jones, Jane Addams, and others. Have students read/research and report about other Women in History.

I AM TO BE WISE & WONDERFUL

Each student needs to express himself/herself in many ways to build their self-esteem. Many times, another child, a teacher, or a tutor needs to work with a child or student to find how that child views/thinks of himself/herself. Each one has a skill/expertise in being a singer, friend, storyteller, reader, math computer, artist, speller, neatest eater, fastest eater, longest ball thrower, play ground cleaner, room cleaner, animal cage cleaner, etc. Each child can write/dictate and illustrate how they are wise and wonderful. This class book could be published and checked out.

WEDNESDAY, WASHDAY

Students love to wash bottles, plastic glasses, spoons, and even doll dresses and clothes. Have students learn the names of the week by saying—

Monday: Mowing the lawn and moving furniture.
Tuesday: Vacuuming (turning the rugs).
Wednesday: Washing dishes/clothes.
Thursday: Ironing, dusting (turning the pictures).
Friday: Cooking, turning food (frying).
Saturday: Sit in the tub and clean ourselves.
Sunday: Sitting in church.

Have sponges, mild soap, and things/items to clean and dry. This is a great ESL Project/game.

WEAVED WEBS

Many spiders spin webs. It is produced by spinnerets. The web consists of a silk-like thread that is strong enough to support the spider. It traps insects so the spider can eat them. It is intricate network of silk. To make a "man-made" web, lay 8" x 8" tissue paper over wax paper. Use glue to draw/weave your web. Let it dry thoroughly over night. When it has hardened, peel away the wax paper. Each spider makes a different web. Compare and contrast different webs of others and yours.

WHO, WHAT, WHEN, WHERE, & WHY

Students in cooperative groups could write a paragraph or short story using all the Ws. After reading, one person from the student group asks the questions and student who has the most correct answers reads their story next. They need to know each news article answers most of these questions, maybe not the why.

WEE STORIES

A small/little thing/person is called a "wee" in Ireland. Each student could make a puppet of a walrus, warthog, wasp, weasel, wolf, whale, wren, wallaroo, woodpecker, white rat, or any animal from the list. In cooperative groups or groups of 3-4 while using their puppets, write a play, Reader's Theater, or skit/story. Each child needs a copy to read from. The plays, stories, or skits could be given to parents also.

W-w — Word Lists

Nouns:

weapon	weather	weather man
web	wedding	wedge
Wednesday	weed	week
weight	wad	wadding
wagon	waif	waist
wain	waiter	waitress
walkie-talkie	wall	wallet
walnut	waltz	wampum
wand	wanigan	war
ward	ware	warehouse
wardrobe	warden	warlock
warlord	warmth	warm-up
warp	warrant	warranty
warrior	warship	wart
washday	washer	washing
washing machine	washroom	washrag
waste basket	wastepaper	watch
watchband	watchdog	water
waterbed	waterfall	watergun
watering place	watering pot	water softener
water spout	watertower	watt
wavelength	wax	we
wealth	woman	wing
wheel	well	wharf
wheat	whelk	whirlwind
whiskey	writer	wrench
wound	world	worker
word	wool	wood
wooden indian	womb	wizard
witness	witch	wisdom
wire	winter	wing
wine	window	windmill
windless	windfall	willow

Verbs:

wade	waddle	waft
wag	wage	wait
waive	wake	walk
wallop	wallow	wamble
wander	want	ward
warm	was	wash
waste	watch	water
wave	wear	weave
wed	weep	weigh
weld	went	wept
were	whang	wheeze
whiff	whimper	whine
whinny	whip	whirl
wry	whisk	whisper
whistle	writing	write
wrinkle	wrist	wring
wriggle	wrestle	wrap
wound	worth	worry
woo	withdraw	wish
wire	wipe	winkle
wind	wilt	will
whiz	whittle	

Descriptive Words:

wonderful	wonderstruck	wrong
wise	worn	working
work-a-day	wordy	woolly
woody	witty	wacky
wandering	waney	warm
wanting	wanton	wave
warm hearted	washable	watchful
watercooled	waxy	way ward
weak	weak-kneed	weak-minded
wealthy	wearable	wearing
weary	weathered	weekly
weeny	weepy	weightless
weighty	weird	welcome
well	well-behaved	well-being
well-done	well-founded	well-known
well-read	well-thought-of	well-wisher
wet	whacked	wireless
wild	willing	willowy
whole	wicked	wiggly

Food Related:

waffles	walnuts	wood sugar
water chestnuts	watercress	watermelon
weakfish	wieners	welsh rarebit
wheat	wheat bran	wheat germ
whey nuts	wheat pilaf	white sauce
white fish	winged bean	wreck fish
wafer	Waldorf salad	wassail
water biscuit	water chestnut	wild rice
wonton	wax bean	wax berry
wax paper	whipped cream	white bread

Areas:

Wagram	Wakayama	Wakefield
Wake Island	Walachia	Walbrzych
Walden Pond	Waldemar	Wall Sey
Wallis and Futuna	Walnut Creek	Walpole
Walthan	Warta	Warsaw
Warwick	Washington	Waterbury
Waterford	Waterloo	Waukegan
Wembley	Weser	West Bengal
West Covina	Westermarch	West Haven
Westminster	West Palm Beach	Westphalia
Wyoming	Wye	Wurttenberg
Worchester	Wonsan	Wisconsin

Animals:

wildcat	wild beast	wombat
wolverine	wolf	wolf spider
wood chuck	woodpecker	wolf fish
wolf-ram	worms	wading bird
wahoo	walrus	weasel
waler	walking stick	wallaby
wallaroo	walleyed pike	wapiti
warble fly	warbler	warthog
wasp	waterbuck	waterbeetle

water buffalo	waterbug	waterdog
water moccasin	water spaniel	wattles
wattlebird	weakfish	web spinner
weevil	weaver	Weimaraner
whale	Welsh corgi	Welsh Terrier
Whale Shark	wheatworm	wheelbug
Whippet	Whippoorwill	Whip Scorpion
Whip snake	Wyandottle	wren
white-tailed deer	white rat	whale

W-w — Reading Resources

Who's Counting? — Nancy Tafuri: Greenwillow, 1983

I Went Walking — Sue Williams Harcourt & Brace Javanovich, 1990

Where's Spot?— Eric Hill, Putnam, 1980

Where Can It Be — Ann Jonas: Greenwillow, 1986

Whose Mouse Are You? — Robert Kraus: Macmillian, 1970

Who Took the Farmer's Hat? — Joan Nodset: Harper & Row, 1936

Who Wants One? — Mary Serfozo: Macmillan, 1989

Who Sank the Boat? — Pam Allen Coward: McCann, 1982

Wiley and the Hairy Man — Molley Garrett Bang: MacMillian, 1976

When It Comes to Bugs — Aileen Fisher: Harper & Row, 1986

Where the Red Fern Grows — Wilson Rawls: Bantam, 1961

The Whingdingdilly — Bill Peet: Houghton Mifflin, 1982

Where the Wild Things Are — Maurice Sendak: Harper Trophy, 1963

Winnie the Pooh — A.A. Milne: Dell Yearling, 1926

The Wind in the Willows — Kenneth Grahame: Scribners, 1908

Where the Buffaloes Begin — Olaf Baker: Puffin, 1981

Will I Have a Friend — Miriam Cohen: Aladdin, 1967

Why Mosquitoes Buzz in People's Ears — Verna Aardema: Pied Piper, 1975

Where Does the Butterfly Go When It Rains — Garelick

Wilfred Gordon McDonald Partridge — Mem Fox

The White Stallion — Elizabeth Shub: Bantam, 1982

How to Eat Fried Worms — T. Rockwell: Del Yearling, 1973

Williams Doll — Charlotte Zolotow: Harper Thropy, 1972

Whales: A First Discovery Book — Gallimard Jeunesse: Scholastic, 1994

Whiff, Sniff, Nibble, and Chew: The Gingerbread Boy — Charlotte Pomerantz

The Witch Who Lives Down the Hill — Donna Guthrie

Wilfred the Rat — James Stevenson: Puffin, 1979

Where the Sidewalk Ends — Shel Silverstein: Harper, 1974

The Wild Baby — Barbro Lindgren Greenwillow, 1981

The Wind Blue — Pat Hutchins, Viking, 1974

The Wolf's Chicken Stew — Keiko Kasza: Putnam, 1987

The Wrong Side of Bed — Edward Ardizzone: Doubleday, 1970

The Walking Stones — Mollie Hunter: Harper, 1970

Weird Henry Berg — Sarah Sargent: Dell, 1981

The Wonderful Wizard of Oz — L. Frank Baum: Dover, 1960 or Ballantine, 1980

Well, I Never — Susan Pearson: Simon & Schuster, 1991

We're Going on a Bear Hunt — Michael Rosen, McElderly, 1990

The Wedding of Brown Bear and White Bear — Martine Beck: Little Brown, 1991

A Wrinkle in Time — Madeleine L. Engle: Dell Yearling, 1963

Wolf Story — William McCleery: Linnet Books/Shoestring Press, 1947

Waiting for Mama — Beatrice Schenk de Regniers: Clarion, 1984

Where Are You Going, Little Mouse? — Robert Kraus, Mulberry, 1986

When We Were Very Young — A.A. Milne: Dell Yearling, 1924

What Ever Happened to Dinosaurs? — Bernard Most: Voyager, 1978

WeaTher — L.B. Hopkins: Harper Collins, 1994

Water — Francois Michel: Lothrop, 1994

Wounded Knee: An Indian History of the American West — Henry Holt, 1994

Wake-Up, Wake-Up: B & R Wildsmith, Harcourt, 1994

X · x

X-x —Recipes

X-cellent X-X Shaped Cookies

Materials:

bowl
electric mixer
3/4 cup sugar
rolling pin
cookie sheets

1 cup sweet butter
8-oz. package cream cheese
4 teaspoons vanilla
3-1/2 cups flour
canned frosting and candies

Directions:

1. Clean hands, area, and equipment.
2. Stir butter in bowl until fluffy using an electric mixer.
3. Add cream cheese to butter and beat.
4. Blend in sugar and vanilla.
5. Add flour.
6. Stir until completely mixed, the dough will be stiff.
7. Roll the dough into, 1/4" thickness on a lightly floured surface.
8. Make strips and lay one strip over the other to create X-shapes.
9. Place cookies on lightly greased cookie sheets about, 1" apart.
10. Bake for, 10-15 minutes at 350 degrees.
11. Allow to cool.
12. Decorate with canned frosting and candies.

X-ceedingly Fun To Make Candy

Materials:

jelly beans
licorice
dried fruit
nuts
aluminum foil
bowl
spoons
colored candy for decorations

1/2 cup light corn syrup
1/2 cup powdered milk
1 teaspoon vanilla or almond extract
2 tablespoons unsalted butter
2 tablespoons water
2 cups flaked coconut
1 cup chopped walnuts

Directions:

1. Clean hands, area, and equipment.
2. Mix corn syrup, powdered milk, extract, butter, and water in large bowl.
3. Mix in coconut.
4. Roll into balls.
5. Shape into desired shapes or X's.
6. Decorate with candy or dried fruit.

X and O Shaped Salad

Materials:

knife	cutting board
saucepan	5-6 red and round potatoes
salted water	3 or 4 stalks of celery
3 eggs	1/2 cup mayonnaise
6 green onions	1 tablespoon vinegar
1/4 cup sugar	1-1/2 tablespoon prepared mustard
pepper	1 tablespoon cilantro
salt	1 tablespoon celery seeds
paprika	seasoning salt

Directions:

1. Clean hands, area, and equipment.
2. Cook potatoes in salted water until tender or until fork can be stuck into potatoes easily.
3. Hard boil eggs for, 15-20 minutes.
4. Refrigerate.
5. Dice, chop celery and green onions.
6. Mix with mayonnaise, sugar, vinegar, mustard, celery seeds, and cilantro.
7. Add seasonings.
8. Cut potatoes lengthwise into strips, 1/4 inch wide.
9. Cut eggs into circles.
10. Blend potato and mayonnaise mixture.
11. Arrange so that either the X's or Os wins.

X-plosive Snack

Materials:

large bowls	1 cup peanuts, salted
wooden spoon	1 microwave oven
paper cups	1 cup raisins and dried fruit

1 light microwave popcorn package

class favorite-wheat, Rice/Corn Chex cereal

1/2 cup chocolate chips or M&M™ Candies

seasoning: garlic/chili powder, seasoned salt, and pepper.

Directions:

1. Clean hands, area, and equipment.
2. Pop popcorn according to directions (about 4 to 5 minutes) in the microwave oven.
3. In large bowl, mix wheat, Rice or Corn ChexÖ cereal, popcorn, peanuts, raisins, dried fruit, and chocolate chips/M&M's™.
4. Mix thoroughly with wooden spoon and season with salt, pepper, garlic, chili, or the class favorite.
5. Divide into small cups or bowls.
6. It is explosive.

X'ED POTATOES

Materials:

powdered garlic
pepper
seasoned salt
salt
knives
foil
1 baking sheet for toaster/conventional oven
flavorings: paprika, garlic powder, salt, pepper, onion powder, and/or celery salt.

8 large baking potatoes, cut lengthwise
1 cup butter (salted or unsalted)
powdered onion
paprika
cutting board
pastry brush

Directions:

1. Clean hands, area, and equipment.
2. Wash/dry potatoes.
3. Cut potatoes on cutting board.
4. Make large "X" on each potato when placed flat side down.
5. Brush with flavored butter (garlic, onion, paprika, pepper, celery salt, salt).
6. Bake at 450 degrees for 35-40 minutes, basting occasionally with butter.

XERACH X-PLOSIVE SANDWICH

This is my family's favorite. Be careful! It may x-plode in your face.

Materials:

electric fry pan
dried chili peppers
2-3 slices of bacon
Garnish: chopped cilantro/onions, tomatoes to add

2 slices of whole grain bread
1 slice of yellow cheese
1 slice of white cheese

Directions:

1. Clean hands, area, and equipment.
2. Fry 2-3 slices of bacon per sandwich. Dry on paper towel.
3. Saute each slice of bread just a bit.
4. Assemble bread, cheese, and bacon. Saute each side.
5. Garnish with cilantro, onions, tomatoes, and your other favorites.
6. It's x-plosive.

X-x Games/Activities

XIT (EXIT) SIGNS/ENTER SIGNS

Students need to be able to read these signs x-tremely fast. One way is to make his/her own signs. Here is how:
1. Clean hands, area, and equipment. Have one loaf of white/ wheat bread, toaster oven, clean small brushes, butter, and food coloring.
2. Toast bread.
3. Mix food coloring with butter or margarine.
4. Make model of Exit/Enter sign or write on board.
6. Allow each child to paint Exit/Enter on the toast.

PRETZELS AND CHEESE X's

Have pretzel stick (straight) handy, plus cubes of cheese. See how many capital and lower case X's each child can make in a half a minute.

XTRA AXLES

Cars, wagons, jeeps, trucks, and trailers each have two axles (A rod on which a wheel turns or one that is connected to a wheel so that they can turn together). To make learning about a complex axle fun, try this:

Each student will need, 1-1/2 hot dogs and two round toothpicks. Cut the half hot dog into four wheels. Attach each wheel to hot dog with wooden toothpick. The axles are the toothpicks. (Hint: The wheels must be the same size, but the uncut hot dog or body of the car could be a carrot or zucchini or even play dough.) After it has been constructed, it may be boiled or fried to eat.

EXACT X-BOARD GAME

There are many board games or teacher/aid/parent can make a board game with places to move a start, a finish, and either a set of dice or a spinner (with numbers, 1-6). The teacher could make cards with the /X-x/ words from the word list. The students either spin the spinner or throw the dice to see how far they moves their marker. Then they must pick up the card and either read it or hear it. Then decide if it has an /x/ sound and if their is correct, they may move.

EXTRAORDINARY X-SENTENCES

The teacher copies flash cards from the word list. The children must take a noun, verb, and can add adjectives, adverbs, and any extra word to make—so that they can verbally state— a complete sentence. Remember that it must make sense. Teacher/aide and then write the sentence and student can then copy and illustrate it. Make a class book or individual books with other letters.

X's AND O's

Students could learn/play X's & O's or tic-tac-toe. A pound key is drawn and each player either places X's or O's, in turn, on the diagram to get three in a row. The row can be vertical, horizontal, or diagonal.

X-TREMELY POSITIVE ESTEEM GAME

Students need to know what a positive statement is. They can be read or stated. The teacher gives examples. When each child understands or can explain what a positive example is, the game can begin. Each student needs a container that will be decorated by that student. Every day, two to three papers are given to each player. Two or three names of the students are drawn (and kept separated so that each student's name is drawn). Each student writes one positive statement for each name written on the board. It can be simple statements like: "I like your dress/shirt/shoes ... I like your smile, barrette, or belt." One student is the delivery person. They deliver and read the positive messages. Books, charts, or silhouettes could be made to house/display the extremely positive, personal text. These would make great Open House/ Back-to-School night displays!

X-RAYS

X-rays can be used. They can be asked for at a hospital or doctor's office if returned. Old ones may be given out if name is cut out. Students could look up information on X-ray and see why/how this machine has helped doctors.

X-MARKS THE SPOT

A child is "Mr./Ms. X" and they look around the room for a Special Spot. The other students have 20 guesses to guess that Special Spot that "Mr./ Ms. X" is thinking about.

X-BOOKS

Students use discarded books, catalogs, magazines, newspapers, or any old pictures to find items with an "x" sound either in the initial, medial, or final position. This can be a cooperative group assignment, individual, or at a center. The student with the most correct pictures wins.

X-x Word Lists

Nouns:

xanthine	xantic acid	xanthein
xanthoma	xeno	xenogenesis
xenophilia	xenophobia	wax
excuse	prefix	suffix
siloxane	xanthophyll	x-axis
box	tax	ax
mixture	axis	index
xebec	xenia	xenolith
xenon	xeroderma	xerography
xerosis	xylophone	xiphisternum
xerosere	xeroradiography	xiphosuran
xerophthalmia	x-ray	x-ray tube
xylograph	xylography	xylan
xyster	text	texture
nexus	index	Lexis
lexeme	axil	axicom
xylem	xylidine	xylotomy
exercise	execution	example
Excaliber	sax	Sext
Sexton	Sextant	lexicon
lox	axle	exit
excuse	excellence	extract
"Xena"		

Verbs:

xerox	fix	relax
mix	exclaim	exaggerate
excel	exist	explain
expand	expect	extract
perplex	except	exchange
exceed	examine	excite
exclaim	exclude	exercising
exhale	exhaust	

Adjective:

xanthochroid	xenophilic	xerach
xeric	expert	six
sixty	extra	exterior
exact	expensive	extinct
extraordinary	xerophilous	xerothermic
xiphoid	xylophagous	complex
textile	textural	extreme

Adverb:

extremely	excessive	vexatious
axially	axile	

Areas:

xhosas	xingu	Lexington
Axminster	Xochimilco	Mexico
Texas		

Musical Instruments/inventions:

xylophone	xyster	xerox
X-ray		

Food:

xigua

X-x Reading Resources

Xio Ming and Katie Visit The Zoo — China Books

Xavier's Fantastic Discovery — Lucinda McQueen

Fox in Love — James Marshall: Pied Piper, 1982

Malcolm X — Arnold Adof (older students) Scholastic Trumpet, 1970

Xioayings Cartoons for Children — Lexiaoying

Xenophons Anabasis — Maurice M. Mather and Hewitt

Earthlets As Explained By Professor Xargle — Jeanne Wills

Father Fox's Pennyrhymes — Clyde Watson: Harper Collins, 1971

The Fox Went Out on a Chilly Night — Peter Spier: Doubleday, 1962

Ox-Cart Man — Donald Hall: Viking, 1979

A Maker of Boxes — W.R. Wright: Holt, 1971

Black Fox of Lorne — Marguerite de Angeli: Doubleday, 1957

Excuses, Excuses: How to Get Out of Practically Anything — John Caldwell Crowell, 1982

An XYZ Adventure in Alphabet Town — Janet McDonnell: Children's Press, 1992

X-Men in the Savage Land — Paul Mantell and Avery Hart: Random House for Young Readers, 1994

X-Men Mask Book — Thompson Brothers: Random House Books for Young Readers, 1994

X-Men Pop-up Book — Thompson Brothers: Random House Books for Young Readers, 1994

X-Men X-tra Large Coloring and Activity Book — Marvel Entertainment Group — Random House for Young Readers, 1994

X-Men: Masquerade — Ron Fontes & Justine Korman: Random House for Young Readers, 1994

X-tinction Agenda — Vicki Kamida: Random House Books for Young Readers, 1994

X-Men: Spellbound — Jim Thomas: Random House Books for Young Readers, 1994

Y · y

Y-y Recipes

YUMMY-YUMMIES

Materials:

1/3 cup butter

16 marshmallows

wooden spoon

waxed paper

refrigerator

teaspoon

6 oz. package chocolate chips

sauce pan/stove or unit burner

1/2 teaspoon vanilla

2 cups rolled oats

1/2 cup chopped nuts

Directions:

1. Clean hands, area, and equipment.
2. Melt chocolate chips, margarine/butter, and marshmallows.
3. Stir until smooth. Remove from heat.
4. Add vanilla, coconut, rolled oats, and nuts.
5. Mix thoroughly.
6. Drop from teaspoon onto waxed paper.
7. Refrigerate.
8. Yummy! Yummy!

YUMMER YAMS

Materials:

casserole pan

potato masher

toaster oven

1 large can of yams

1 tablespoon margarine

1 small can pineapple chunks and juice

12 large marshmallows

Directions:

1. Clean hands, area, and equipment.
2. Drain yams and put into a greased casserole pan (that fits into toaster oven).
3. Add pineapple and juice.
4. Mash pineapple and yams gently.
5. Cover with one tablespoon of margarine and, 12 large marshmallows.
6. Bake uncovered for 20 minutes at 350 degrees.
7. Enjoy.

Yoo-hoo Yogurt Salad

Materials:

measuring cups

measuring spoons

wooden spoon

can opener

refrigerator

bowl 1/2 cup of broken walnuts

3/4 cup of vanilla yogurt

1/2 tablespoon powdered sugar (optional)

1/2 cup of canned Queen Anne cherries, pitted

1 can of pineapple chunks

1 can of Mandarin orange segments

1-1/2 cups of seedless grapes

1 cup of miniature marshmallows

1 cup of flaked coconut

Directions:

1. Clean hands, area, and equipment.
2. Drain pineapple, oranges, and cherries.
3. Combine pineapples, oranges, grapes, marshmallows, coconut, walnuts, and cherries.
4. Mix yogurt with sugar.
5. Fold yogurt mixture with fruit and nuts.
6. Chill for one hour.
7. Yoo-hoo.

Yucky-Yuck Treats
(No Bake)

Materials:

wooden spoon

saucepan

wax paper

bowl

1/4 cup of cocoa

stove/hot plate, unit burner

measuring cups and spoons

5 cups of marshmallows

1 stick of butter

1/4 cup of milk

additives: peanut butter, raisins, nuts, coconut, and cereal.

Directions:

1. Clean hands, area, and equipment.
2. Stir marshmallows, milk, butter, and cocoa over low to medium heat until all is smooth.
3. Add any of the additives and stir (taste).
4. Wet hands with water before placing scoop of ingredients on waxed paper.
5. Allow children to sculpt and form yucky-yucks.
6. Cool.
7. Yucky!

Yo-Yo Muffins
My Daughter Called Yogurt "Yo-Yo".

Materials:

bowls	measuring spoons/cups
2 cups flour	2 teaspoons baking powder
1/2 teaspoon salt	1/4 teaspoon cinnamon
2 large eggs	1/4 teaspoon ground nutmeg
1/3 cup honey	1/4 teaspoon all-spice
1/4 cup oil	1 carton of yogurt
oven	

lemon, peach, strawberry, and muffin tin/cup cake holders

Directions:

1. Clean hands, area, and equipment.
2. Stir flour, baking powder, salt, nutmeg, cinnamon, and all of the spices into medium bowl.
3. Combine eggs, honey, oil, and yogurt (yo-yo) in large bowl.
4. Combine yo-yo mixture (large bowl) with dry mixture (medium bowl).
5. Stir until just moistened.
6. Spoon batter into cupcake holders (3/4 filled). Then place cup cake holders into muffin tin.
7. Bake at 400 degrees for, 18-20 minutes or until golden brown.

Yummy Yankee Gingerbread

Fancy recipe made in about the, 1700s at that time. Maple syrup was used for sweetness. When boiled down, a sort of sugar was left.

Materials:

pan for baking	measuring cups and spoons
Toaster oven	spoons
bowls	2 cups flour
1 teaspoon soda	1/2 teaspoon salt
1 teaspoon ground ginger	1 egg beater
1 cup sour cream	butter for pan
1 cup maple syrup	whipping cream can be used for topping

Directions:

1. Clean hands, area, and equipment.
2. In large bowl, measure and combine flour, soda, salt, and ginger.
3. In small bowl, combine sour cream and maple syrup.
4. Combine ingredients in large and small bowl.
5. Bake in buttered pan in toaster over for 40 minutes at 350 degrees.

YEAST BREAD

Yeast-a leavening agent is a living plant, which grows in warm, moist dough. It gives off bubbles of gas, causing the dough to rise. If the liquid is too hot, it will kill the yeast. The temperature for yeast should not be above, 100 degrees. (Dough can be put it into plastic-air tight containers.) Have students knead/sculpt and allow to rise. Then bake and decorate. (Rule: Dough made with at least two cups of liquid doubles in three hours.)

Materials:

1 tablespoon salt
2 towels
aluminum foil
bowls
1 egg
plastic wrap
1-1/2 to 2 cups warm milk (for richness)
2 teaspoons granulated sugar (yeast food)

1 pkg.. active dry yeast
5 to 6 cups all-purpose flour
1/4 cup softened butter
measuring cups/spoons
clean pastry brush
wooden spoon

Directions:

1. Clean hands, area, and equipment.
2. Add yeast to warm milk and sugar.
3. Stir until dissolved.
4. Allow yeast to proof (see fermentation by bubbles appearing and mixture gets larger). When proofed, add butter.
5. Measure and combine flour and salt.
6. Combine flour mixture with yeast mixture and butter in big bowl, a little at a time. (It will be firm.)
7. Put mixture on floured board or slab and knead until no longer sticky (10 minutes). Add just enough flour to to knead; it gets tough when you add too much flour to the board/hands.
8. Butter bowl.
9. Cover with towels.
10. Allow to rise in warm spot (two hours).
11. Punch dough down (Teachers: refrigerate at this point, and then take to school).
12. Flour bread board/hands and knead 4-5 more minutes.
13. Shape or place in a 9"x5" inch loaf pan.
14. Cover with towels or plastic wrap.
15. Let rise until doubled in size (40-45 minutes).
16. Brush with egg glaze (raw egg mixed with water).
17. Bake at 350 degrees until golden brown (for loaf about 40 minutes).

Y-y Games/Activities

YEAH GAME BOARD

The teacher can transfer/write words from word list to flash cards. The board could look like a yardstick. Each player rolls the dice, then must hear/ read the word and use it in a sentence. If able, they states "yeah" and move the spaces that correspond to the number on the dice. The first player from start to finish is the winner.

Y-Y FLASH CARDS

Y-y flash cards can be used within a writing center for sentence building/forming and as dictionary work to find the meanings of these words. "Around The World" could be played by reading groups/cooperative learning groups/whole class game. The student must read the word and use it in a sentence or tell if it is a noun or verb, animal, area, etc.

IT'S YOUR TURN

Students in cooperative learning groups each watch a TV video, TV show, read a book, decide on sharing an incident they saw, or choose a school lunch. The group must talk about and decide upon one item. Decide if they liked it or not. They present it to the class and state what the reasons were for their decision. Then each member of the class makes up their own mind or takes their turn to decide and vote. A chart/graph can be kept as "our turn" or "your turn."

YARD WORK

Several students trace yardsticks onto heavy tag board or railroad board. They then measure (in yards) the classroom, the schoolyard, the buildings, and cafeteria/auditorium. They could also measure their own house and yard. A comparison could be graphed/charted to see the size in yards. A piece of yarn the size of a yardstick would also work.

YAWNING

Students need to learn the importance of yawning. It reduces the pressure in the ears and sinuses. A sinus is an air cavity in the skull, which leads to the nasal cavities. By yawning, we reduce pressure. We should yawn when there is a change in altitude or if we feel drowsy, dull, or fatigue. This is because we need oxygen.

YOLK'S ON YOU

A yolk is the yellow substance of an egg and it is the protein and fat, which serves as nourishment for the growing embryo. Teacher could collect eggs and compare size of eggs, plus the coloring of the eggshells. Besides birds, the animals that lay eggs are turtles, lizards, frogs, and most reptiles and amphibians. Students can also do research and draw pictures of animals that lay eggs. It will hatch only if fertilized.

YUMMY YOGURT

Students can make their own yogurt using electric yogurt makers or milk in a gas oven overnight. Another way is to buy plain yogurt. A taste test could be fun. Yogurt with flavors could be sampled and students register their favorite flavor. A chart/graph could be made and a letter could be sent to the manufacturer, which expresses the class favorite.

YARN PICTURES

Using tag or railroad board let students draw a picture. Then use glue and yarn to color (paint) the colors and details. These pictures are like pictures sold in Mexico. This could be done around Cinco de Mayo (May, 15th) or September, 16th.

YAM CONTESTS

Each child/cooperative learning group could have yam (sweet potato) and a jar with four or five toothpicks. This needs to start in a dark area. Then when the yam has started to grow, transfer close to sun. Students can have a contest to see which yam grows the longest, the most leaves, the darkest, the best. The contest could also include using plant food and sugar in the water.

Y-y Word Lists

Nouns:

yarrow	yule	yarn
yogurt	yacht	yachtsman
Yagi antenna	yank	yankee
yawn	year	Yule log
Yuletide	yucca	yo-yo
youth	youngster	you
York	yolk	yokel
yoke	yohinibine	Yogi
yesterday	yoga	ylang-ylang
Yeoman	yenta	yen
yeast	yearling	yearbook
year	yeanling	y-axis
yarn	yard stick	yard work
yard master	yard man	yard
yolk-stalk	yohimbine	

Verbs:

yakked	yakking	Yammer
yank	yap	yodel
yipped	yipping	yield
yelp	yell	yearn
yean	yawp	yawn
yaw	yatter	

Animals:

yak	yeanling yapook	yellow warbler
yellow tail	yellow jacket	yellow throat
yellow hammer	yellow-green algae	yellow bird
yellow-bellied sapsucker		

Food:

Yorkshire pudding	yam	yeast
yoghurtor	yogurt	yolk
yolk sac	yellow squash	yaupon

Areas/Mountains/Rivers:

Yunnan	Yemen	Yangtze
Yukon	Yosemite	York
Yorkshire	Yokosuka	Yemen
Yellowstone	Yellowknife	Yazoo
Yawata	Yablonovyy Range	Yadkin
Yakima	Yakutsk	Yalta
Yalo		

Describing Words:

Yonder	yeomanly	yummy
yellowy	youthful	young
young-eyed	young-ish	yucky

Y-y Reading Resources

You Read to Me, I'll Read to You — John Ciardi: Harper Trophy, 1981

Young Owl — Bill Martin: Henry Holt, 1986

Yummers — James Marshall: Houghton Mifflin, 1973

Yearwalk — Ann Nolan Clark: Puffin, 1952

Yeh Shen — Cinerella Story from China — Al-Ling Louie

You Come Too — Robert Frost

Yearling — Marjorie Rawling: Collier, 1938

Year at Maple Hill Farm — Alice Prorensen: Aladdin, 1978

Baba Yoga — Earnest Small

You've Come a Long Way Kitty — Carolyn Duckworth

Little Blue and Little Yellow — Leo Lionni, Knopf, 1963

Young Mark Twain and the Mississippi — Harnett Kane

Yummers Too — James Marshall: Houghton Mifflin

Yo-Hungry Wolf: A Nursery Rap — David Vozar: Delacorte Press, 1995

Yo! It's Captain Yo-Yo — Jon Buller & Susan Schade: Put- nam Publishing Group, 1993

You Can Write Chinese — Kurt Wise: Viking, 1946

Y Basketball Passers Manual: For 3rd -4th Grade Players — Robert Levin: Human Kinetics Pub., 1984

Yurtle the Turtle and Other Stories — Dr. Seuss: Random House, 1958

Yellow and Pink — William Steig: Farrar, Straus, & Giroux, 1984

Yonder — Tony Johnston: Pied Piper, 1988

You Be Good and I'll Be Night — Eve Merriam: Morrow Jr. Books, 1989

Young Fu Of The Upper Yangtze — Henry Holt,, 1932

Year Without Michael — Susan Beth Pfeffer: Bantam, 1987

The Year of the Black Pony — Walt Morey: Dutton, 1972

The Year of the Perfect Christmas Tree: An Appalachian Story — Gloria Houston: Pied Piper, 1988

The Yellow Umbrella — Henrik Prescher: Bradbury, 1987

Your Old Pal, Al — Constance Greene: Puffin, 1969

You Are Much Too Small — Betty D. Boegehold: Bantam, 1991

Young Lions — Toshi Yoshida: Philomel, 1990

Young Merlin — Robert D. Sansouci: Doubleday, 1991

Y Aun Podria Ser Aqua - It Could Still Be Water — Allan Fowler: Children's Press, 1993

Y Tu Donde Vives? — Ina Cumpiano: Hampton Brown Co., 1992

Y Domingo, Siete — Robert Baden, Albert Whitman & Co., 1990

You Ought To See Herbert's House — Doris Lund: Franklin Watts, 1973

Yonie Wondernose — Marguerite de Angeli: Doubleday, 1945

Yagua Days — Cruz Martel: Dial, 1976

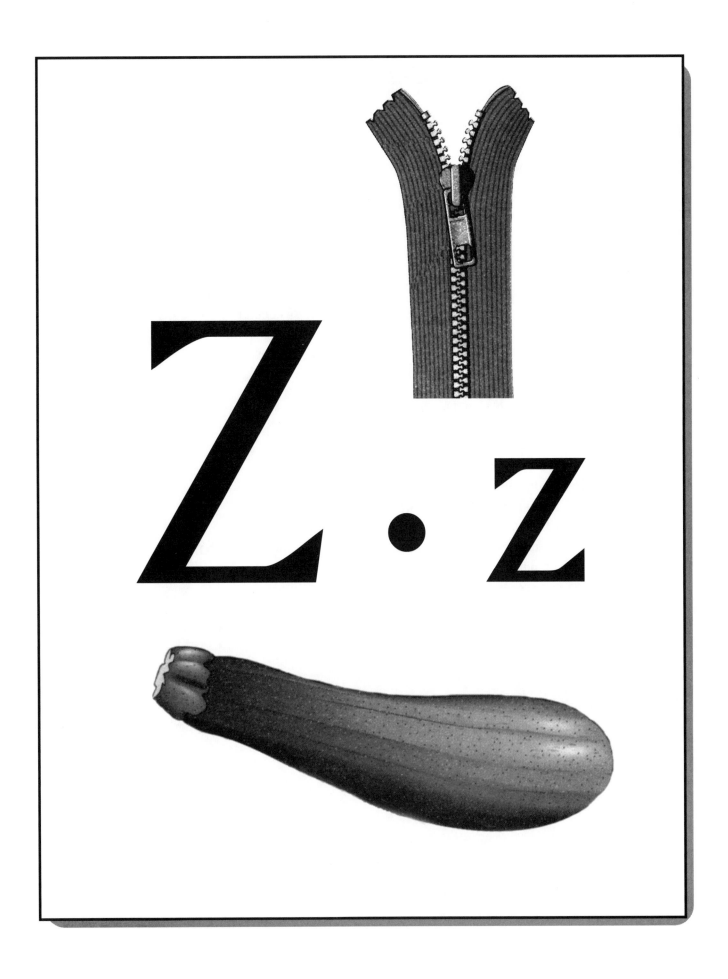

Z · z

Z-z Recipes

ZENITH ZUCCHINI MUFFINS #1

Materials:

muffin tin
masher
bowls
spoons
measuring cups
can opener
1 teaspoon salt
3 large eggs
1/2 cup vegetable
toaster oven/oven

3 very ripe bananas
3-1/2 cups all purpose flour
2 cups chopped walnuts
1/2 cup crushed pineapple
2 teaspoons baking soda
1/2 teaspoon baking powder
2 teaspoons vanilla extract
1 can cream of coconut
2 cups shredded zucchini
2 cups brown sugar

Directions:

1. Clean hands, area, and equipment.
2. Mash bananas.
3. Combine bananas and brown sugar in large bowl.
4. Mix flour, baking soda, baking powder, and salt in medium bowl.
5. Beat three eggs and add to large bowl.
6. Beat in oil, vanilla, and cream of coconut in large bowl.
7. Combine in flour mixture from medium bowl into large bowl.
8. Add to this mixture to the shredded zucchini and chopped walnuts.
9. Add crushed pineapple.
10. Pour into cupcake holders and put in muffin tins.
11. Fill 3/4 full.
12. Bake At 350 degrees for 20-25 minutes or until golden brown.

Zenith Zucchini Muffins #2

Materials:

muffin tin
spoons
masher
1/2 cup oil
bowls
measuring cups
can opener
3 large eggs
1/2 cup vegetable
1 teaspoon salt
1/2 cup crushed pineapple

toaster oven or oven
1/2 teaspoon baking powder
3-1/2 cups all-purpose flour
2 cups brown sugar
2 teaspoons vanilla extract
2 teaspoons baking soda
3 very ripe bananas
2 cups shredded zucchini
1 can of cream coconut
2 cups chopped walnuts

Directions:

1. Clean hands, area, and equipment.
2. Mash bananas.
3. Combine bananas and brown sugar in large bowl.
4. Mix flour, baking soda, baking powder, salt in medium bowl.
5. Beat three eggs and add to large bowl.
6. Beat in oil, vanilla, and cream of coconut in large bowl.
7. Combine in flour mixture from medium bowl into large bowl.
8. Add to this mixture shredded zucchini and chopped walnuts.
9. Add crushed pineapple.
10. Pour into cupcake holders and put in muffin tins.
11. Fill 3/4 full.
12. Bake At 350 degrees for 20-25 minutes or until golden brown.

Zucchini Casserole

Materials:

shallow baking dish that fits into toaster oven

2 zucchinis

salt

garlic salt

2 sliced tomatoes

toaster oven

Parmesan cheese

seasoning salt

pepper

1/4 onion, chopped

cooked crumbled bacon

Directions:

1. Clean hands, area, and equipment.
2. Slice zucchini thinly.
3. Place in greased (buttered) shallow baking dish.
4. Add Parmesan cheese, salt, pepper, garlic salt, and seasoning salt.
5. Spread onion and sliced tomatoes over the cheese.
6. Layer crumbled bacon over onion and tomatoes.
7. Sprinkle with additional Parmesan cheese.
8. Bake At 400 degrees for, 15-20 minutes or until cheese Is golden brown.

Zany Zucchini Zoo

Materials:

2 zucchini (clean, scrubbed, and cut into 2" pieces)

cheddar cheese

cream cheese

cutting board

knife

celery

raisins

noodles

pickles

1 carrot cut into, 1/2 inch slices

round toothpicks

olives, oranges

banana

nuts

chow mien

Cheerios

Directions:

1. Clean hands, area, and equipment.
2. Clean vegetables and cut fruits and vegetables into slices. Cut cheese into cubes.
3. Allow each student to make/construct animals with ingredients. Make sure he/she realizes the cream cheese is the "cement".
4. The animal must fit into the cage. The animal must have A name and A small description about it.
5. A zoo/animal cage can be made with 2 orange slices and toothpicks around the edges. Glue may be used for the cages.

ZOWIE ZUCCHINI BREAD

Materials:

9"x5" loaf pan
wooden spoon
bowl
1/2 cup oil
butter
1/2 teaspoon salt
2 eggs
1 cup sugar
1/8 teaspoons ground coriander
1/2 teaspoon baking soda

measuring cup and spoons
1 cup shredded zucchini
1-1/2 cups all-purpose flour
1/4 teaspoons ground cloves
1/4 teaspoon baking powder
2 teaspoons ground cinnamon
1/2 cup chopped walnuts
1/4 teaspoons ground nutmeg
2 tablespoons vanilla, extract

Directions:

1. Clean hands, area, and equipment.
2. Beat eggs.
3. Add sugar, oil, and vanilla.
4. Beat until well-blended.
5. Add zucchini, flour, salt, baking powder, and spices.
6. Mix until blended.
7. Stir in nuts.
8. Spoon batter into greased (butter) and floured 9"x5" pan.
9. Bake At 350 degrees for 50-60 minutes or until cake tester comes out clean.
10. Allow to cool.
11. Zowie!

ZWINNER ZWIEBEL

A zesty taste for Passover, A Jewish Holiday around Easter.

Materials:

matzos

onionoven/toaster oven

butter

salt and pepper (also hot pepper)

Directions:

1. Clean hands, area, and equipment.
2. Rub matzo with raw onion.
3. Spread with butter and serve hot.
4. Sprinkle with salt, pepper, hot pepper, and other seasonings you like.
5. Place in oven to dry.
6. Serve this zwinner.

ZANIEST ZERO-GROWTH GARDEN

(This is a great dessert.)

Materials:

2 small packages of instant vanilla pudding

8 oz cool whip

2-3/4 cups milk

bowls

paper cups

gummy worms

8 oz. package of cream cheese.

1 package of Oreo™ cookies

measuring cups/spoons

plastic flowers

Directions:

1. Clean hands, area, and equipment.
2. Mix together cream cheese, pudding, cool whip, and milk.
3. Chill for, 1/2 to, 1 hour.
4. Remove centers of cookies (cream) and crush chocolate cookies into fine crumbs (put cookies in plastic bag and crush with book/block).
5. Fill cups 3/4 full with chilled mixture.
6. Sprinkle cookie dust like top onto the soil in the garden.
7. Place plastic flower in the center.
8. Put Gummy™ worms in each planter.

Z-z Games/Activities

ZINGY FLASH BASEBALL

The teacher writes out words onto flash cards. A student must read the word/and if able, use the word in a sentence. If the student can read the word and use it in a sentence, he then walks to first base. The next person on the team either gets a hit or is out. The team remains up until it makes three outs. Then the other team is up. Teacher designates, 1st, 2nd, 3rd base and home. The team with the most points wins. The flash cards may also contain other consonants and the student then tells the beginning sound.

ZESTFUL TASTINGS

Plates of zucchini, Zwieback™ toast, Zingers™, Screaming Yellow Zonkers™, & zoo cookies/crackers. Each student tastes each item mentioned, plus other items starting with z, and is given a marker. They place the marker with their name on the back of the designated area next to the plate. The plate with the most markers wins. This needs to be charted and graphed.

ZERO GAME

Mr./Ms. "Zero" gets to look around the room and find an item that starts with the "z" sound. The group then has, 10-20 chances to guess what the item could be: a zipper, zinnia, zebra, zoo, zero, zillion, zone, zip code, Zeppelin, Z Books, etc.

Z-SNACKS

Zucchini, carrots, celery, jicama, brocoflower, cauliflower, cherry, tomatoes, and broccoli could be placed around a "dip." A dip recipe could be made out of 2 cups yogurt, 2 cups cottage cheese, 2 tablespoons minced lemon zest, 2 teaspoons ground coriander, 4 tablespoons lemon juice, and, 1/2 teaspoon chopped fresh dill. Mix well. Children need to know snacks can be/should be healthy, not fatty and bad for them.

ZOO ANIMALS

Pictures/realia of animals could be shown and students determine whether the animals live in a zoo, farm, city, pet shop, or jungle. The pictures could be given to cooperative learning groups and each group determines/decides how to classify/sort them.

ZOO TRIP

Shoe boxes can be made into zoo-o-ramas. Each student could use clay, plaster of paris, or play dough to sculpt an animal. Pipe cleaners can make/form the bars. Each student names and writes the description of each animal. A book may be written about each animal. The zoo can then be visited by parents, other teachers, or classes. The book could contain information about food, environment, special needs, reproduction, and skin. This can be true/real or make believe zoo animals.

ZANNY ZONES

Duct/Masking tape can be used to section off zones. Each zone could be labeled quiet, singing, standing, hopping, jumping, sitting, right hand on head, eyes blinking, etc. Each student starts on "Start" and walks from zone to zone, doing what the sign says At each zanny zone. The students will want to go through the zones several times.

ZOTHER, MAY I?

Students line up on line. Zother is "it." Student says, "Zother may I take ... A baby step, umbrella step, giant step, zig-zag step, etc.?" Zother either says "Yes" or "No." If the answer is "Yes," the student moves that move only. If the answer Is "No," the student may not move. The student that reaches Zother first, is the new Zother.

ZOMBIES

A zombie (West Indies) is a speechless, will-less body that believes in the power of Black Magic. It's capable only of an automatic-trance-like movement and was supposed to have died, but instead was reanimated. Students could make a capital Z, then use markers to create a "Zombie" or A supernatural snake that was supposed to enter the zombie's body. (This is a legend from the West Indies' African Voodoo Cult).

ZONKED MUSIC

A tape or record could be played of a march or classical music and students march on the Giant Z. When the music stops, they must stop on the "Z." If they are zonked ... they are put in the zonked pot. The last one up is the zonk winner. Students march or walk on a duct tape Giant Z.

WATCH THOSE ZINNIAS

Children need to save milk cartons or paper cups. Fill 3/4ths full with potting soil. Make three holes. Plant zinnia seed in soil, then water it and place it in the sun. This is a great project around Mother's Day or spring. The students can measure and compare size. The growth can be charted/graphed.

Z-z Word Lists

Nouns:

zinnia	zombie	zinger
zinfandel	zineb	zaffer
zamia	zag	zamindar
zany	Zapotec	zaratite
zarf	zarzuela	zax
z-axis	zeal	zealot
zebra wood	zedoary	zonule
zein	Zen	Zenith
zeolite	zephyr	Zeppelin
zero	zest	zeugma
zig	ziggurat	zig zag
zilch	zillion	zinc
zincate	zinc chloride	zincite
zincography	zinc ointment	zinc oxide
zing	zone	zoo
Zwitterion	Zori	Zinc White
Ziram	zooid	Zinjanthropus
Zircaloy	zoology	zinkenite
zircon	zooming	zipper
zirconium	zoometry	zip code
zodiac	zoom lens	zip gun
zoo geography	zoonosis	zoography
zoophilism	zoophyte	zoospore
zoophobia	zoosterol	zootomy
zootsuit	zymurgy	zymotic
zymosis	zymometer	zygote
zygospore		

Verbs:

zap	zincked	zinced
zinking	zing	zipped
zipping	zoned	zoing
zoom		

Adjectives:

zonked	zygodactyl	zoogenic
zanier	zaniest	zealous
zero	zero base	zero gravity
zero-zero	zero-sum	zero hour
zero growth	zestfully	zibeline
zingier	zingiest	zippy
zodical	zoographical	

Areas/rivers/mountains:

zabrze	zagreb	Zug
Zagros Mountains	Zaire	Zakinthos
Zambezi	Zanzibar	Zaporozhe
Zealand	Zeeland	Zend
Zetland	Zhdanov	Zhukov
Zimbabwe	Zulu	Zweig
Zurich		

Animals:

zorilla	zebu	zebra
zebra butterfly	zebra finch	zebra fish
zebrass	zoea	zooparasite
zooplankton		

Food:

zabaglione	zinger	zyme
zucchini	zwieback	ziti

Adverbs:

zesty	zincy

Z-z Reading Resources

Animals A to Z — David McPhail

Z Was Zapped — Chris Van Allsburg: Mifflin Co., 1987

Zucchini — B. Dana

Zamai Goes to Market — Mariel Feeling

Zoo Doings (poem) — Jack Prelutcky: Trumpet, 1983

Zeralda's Ogre — tomi Ungerer: Aladdin/Sunburst, 1971

Zlateh the Goat and Other Stories — Issac B. Singer: Harper, 1967

Zeely — Virginia Hamilton: Macmillian Children's Book Group, 1993

Zia — Scott O'Dell: Houghton Mifflin, 1990

Z Is for Zachariah — Robert O'Brien: Athenum, 1965

If I Ran the Zoo — Dr. Seuss: Random, 1951

Z Is for Zebra — Pam Schmacker: Storytime Publishing, 1992

Zack's Alligator — Shirley Mozelle: Harper Collins' Children's Books, 1995

Zack in Action — Beth Cruise: Macmillian Children's Book, 1994

Zeke Pippin — William Steig: Harper Collins Children's Books, 1994

Zoodles — Bernard Most: Harcourt Brace and Co., 1994

Zeee — Elizabeth Enright: Harcourt Brace and Co., 1994

Zoom at Sea — Tim Wynne-Jones: Harper Collins Children's Books, 1993

Zoom Away — Tim Wynne-Jones: Harper Collins Publishers inc., 1993

Zoom Rimes: Poems About Things That Go — Sylvia Cassedy: Harper Collins Children's Book, 1993

The Zebra-Riding Cowboy: A Folk Song of the Old West — Angela Medearis: Holt, Henry, and Co., 1992

Zipping Zippers Save the Zoo — Elaine Weimann and Rita Friedman: New Dimensions in Education, 1986

The Zebra Wall — Kevin Henkes: Puffin Books, 1989

Zack's Alligator — Shirley Mozelle: Harper Collins, 1989

Zebo and the Dirty Planet — Kim Fernandes & Pat Lacroix: Firefly Books, 1991

Zip, Whiz, Zoom! — Stephanie Calmenson: Little, Brown, & Co., 1992

Zinnia and Dot — Lisa Ernst: Viking Children's Books, 1992

Z Is for Zombie — Mel Gilden: Avon Books, 1988

A Zoo in Our House — Heather Eyles Warner, 1989

The Carsick Zebra and Other Animal Riddles — David Adler: Holiday, 1993

The Accidental Zucchini — Max Grover: Browndeer Press, Harcourt Brace & Co., 1993

Appendix A

Techniques & Strategies that Work

1. Presenting a letter in both upper (capital) and lower case form, with a dot or dash in between, saves time in teaching the association of capital with lower case. Be sure and go over which is which several times.

2. Teachers and parents still need to teach writing of the letter in the air (if the child is unable to write it properly), independently. The teacher stands behind the child and helps the child. Children need to "see" the letter on the blackboard, "hear" the sound, and "feel" the letter. The first step is writing it in the air. Then the children could print it, use beans, macaroni, Alpha-Bits™, rice, or whatever is available and/or inexpensive to paste or glue the material into a large alphabet letter-strapped tag board. When it dries, the children can then "feel" it. Also, duct tape could be put on the floor and the children could then walk on the shape of the letter. Another suggestion, besides those in the chapters, is to use soft, fine sandpaper to cut out the shape of the letters. The last suggestion is to put rice or sand in a tray and allow students to use their finger to "write" the letter.

3. Another way to "see" and "feel" the letter is to make the letter out of one of the dough recipes listed in the book. Several are under the letter "D-d." Cookies also help.

4. It is very important to have children paint letters on an easel, finger paint letters, or use markers. While the child is "seeing" the letter, the child should be associating the letter with the sound of the letter. Have the child say the sound while writing/painting.

5. A great way to introduce a letter is to associate it with a child's name. Have children state names of friends, siblings, or themselves—people whose first or last name begins with that letter—to reinforce the shape and sound.

6. There are many, many words for each letter in the "word list." These can be used to make memory games, sight word games, and even reports. All of this depends upon the age, skill or ability level of your children/students. Flash cards could go home with the students to reinforce the concept and strengthen the school/home relationship.

7. Associating an animal, food with a letter is a great way to reinforce reading skills. The animal name could be a clue to help the student remember the letter and sound.

8. Words can be combined to become sentences. Or, words can be combined with pictures for memory games. Words can also be combined into a story or sentence. Each child can use the word to form a sentence, then the sentences can be sequenced onto a strip, which when viewed through a box or holder, becomes a story. The story can also be printed on a computer to be sequenced and read at home.

9. Another way to use the words is to write 20 of the words on the board. (The words from only one letter.) Then, put an actual object into a bag and have the children try to guess the object after giving three clues.

10. Certain music can be associated with certain letters. *Teddy Bear Picnic* could be danced or played when learning the "B-b" sound, for instance. *Incy Wency Spider* could be sung

during the I-I letter.

11. Each letter can be "masked" to bring the students' attention/focus on that particular letter in the word, or that little word in a sentence. A 3 x 5 inch index card could be cut to provide an outline. (Cut a small square "window" in the card.)This outline/square could be used to find all of the D's in this poem or morning journal entry, or paragraph. The student could then mask or point to that letter. This could be done after a Language-Experience Approach Paragraph/Sentence or Oral Dictation. the teacher could make the sound, the child must find the letter and mask or put the square-shaped card around it, to associate the sound/symbol.

12. Many teachers are required to assign and collect homework. Many of the children need more reinforcement on finding items/objects/things that begin with that sound, or have a desired sound in the name of the object. The object could be brought to school in a bag and children have to guess what the object is. "Name that object." A paper could be placed and the objects could be classified and then sorted. It is very easy to combine math and science with reading.

13. There are many home-made/teacher-made board games that can use the words from the word lists in each chapter. The words can be manipulated many ways to teach sight words and/or sounds. Some words have only one syllable and others have more. So pick the words at *your* students' abilities. The words could be used for encoding as well, or spelling. The encoded (written) word could be written on individual chalk boards and a game of "how many words can I spell/write" could be played. Be sure to emphasize the vowel sound.

14. Publishing the individual's or class' work is very important. Books can be made such as: "*C-c is for C-a-t* and *C-c is for*...." This could be dictated to the teacher, aide, or parent and written down. It could then be typed on a word processor and printed. Each child can have their own copy to read and a class book can be given to the class library. This could also go home to share with all the families. Also, a class newspaper could be published with the "letter of the week" and each child tells about an object that is real or imaginary, and the paper is read at home. This keeps a close contact with the home and child, and allows the families to help the children.

15. Flash cards can be made on small tag-board-like cards. A hole is punched and a ring is put through the holes so that the child now has a ring of words per letter, or three to four words per letter of the alphabet, that the child has selected. The child can then illustrate the word on the back of the card. Many times, students become "teachers" at home.

16. The letters in this collection are in alphabetical order, but many programs teach the consonants, plus vowels, in this order: m, f, r, s, n, t, a, c, l, h, b, i, g, d, e, j, o, k, q, p, z, v, w, y, x, y. This allows for initial, final consonant (plus a vowel) to make c-v-c words. Another program presents its letters like this: (initial consonants): b, c, d, f, g, h, j, k, l, m, n, p, r, s, t, w, and y. It then teaches the letters: a, k, l, m, n, p, r, t, and x as final consonants. Most programs then teach short vowels, then long. Children can learn to associate sounds, but it does not help them blend or decode until they hear and can sequence the sounds of the words. Children need to hear the sounds of the short /e/

and short "i" and these sounds must be fully exaggerated for the students to discriminate between the two. This enables the student to decode (read) and encode (spell). What students need to know about phonics is that phonics is a tool for reading. The basic concepts of phonics are:

A. Students need to know the relationship between the letter and the sound. This is the same sound associated with the letter no matter when the student reads and writes. Many teachers teach the sound of the 21 consonants first, because the symbol represents one sound (except for /c/ and /g/, which have two sounds). Consonants can be felt within the mouth, because consonants stop the flow of air.

B. Vowels, on the other hand, need to be sung elongated. The child can hear the initial consonant, vowel, and then the final consonant. Students need to know the sounds of the first letter. Many times, the first two letters, or a consonant, comes before the vowel.

C. Many students learn to read by using "word families" like: ack, ain, ake, all, ame, an, ank, ap, ash, at, ate, aw, ay, eat, ell, est, ice, ick, ide, ight, ill, in, ine, ing, ink, ip, ir, ock, oke, or, ore, uck, ug, ump, unk Then, they learn to attach an initial consonant to it and then decode the word. (About 450-500 words can be made from these 37 families.)

D. When the <u>V</u>owel is in the middle of two <u>C</u>onsonants (or a C-V-C pattern), it is a short vowel sound about 60 percent of the time.

E. "When two vowels go walking, the first one does the talking," means the first vowel is long and the second one is silent. (To be long, it says the name.) This is true about 40 percent of the time. * It works for ee, oa, and ay. * Sometimes it works for ea and ai. * However, it doesn't work consistently for ei, ie, or oo. * It doesn't work at all for dipthongs like oi, oy, and ou. * It is best to learn word families for oat, eet, eat, ay, ain, oot, ound, out, owl, and oil.

F. When two vowels are in one word and the last one is a silent "e" or magic "e", it makes the first vowel long and is also silent. (This works about 55-65 percent of the time.)

G. Vowels that come before the letter "r" are controlled by the "r" sound, like: /ar/, /er/, /ir/, /or/, and /ur/.

H. If a word/syllable ends in a consonant and it has only one vowel, the vowel is short. If the word ends in a vowel, the sound is long. Every syllable contains a vowel and the number of syllables is controlled by vowel sounds. If two or more consonants follow a vowel, the word is divided between the consonants.

I. If a consonant has a le with it, it becomes just one syllable, like the word beetle. If the word ends in d or t, the suffix ed becomes a separate syllable. If the word ends with any other consonant or vowel, it forms a single syllable. Phonics helps make sense of print. Phonics will allow students to put their own speech into print. Phonics gives students a way to make sense/meaning of print. Phonics needs to be combined with relevant context (i.e. useful, interesting, functional).

17. Cut up sentences or words. Have each child dictate a sentence by using the words in the alphabet word list in each chapter, or any word that begins with that letter. The teacher/aide writes the sentence on a Sentence Strip. The child reads it back several

times. The teacher then cuts it up and the child must sequence the words into the correct order. This works for words cut into letters to sequence into the correct order. The letters on the words could be written in blue for consonants and red for vowels.

18. A sight vocabulary is built and increased by reading and writing words. Making signs to identify the objects in a child/students room helps a lot. Sight vocabulary can begin using high-frequency words—which are words used often in stories/books. These are written and read often and many cannot be decoded by using the decoding rules. Here are 100 high-frequency words:a about, after, all, an, and, are, as, at, be, been, but, by, called, can, come, could, day, did, do, down, each, find, first, for, from, get, go, had, has, have, he, her, here, him, his, how, if, in, into, is, it, its, like, look, long, made, many, may, more, my, new, no, not, now, number, of, oil, on, one, or, other, out, part, people, said, she, see, so, some, than, that, the, their, them, then, these, this, time, there, to, two, up, use, was, water, way, we, were, what, when, which, who, will, with, words, would, write, you, your—when students know these words, reading and writing is more fluent.

19. "Words-in-a-Bag"This could be played at a center or in small reading groups. One child holds the bag of flash cards and is "it." Another child pulls out a card and hands it to "it." "It" must read the word. If correct, another student selects/draws out a word. "It" is the reader or "it" until he/she misses. Another way this could be played is "it" draws the card, then reads it. The other students encode/write/spell it on individual chalkboards with chalk. They keep score in a little group on their boards.

20. Body Alphabet Letters: Each group consists of one pair of students. When the bell rings, or music begins, the students communicate/think/plan on how to make their bodies form either a capital or lowercase letter, as stated by the teacher. The first pair that is correct gets three points, the second pair two, the third group gets one point. The team with the most points wins.

21. We need to check and see if the children are learning what we want them to learn or master. A suggested sequence of steps is: 1) writing in the air, 2) writing on a tray (with rice or sand), 3) writing with markers and then with pencils, and 4) writing on large-lined paper. Have students say the sound the letter makes each time. Check to see if the child is correctly forming the letter. If not, this is the time to hold his or her hand and assist the letter writing formation. You can use a green dot to show the student where the letter begins, a series on dots, and then a red dot where that child writing the letter should stop. You may need to do this five to ten times until the child writes the letter correctly. I always mark the paper with a "Happy Face" sticker for an attempt. This could also be homework. The second thing I need to say is that one piece of paper is never enough. If the letter is "M", have the child do activities, recipes, and spend sufficient time needed to learn that sound, associate with the letter, and write that letter. Then go back and review the letter learned before. Children need to learn and review/go over the concept until it is firmly/thoroughly learned. If the child is not learning after that time, more time is needed to review and use other activities to reinforce that letter concept. The child needs to reinforce that skill while a new one is learned. After the letter is learned, it must be constantly reviewed. Pair two consonants

and a vowel together so that a student can actually learn a word and recognize it while reading, or use it in a story, sentence and/or book. Remember to check and re-check to make sure the letter is written correctly. It is easier to correct the letter when the pattern has not been learned.

22. Using the word families in strategies/techniques #17c: a circle is made. On the circle, write the word families. The second circle which is attached by a brad could have consonants. The child spins the top paper and blends words like "ick" blended with a "p" to become "pick" or with an "s" to become "sick." Write words with consonants in blue and vowels in red. Children will decode/encode faster. Place letters (magnetic) on baking sheet and have students sequence letters to spell words.

23. Keep your eyes open for Alphabet Cookie Cutters. These can cut Jell-O™, cookies, play dough, bread, or any material to make words/letters which can be eaten or manipulated/felt to reinforce the letter recognition.

24. I always, if possible, combine reading with writing as it reinforces the concepts and helps in so many ways. Writing makes students better thinkers and readers. If a student can not write inventively (any sounds that he hears in the word), allow him or her to dictate to a parent, teacher, or aide and copy it. It's the student's words and they remember the lesson and their words become important.

25. Remember that letter recognition is first. The child must see the letter symbol as an individual letter, which is different from any other letter. When letter recognition is achieved—capital and lower case—then the sound can be established/connected to it. Phonemic awareness and letter recognition is a good predictor of early progress in reading. This letter recognition or discrimination is necessary for reading progress. That is why I have given you several cookie dough games and fun activities to teach letter discrimination/recognition and then attach a sound to the letters. Metal trays with magnetic letters are another great manipulative, which can be used at home/school to assist letter recognition/discrimination.

26. While in Russia, I saw children playing with manipulatives that helped with their phonemic awareness, and phonics-plus-sequencing, which is a big part of the problem with learning disabled students—and any students learning how to read. Squares can be made of all the consonants written upon each one. The squares of consonants could be blue or red. The vowels could be the opposite. for reading/center work/even spelling or seatwork, students could hear the word and try to use the manipulatives, in order to spell c-a-t, c-a-n, b-a-g, etc. The teacher will want to circulate to make sure the word is spelled correctly. (They had flannel boards and the child cam up and spelled the word using a flannel board. Some ideas just go around the world.)

Appendix B

A Sample Lesson to Be Used with Any Letter of the Alphabet

1. The teacher says the sound of the letter, then writes the capital and lower case letter on the board. The teacher then asks students if they know a word or name that begins with this letter. The teacher writes down all answers. The class helps cross out any that are incorrect.

2. On display are books with the letter sound in the name. Several are listed in the back of each letter/chapter in this book.

3. The teacher then names or chants Consonant-Vowel-Consonant words or any words that start with that sound. Many suggestions are placed in the word list on each letter. Students then chant the words with the teacher.

4. The teacher then asks what sound is the initial/beginning sound of all of the words you have just said. The students reply. The teacher points to the capital and lower case letters and states the correct way to say the sound of that letter.

5. The teacher then asks students to read or chant the words again and say the sound that is associated with that letter.

6. The teacher then models, or demonstrates, how to write the letter in the air. Students then write the letter in the air. (If the capital is different than the lower case letter, both are made.)

7. Individual chalkboards may be passed out and students instructed to make the capital letter on the board with chalk. If the child is correct, the teacher could put a star over that letter; if not, the teacher needs to help the child right then and there. The teacher could make dotted lines, so the student traces over the letter, or the teacher could use a different color of chalk, so that the student can trace the letter several times, and then write the letter correctly in the beginning. Some students will need the teacher or aide to hold his or her hand several times until the student can correctly write the letter. A star is written on top of the letters that are correct.

8. Pieces of yarn, construction paper, and glue or paste are passed out. The student manipulates the yarn so that it copies the letter on the board. If correct, the child then glues or pastes it on the paper. Another activity could be that a capital and lower case letter could be traced and cut. Then corn glued for /c/, Applejacks™ for /a/, seeds for /s/. Many ideas are listed under the Activities section for each letter. The teacher must make sure that the child writes from the top down and follows the correct way to write the letter.

9. Play Dough™ is another way students can manipulate a letter and then "feel" the shape or configuration. This is important. Make sure the student starts from the beginning and feels the letter as it should be written.

10. The teacher then faces the letter on the board and moves his or her hand as if writing the letter, or writes the letter in the air. The students then write the letter in the air.

11. The teacher then makes the sound associated with the letter, or the sound the letter

makes. As students are writing in the air, they are now saying the sound also.

12. The teacher then focuses their attention either to their chalkboards or large sheets of paper with large felt tip markers. The students then write the letter as they say the sound, associating the sound with the letter as they write. Again, the teacher is circulating and helping those who need help, and putting stars or happy faces on top of the correct letters.

13. The students could look around the room and find objects that start with that letter sound. A grab bag could be filled with objects that do and do not start with that letter sound and students would have to identify the matching objects.

14. At this time, even if it has taken two or three days, a recipe should be chosen for the students to make. (Some require cooking and some do not.) Now students have seen the letter, have heard the sound the letter makes, can discriminate that sound from others, and now will taste a recipe. The recipe is made and can be copied for the students to share with their families. This is a way for families to bond with the school.

15. Students can be assigned homework: Bring objects to school from home to be shared and then brought back home. The class decides if the object's name begins with the sound of that letter. The object could also become a game with several clues given and the class has to name the object.

16. Students now have large lined paper and pencils and can write the letter and say the sound associated with the letter. There are many activities listed and many recipes, plus books and vocabulary words. If the students are capable, and this is not your first letter, then words could be spelled by using square cards with consonants and vowels made up on differently colored paper. I teach the letters s, m, b, t, and n, right away. I would then add a vowel, so that you are spelling words and the material is not just "drill and kill", but meaningful. The teacher must check constantly to make sure that the student is writing and saying the sounds correctly. Try many of the activities as it reinforces the skill.

17. Students get to choose a book that has been selected that has the letter in the title. The book can be read several times or several books can be read one time. Children can then check out the books from the library and read them at home. Suggestion: never spend just one week on each letter, and if the child is absent, please go over the letter with him or her, so they will not be lost. Also go back and review the letters, so that students will not forget what they have learned.